SON OF
THE 100 BEST
Movies You've
NEVER Seen

SON OF THE 100 BEST Movies You've NEVER Seen

RICHARD CROUSE

ECW PRESS

Published by ECW PRESS
2120 Queen Street East, Suite 200, Toronto, Ontario, Canada M4E 1E2
info@ecwpress.com / 416.694.3348

LIBRARY AND ARCHIVES CANADA CATALOGUING IN PUBLICATION

Crouse, Richard, 1963-
Son of the 100 best movies you've never seen / Richard Crouse.

ISBN 978-1-55022-840-3

1. Motion pictures—Reviews.   I. Title.   II. Title: Son of the one hundred best movies you've never seen.

PN1993.5.A1C865 2008   791.43'75   C2008-902380-3

Editor: Jennifer Hale
Cover, Photo Section and Text Design: Tania Craan
Cover Photographs: Richard Beland
Production & Typesetting: Gail Nina
Printing: Transcontinental

This book is set in Akzidenz Grotesk and Minion

The publication of *Son of the 100 Best Movies You've Never Seen* has been generously supported by the Government of Ontario through the Ontario Book Publishing Tax Credit, by the OMDC Book Fund, an initiative of the Ontario Media Development Corporation, and by the Government of Canada through the Book Publishing Industry Development Program (BPIDP).

Canadä

PRINTED AND BOUND IN CANADA

ECW PRESS
ecwpress.com

*"Part of the love of movies is
going through the rummage bin
and finding the jewels."*

— Quentin Tarantino

Thanks to . . .

Andrea Bodnar; Jen Hale, Jack David, Tania Craan and everyone at ECW Press; Claudio Castro; Geoff Pevere; Ed, Norma, Gary, Christian and Nicholas; everyone who contributed their time and material to this book: Glenn O'Brien, Rodney Bingenheimer, Thelma Schoonmaker, Danny Boyle, Albert Maysles, Stuart Gordon, Ken Loach, Nick Broomfield, Peter Greenaway, Charles Dutton, John Sayles, Deepa Metha, Ron Mann, Herschell Gordon Lewis, Lloyd Kaufman; all those at CANADA AM, Seamus O'Regan, Beverly Thompson, Liz Travers, Jeff Tam, Karning Hum, Melissa LeBlanc, Phil, Vicki and little Rachel; Steve Kowch, Bill Carroll, Ryan Doyle and Jeff Moss and everyone at CFRB; my GROOVE SHINNY pals Pedro Mendes, Kai Black, David Carroll and Brent Bambury; Frances and everyone at Southern Accent; Ron "Do you remember when you were two?" Bodnar; Angela Bodnar; Susan Smythe; Laura Quinn; Virginia Kelly; Nancy Yu; Angie Burns; Bonne Smith; Dara Rowland; Shelly Chagnon; Bryan Peters; Charles Wechsler; and everyone who watched REEL TO REAL each week.

Table of Contents

Introduction **xi**

Ace in the Hole (1951) **1**

A Child Is Waiting (1963) **4**

Advise & Consent (1962) **7**

Akeelah and the Bee (2006) **9**

A Matter of Life and Death (1946) **11**

Amphibian Man (1962) **13**

The Astronaut Farmer (2006) **17**

Baadasssss! (2003) **19**

La Belle et la Bête (1946) **23**

Bigger Than Life (1956) **25**

Black Christmas (1974) **27**

Bloody Mama (1970) **32**

Richard's Favorite Advertising Taglines for Horror Films with Christmas Themes **33**

Roger Corman Appreciation Society: Richard's Favorite Appearances of the Director on Film, Part One **38**

Boom! (1968) **39**

The Boondock Saints (1999) **42**

Bride of the Monster (1955) **45**

The Brothers Grimm (2005) **50**

The Brown Bunny (2003) **52**

Caged! (1950) **55**

The Cameraman's Revenge (1912) **58**

The Cars That Ate Paris (1974) **60**

Ciao! Manhattan (1972) **63**

Confessions of a Dangerous Mind (2002) **68**

The Crime of Dr. Crespi (1935) **71**

Richard's Favorite Casting Stories **74**

Day of Wrath (1943) **77**

My Favorite Movie You've Never Seen: Deepa Mehta **79**

Dear Frankie (2004) **80**

The Descent (2005) **81**

Downtown 81 (1981) **83**

The Duellists (1977) **86**

El Topo (1970) **89**

My Favorite Movie You've Never Seen: Ron Mann **93**

Evil Roy Slade (1972) **94**

Fantastic Voyage (1966) **96**

Richard's Favorite Mad Movie Science **100**

Faster, Pussycat! Kill! Kill! (1965) **102**

F for Fake (1974) **107**

Flame (1975) **109**

The Game (1997) **112**

The Girl from Mexico (1939) **116**

Godspeed You! Black Emperor (1976) **119**

Grey Gardens (1975) **121**

My Favorite Movie You've Never Seen: Albert Maysles **124**

The Heart of the Game (2005) **124**

Hearts of the West (1975) **126**

The Hidden Fortress (1958) **128**

The Horn Blows at Midnight (1945) **130**

Idlewild (2006) **133**

I'll Never Forget What's 'Isname (1967)
 135

The Intruder (1962) **139**

Roger Corman Appreciation Society: Richard's
 Favorite Appearances of the Director on
 Film, Part Two **142**

I Woke Up Early the Day I Died (1998)
 143

The Junky's Christmas (1993) **146**

Killer of Sheep (1977) **148**

The Killing (1956) **150**

The Last Laugh (1924) **153**

The Little Kidnappers (1953) **156**

My Favorite Movie You've Never Seen: Ken
 Loach **159**

The Loneliness of the Long Distance Runner
 (1962) **159**

Maidstone (1970) **162**

Marie Antoinette (2006) **164**

Martin (1977) **167**

Mayor of Sunset Strip (2003) **169**

My Favorite Movie You've Never Seen: John
 Sayles **173**

Microcosmos: Le peuple de l'herbe (1996)
 173

Richard's Favorite Big Bug Movies **175**

The Monster Squad (1987) **177**

Narc (2002) **181**

Night Moves (1975) **183**

On Dangerous Ground (1952) **185**

One from the Heart (1982) **188**

Richard's Favorite Actors Turned Singers
 193

Operation Kid Brother (1967) **196**

The Painted Veil (2006) **198**

Panic in the Streets (1950) **201**

Park Row (1952) **206**

Passport to Pimlico (1949) **209**

My Favorite Movie You've Never Seen: Thelma
 Schoonmaker **211**

Performance (1970) **211**

Perfume: The Story of a Murderer (2006)
 215

Planet of the Vampires (1965) **217**

Plein soleil (1960) **221**

Pulp (1972) **223**

My Favorite Movie You've Never Seen: Peter
 Greenaway **224**

The Rebel (1961) **227**

Respiro (2002) **229**

Rififi (1955) **231**

The Roaring Twenties (1939) **233**

My Favorite Movie You've Never Seen: Stuart
 Gordon **237**

Rolling Thunder (1977) **238**

Safety Last! (1923) **241**

The Saragossa Manuscript (1965)
 243

Serenity (2005) **245**

Seven Thieves (1960) **247**

Sherman's March (1986) **249**

Stalker: A Film by Andrei Tarkovsky (1979)
 251

My (Three) Favorite Movies You've Never Seen:
 Danny Boyle **253**

Straight to Hell (1987) **255**

My Favorite Movie You've Never Seen: Charles
 Dutton **258**

Sullivan's Travels (1941) **258**

Switchblade Sisters (1975) **262**

Tampopo (1985) **264**

Theremin: An Electronic Odyssey (1994) **265**

Titicut Follies (1967) **267**

Twentieth Century (1934) **269**

My Favorite Movie You've Never Seen: Lloyd Kaufman **271**

The Twonky (1953) **271**

My Favorite Movie You've Never Seen: Herschell Gordon Lewis **274**

Venus in Furs (1969) **275**

Viva la muerte (1971) **277**

The Well (1951) **279**

We Were Strangers (1949) **281**

My Favorite Movie You've Never Seen: Nick Broomfield **286**

When the Wind Blows (1986) **287**

The Wild Dogs (2002) **289**

Who Killed Teddy Bear? (1965) **291**

The Yellow Rolls-Royce (1964) **295**

Zathura: A Space Adventure (2005) **297**

Bibliography **301**

INTRODUCTION

What makes a good movie? There are as many definitions as there are films. Italian critic and screenwriter Cesare Zavattini said, "The ideal film would be 90 minutes of the life of a man to whom nothing happens." Another writer suggested that "movies should be punishment inflicted on people seeking entertainment." My girlfriend says a good movie is any movie starring Adam Sandler.

Me? I fall somewhere in the middle.

I like movies that push the boundaries of art and taste as much as I like empty-headed eye candy. Andrei Tarkovsky or Carl Theodor Dreyer may make me think, but George A. Romero scares me and Fernando Arrabal freaks me out while Jess Franco blows my mind and Ladislas Starevich can fill me with wonder. All are different and all are included here because through their lenses each of these directors (and the other 94 included in the book) has effectively conjured up something that, for me, is memorable or moving in some way.

Are all the movies in this book on the American Film Institute "Best of" lists? No. Some will be, but it's unlikely that the made-for-television movie *Evil Roy Slade* is going to pop up on any serious "Best of" inventory. That is unless the list includes movies guaranteed to make you laugh. I chose these movies not with an eye toward impressing other film critics with my depth of knowledge or ability to dig up obscurities, but with the goal of binding together 100 personal choices that I think are worth a second and third look. Many of these movies were released as mainstream commercial fare only to be labeled obscure after audiences stayed away or the passing of time saw them fall out of favor. This book should act as a reminder that there are great films to be found past the new releases rack at your local video store.

Along the way I asked for some help from some famous film directors. The question was simple, "Can you give me the name of a movie that you love that may not have gotten the attention it deserved?" Some, like Danny Boyle and Peter Greenaway, barely paused for a breath before launching into detailed descriptions of their favorite overlooked gems.

Others, like Paul Haggis, had a harder time with the question. The director of *Crash* and *In the Valley of Elah* hemmed and hawed before suggesting *The Three Burials of Melquiades Estrada*, and I think that film (great though it is) only sprung to mind because we had just been discussing the film's director Tommy Lee Jones. So many great pictures get overlooked that it's hard to boil down a lifetime of watching and loving movies to just one title. Luckily, my job was easier. I got to pick 100.

Another filmmaker, visionary French director Michel Gondry, wouldn't even venture a title, instead he said, "Oh, there are millions . . . it would be hard to choose just one. If people would stop making films now we could watch what already exists for 100 years and we'd hardly see the difference."

I love that.

I'm not suggesting that people stop making movies (although I wish Michael Bay would), but that people take a little time and appreciate what we already have — an ever-growing archive of great movies just down the street at their local video store.

So, with no apologies, here are 100 movies I love. . . .

ACE IN THE HOLE (1951)

Billy Wilder, the storied director of *Double Indemnity* and *The Lost Weekend,* was at the top of his game in 1951. His film, *Sunset Boulevard,* despite earning the ire of Hollywood insiders — MGM head honcho Louis B. Mayer suggested Wilder be tarred, feathered and horse-whipped for portraying his profession with such a jaundiced eye — was a huge hit, nominated for 11 Academy Awards, taking home three, including one for Wilder in the category of Best Writing, Story and Screenplay.

Perhaps it was the success of that film, despite the backlash from the industry, which gave Wilder the courage to go ahead with a film that was sure to alienate a powerful group of Tinseltown insiders — the Hollywood press. *Ace in the Hole*, his scathing exposé of shady journalism, put him at odds with the frontline scribes who would write about the movie and hopefully stir up interest with audiences. Their rejection of the film doomed it to failure.

"Fuck them all," Wilder said after the movie tanked. "It is the best picture I ever made."

Wilder picked up the idea for *Ace in the Hole* from a 20-year-old radio writer named Walter Newman. Newman pitched the director a treatment called *The Human Interest Story* based on the 1925 case of spelunker Floyd Collins, the self-proclaimed greatest cave explorer ever known. Collins had been investigating a Kentucky cave in hopes of turning it into a profitable tourist attraction when a 27-pound rock collapsed on his foot, trapping him in a narrow, wet hole. He remained wedged in the space for 17 days, before he succumbed to starvation and exposure. The part of the story that grabbed Newman was the media circus that grew around the event.

Collins was pinned in an inaccessible fissure only 150 feet from the mouth of the cave, so he was able to banter back and forth with rescuers and journalists. William Burke "Skeets" Miller, a cub reporter for the *Louisville Courier-Journal* played up the story in a series of dramatic articles, turning the local misfortune into a national event. His melo-dramatic reportage earned him a Pulitzer Prize and drew tens of thousands of people — disaster tourists — to the area, turning this unfortunate set of circumstances into the third biggest media event between the World Wars (next to Charles Lindbergh's transatlantic flight and his son's kidnapping).

In the film Kirk Douglas stars as Charles Tatum, a former ace reporter now on the skids. "I can handle big news and little news. And if there's no news," he says, "I'll go out and bite a dog." Tatum has been fired from every major newspaper in the country, and in a desperate bid to rebuild his sidetracked career he offers his services to a small Albuquerque, New Mexico, daily. Outside the editor's office hangs an embroidered sign that reads "Tell the Truth."

"Wish I could coin 'em like that," Tatum says to a secretary. "If I ever do, will you embroider it for me?"

Assigned to covering rattlesnake hunts and other small town news, one day Tatum stumbles across the story he thinks will vault him back to the big time. In the nearby Mountain of the Seven Vultures, Leo Minosa, an ex-GI, has been trapped by falling debris while hunting for artifacts. Tatum seizes the chance to cover the story, recalling another reporter who "crawled in for the story and crawled out with a Pulitzer Prize."

Tatum spices the story with histrionic hokum ("Ancient Curse Entombs Man!") to create a national buzz for his scoop, but it isn't until he conspires with a corrupt sheriff (Ray Teal), the GI's wife (Jan Sterling) and a gutless contractor (Lewis Martin) to prolong the story by keeping Leo buried under the rubble that the movie reveals its true dark heart.

Cynical, bitter and uncompromising, *Ace in the Hole* is a no-holds-barred indictment of yellow journalism, unfettered greed, ambition and opportunism. Other films have tread the same ground, 1957's *A Face in the Crowd* and from 1976 *Network* to name a couple, but neither of those movies has the same cutting edge, the underlying flavor of arsenic.

Wilder wastes no opportunity to pour vitriol on the idea that human suffering can be treated as a spectator sport. Even the carnival trailers at the scene are used as a metaphor. Their name? S&M Amusement Services.

In the lead role of Tatum, Kirk Douglas personifies ruthless ambition coupled with a complete disregard for humanity. His indifference for the safety of the trapped man is a microcosm of the larger issue regarding the warped relationship between the American media and its public. He's a sociopath who gives the people what they want — vivid human interest stories — no matter what the cost.

Douglas's work here rates among his best, alongside Vincente Minnelli's *The Bad and the Beautiful*, Stanley Kubrick's *Paths of Glory* and Mark Robson's *Champion* for which he was nominated for an Oscar. Douglas drips with confidence, chewing up and spitting out the dialogue. In his hands Tatum is a despicable character, but he's a compelling one.

When a group of big-time reporters descend on his story, trying to find a way to muzzle in on his scoop, it's a moment with the kind of zippy dialogue that could only exist in a Wilder noir — and Douglas makes the best of it.

"We're all buddies in the same boat," says one frantic correspondent.

"I'm in the boat. You're in the water," Tatum spits back. "Now let's see you swim, buddies."

It's great stuff and Douglas seems to relish every manic, brutal syllable.

Ace in the Hole was (predictably) beaten up by the press and despite winning an award at the Venice Film Festival, failed to find an audience in 1951. Paramount, ignoring Wilder's contractual right of title and final cut, went behind his back and re-released an edited version of the film titled *The Big Carnival*, which didn't fare much better than the original. Disheartened by the movie's failure Wilder played it safe for the next few years, mostly adapting Broadway plays for the screen.

In 1997 the film was remade as *Mad City* by politically charged film-maker Costa-Gavras, but audiences didn't get a chance to see Wilder's original unsung masterpiece again until it earned a limited theatrical release in 2002. This time critics lobbed laurels at the 50-year-old film, praising its prescient view of the out-of-control tabloid media. Critical response to the re-release led to a handsome DVD package from Criterion in 2007.

"It was a totally uncompromising film at a time when the movies were said to be totally compromised," wrote Maurice Zolotow in *Billy Wilder in Hollywood*. "It is shocking even now."

Availability: On Criterion DVD

"A child can be so many things – warmth, love, laughter – and sometimes a child can be . . . heartbreak."
– NARRATION FROM THE TRAILER OF *A CHILD IS WAITING*

A CHILD IS WAITING (1963)

Filmmaker John Cassavetes disowned the final cut of his 1963 film *A Child Is Waiting* after producer Stanley Kramer wrestled control of the movie away from him and did a re-edit. "I didn't think his film — and that's what I consider it to be, his film — was so bad," said Cassavetes, "just a lot more sentimental than mine."

Cassavetes had a reputation for being uncompromising. He raised the money for his first film, *Shadows*, during a radio appearance to promote another picture. Booked on *Jean Shepherd's Night People* to pump up a 1957 Martin Ritt film called *Edge of the City* (co-starring Sidney Poitier), Cassavetes instead railed against Hollywood movies, particularly the one he was there to promote, and said that if everyone listening sent him one dollar he could make a "real" film. The radio show netted him $2,000 which became the seed money for his directorial debut. From that point on he did things his way or not at all.

Working with Kramer on his third picture, Cassavetes clashed with the producer, and his stars Judy Garland and Burt Lancaster who both wanted more structure on set (and less improvisation) than Cassavetes was willing to provide. Kramer, a seasoned director and producer with an impressive list of credits like *Judgment at Nuremberg* and *The Defiant Ones*, exerted pressure on the director to deliver a slick movie, even going so far as to order reshoots of scenes he dubbed too grainy.

"My God," said Cassavetes, "you damn Hollywood people. All you can think of is smoothness of camera. What we want is to get some rough edges in here."

Cassavetes may have felt stifled by Kramer's interference, but the resulting picture, even in its edited and altered state, still feels like a Cassavetes film — intelligent, devoid of self pity and socially aware.

Dr. Matthew Clark (Burt Lancaster) runs the Crawthorne State Mental Hospital (modeled on the Vineland Training School in New Jersey), a state institution for mentally challenged children. His authority is challenged by Jean Hansen (Judy Garland), a former music teacher who is skeptical of Clark's strict methods. She feels that love, not rules or discipline, is all the children need to lead happy, productive lives.

After becoming emotionally involved with 12-year-old Reuben Widdicombe (Bruce Ritchey), a troubled boy who has been abandoned by his parents, Hansen goes behind Clark's back and asks the young patient's parents to come and visit, thinking it will help calm the youngster's behavioral problems. Surprisingly, however, Sophie Widdicombe

(Gena Rowlands) agrees with Clark, that it would be too disruptive for Reuben to see his parents.

As she is on her way out, Reuben catches a glimpse of her and chases her car. The encounter has severe emotional repercussions on Reuben, who, distraught, runs away from the institution. When Clark finds the child and returns him to the hospital the next morning, Hansen, realizing she was wrong to take matters into her own hands, tenders her resignation.

Clark refuses to let her go, asking her to stay on-board at least long enough to help stage the institute's big Thanksgiving show for the parents. In the ending that rankled Cassavetes, Reuben's father arrives at the hospital to cart his son off to a private school, but is so moved when he hears Reuben recite a poem onstage that he changes his mind, deciding that the institutional life is the best way for his boy to function.

"The difference in the two versions is that Stanley's picture said that retarded children belong in institutions and the picture I shot said retarded children are better in their own way than supposedly healthy adults," says Cassavetes in *Cassavetes on Cassavetes*. "The philosophy of his film was that retarded children are separate and alone and therefore should be in institutions with others of their kind. My film said that retarded children could be anywhere, any time, and that the problem is that we're a bunch of dopes, that it's our problem more than the kids'. The point of the original picture that we made was that there was no fault, that there was nothing wrong with these children except that their mentality was lower."

"We had just come up from New York," Gena Rowlands told me in 2008. "I don't think we had ever heard the fact that the director didn't have the final cut. To us it was an assumption that he did. We found out the hard way. So there was a great deal of controversy about that."

That being said, *A Child Is Waiting* is still a powerful drama that draws on the humanity that Cassavetes brought to all his directorial efforts as well as Stanley Kramer's socially aware stance. The result is a film that, while dated, is a provocative and moving study of the predicament of mentally challenged children.

Written by Abby Mann, who also penned *Judgment at Nuremberg* and later *Ship of Fools*, and shot in the loose style that was Cassavetes' trademark, *A Child Is Waiting* has an almost documentary feel. Much of the authenticity of the film comes from the fact that — save for Bruce Ritchey who played Reuben — all the children in the film were patients from the Pacific State Hospital in Pomona, California.

A Child Is Waiting isn't pure Cassavetes, but it is a fascinating mix of his singular emotional density as filtered through the Hollywood studio system. "I thought the picture was pretty terrific from either point of view," said Rowlands, "I liked John's better, but I didn't hate Stanley's."

Availability: Out of Print VHS

"Son, this is a Washington, D.C., kind of lie. It's when the other person knows you're lying and also knows you know he knows."
— ROBERT A. LEFFINGWELL (HENRY FONDA) IN *ADVISE & CONSENT*

ADVISE & CONSENT (1962)

Director Otto Preminger almost pulled off what could have been one of the great casting coups of the 1960s when he offered civil rights leader Martin Luther King Jr. a role in his politically charged drama *Advise & Consent*. Preminger, the mercurial director of *Exodus* and *Saint Joan*, thought King would be perfect for the role of a southern Senator, despite the fact that no African Americans were serving in Senate at the time. King gave the offer some thought, but declined, fearing the backlash and possible harm to the Civil Rights movement.

Even without King, Preminger still assembled an impressive cast —

Henry Fonda, Charles Laughton (in his last film role), Gene Tierney and Kennedy insider Peter Lawford — to portray former *New York Times* congressional correspondent Allen Drury's Pulitzer Prize–winning novel about the ratification of a secretary of state and the dirty little secrets that people in public life must keep hidden.

As the action gets underway a political firestorm is looming. The ailing U.S. president (Franchot Tone playing a thinly veiled Franklin Delano Roosevelt) has nominated a self-proclaimed "egghead" and former Communist Party member named Robert A. Leffingwell (Henry Fonda) for the office of secretary of state. He's not only a former commie, but also an outspoken intellectual with the reputation of having "more enemies in Congress than any other man in government."

A small group of Capitol Hill loyalists — including Fred Van Ackerman (George Grizzard as a character based on Joseph McCarthy), a junior senator from Wyoming — struggle to line up the necessary votes to secure Leffingwell's post, but they face massive opposition from powerful, entrenched players like Seabright Cooley (Charles Laughton) who hates Leffingwell's politics almost as much as he hates the man himself.

Political battle lines are drawn as a full frontal attack is launched on the character and credentials of the new nominee.

Preminger spends the first twenty minutes of the film introducing the characters and making sure the viewer understands just who these people are and where they are coming from. It's a risky move that threatens to kill the movie's momentum before it even gets started, but once Laughton opens his mouth the story takes off like a rocket, and you'll be glad you know who's who.

The film's title is a play on the United States Constitution's Article II, Sec. 2, cl. 2, which says that the President of the United States "shall nominate, and by and with the Advice and Consent of the Senate, shall appoint Ambassadors, other public Ministers and Consults, Judges of the Supreme Court, and all other Officers of the United States . . ." Preminger dropped much of the satire contained in the book — he didn't bother with a liberal peace organization called COMFORT: The Committee On Making Further Offers for a Russian Truce, for instance — but he did keep the book's controversial gay subplot.

In its day the film was praised for its homosexual storyline in which one of the senators visits a gay bar. Today the gay content seems dated, but what still feels fresh is its portrayal of how Washington works. Post-Watergate we're used to seeing the unsavory inner workings of Capitol Hill on the big screen, but Preminger lifted that curtain in 1962, showing off the soft underbelly of the Senate complete with corruption, malice and pettiness.

At the same time the film doesn't judge its characters. No one is portrayed as an all out hero or villain — despite a couple of star-turn performances by Laughton and Fonda. Instead Preminger allows the story to be the star.

Advise & Consent is talky and slow paced, but fascinating in its ability to gradually draw the viewer into the intrigue of the political process.

Availability: On DVD

"Our greatest fear is not that we are inadequate; our greatest fear is that we are powerful beyond measure."
– AKEELAH (KEKE PALMER) IN *AKEELAH AND THE BEE*

AKEELAH AND THE BEE (2006)

Akeelah and the Bee plays like *Rocky* crossed with *Good Will Hunting*. A spelling bee movie — is there a stranger genre? — which came hot on the heels of the hit documentary *Spellbound* and the drama *Bee Season*, *Akeelah and the Bee* is a story designed to make you cheer for the underdog.

Akeelah is a shy young girl from South Central Los Angeles who has a gift for spelling. It seems her late father instilled in her a love of language and word games — don't bet against her in a Scrabble match — but she tries to keep her etymologic endowment a secret in school, explaining that if she appears to be too smart the only word she'll have to know how to spell is n-e-r-d. With some encouragement from her principal — the guy who played Booger in the *Revenge of the Nerds* movies — she enters the school's spelling bee. After an easy win at her school she takes on a tutor — the brusque Laurence Fishburne — a former champ who trains her for the national bee.

Akeelah and the Bee is a sentimental story that occasionally feels overcalculated, as though writer/director Doug Atchison is trying to cram every after-school special cliché into one story — we have the virtues of hard work, good sportsmanship, following one's dreams and of course the ever popular love conquers all, to name just a few. The story is emotionally uncomplicated, some of the characters come directly from central casting and it doesn't have the clout of *Spellbound*, but there are a couple of elements that elevate this film, making it worthy of a big-screen treatment. The movie does have good messages for young people. Akeelah starts her journey as a shy young girl and gradually gains confidence in her abilities, leaning to trust not only herself, but those around her. Her character teaches kids that they can opt for any path in life and work toward any destination they choose.

The movie's secret weapon is Keke Palmer as the wonderful wordsmith. Palmer is a natural talent who brings new life to a character that we've seen onscreen many times. Her performance is so guileless that it feels like you are watching a real kid working through Akeelah's issues. Her authentic sensitivity blunts some of the more obvious emotional manipulations and earns the film a recommendation.

Availability: On DVD

A MATTER OF LIFE AND DEATH
(A.K.A. STAIRWAY TO HEAVEN) (1946)

Produced by the ingenious English filmmaking duo known as the Archers — Michael Powell and Emeric Pressburger — *A Matter of Life and Death* is a supernatural love story set against the backdrop of World War II.

We join the story in May 1945 just as squadron leader Peter Carter's (David Niven) British bomber is engulfed in flames and about to crash after a reconnaissance raid over Germany. His crew has bailed out to safety, unfortunately taking all the parachutes with them. Forced to make a grim choice, he bravely declares, "I'd rather jump than fry."

Faced with certain death, he speaks his last words to June (Kim Hunter), an American-born Royal Air Force ground controller. Establishing an immediate rapport, Peter uses the last moments of his life to flirt with the lovely voice on the other side of the radio. Moved by his courage she says, "I could love a man like you, Peter."

"I love you, June," Peter replies before he leaps out of the plane. "You're life and I'm leaving you."

It's curtains for Peter, but then something remarkable happens; he washes ashore, confused but unhurt save for a scratch on his forehead. It must be his lucky day because not only did he survive the tremendous fall, but in the distance he sees June on a bicycle. They meet and fall in love and all is well. All, except that a mistake was made by a higher power: Peter was not meant to live.

It seems that due to thick fog Peter's guide into the next world, Heavenly Conductor 71 (Maurice Goring), a French aristocrat executed during the Revolution, lost track of Peter and failed to collect his soul. Now the conductor is charged with bringing the pilot back to his intended celestial home. Peter, of course, doesn't want to leave Earth so a Heavenly tribunal is convened to decide his fate.

First and foremost *A Matter of Life and Death*, renamed *Stairway to Heaven* for its American release, is a treat for the eyes. Powell and Pressburger (who always went 50-50 with the writing, directing and producing credits) flip-flop the *Wizard of Oz* technique of using color for the fantasy sequences and black and white for reality by shooting the film's Earth-bound scenes in glorious Technicolor, while using stark black and white for Heaven's panoramas. Heaven is an immense but cold and clinical place, run by bureaucrats. It's here though where much of the film's sly visual humor lurks; to make Americans feel welcome in the hereafter a Coke machine is placed by Heaven's door and newly minted angels carry their wings in dry cleaning bags. The film's most famous image involves a stairway to the otherworld, upon which Carter is unknowingly transported to his reward.

As per usual the handsome Niven hands in a suave and cool performance, supported by a strong love interest played by Kim Hunter. Hunter, an Oscar winner for *A Streetcar Named Desire*, although probably best known as Zira in the *Planet of the Apes* movies, brings a gentle nobility to the role of June and through her relationship with the veddy English Niven provides a wartime subtext of the importance of Britain and America standing together and overcoming cultural differences.

Inventively conceived and lushly produced, *A Matter of Life and Death* succeeds because it avoids the pitfalls of some of its magic realist brethren. It sidesteps the love-conquers-death clichés of *Ghost* and underplays the saccharine content so prevalent in *It's a Wonderful Life*, another 1940s angel-on-Earth story. The Archers unerringly calibrate the film's tone toward the witty, profound and playful, and use eye-popping special effects to create a stylish film that celebrates life and love.

Availability: Out of Print VHS

"Tarzan des mer"
— UNUSED FRENCH TITLE FOR *AMPHIBIAN MAN*

AMPHIBIAN MAN (CHELOVEK-AMFIBIYA) (1962)

At the time of its release in Russia *Amphibian Man* was the most popular movie to date. Something of a pop culture phenomenon, the movie brought in 65 million admissions in 1962 — roughly the equivalent of a $520 million box office take in today's dollars — and spawned a hit song, "The Sea Devil." Based on the novel *Chelovek-Amfibiya* by the man called "the Russian Jules Verne," author Alexander Belyayev, it is usually classified as science fiction, but at its heart it is a romance.

Set in a Mexican fishing community where rumors of a strange underwater creature are whispered by the locals, *Amphibian Man* revs up when some pearl divers come across the strange sub aqua being. The creature is quite a sight, complete with silvery fish skin, gills and enormous eyes. Freaked out, the divers race back to their boat where they jabber about their discovery to their boss, Don Pedro Zurita (Mikhail Kozakov).

Don Pedro, unimpressed that they didn't capture the "sea beast," scolds them. Calling them cowards, he angrily shoves one of the divers back into the water. Too bad for Don Pedro that his reluctant girlfriend, Gutiere (Anastasiya Vertinskaya), witnesses his tantrum and is disgusted by his behavior. When Pedro forcibly tries to kiss the girl she dives into the water to get away from his unwanted embrace.

As she hurriedly swims away Don Pedro sees a shark making a bee-line for her. As he leaps into a row boat to come to her rescue he is unaware that someone — or something — else is coming to her aid. In an amazing display of aquatic dexterity the Sea Devil wrestles with and kills the shark, saves the unconscious Gutiere from drowning before depositing her limp body on Don Pedro's boat and disappearing beneath the waves.

A stunned Don Pedro can't believe the Sea Devil saved Gutiere, but sees a way to turn the situation to his favor. Back on the main ship he tells everyone, including Gutiere's father, that he battled the shark and rescued the damsel in distress. The girl's father, eager to repay his debt to his daughter's savior, convinces Gutiere to marry Don Pedro even though she doesn't love him.

Meanwhile a journalist, Olsen (Vladlen Davydov), is doing some research on the Sea Devil at the home of Dr. Salvator (Nikolai Simonov) who, at first dismisses the idea of the beast as superstition and myth. Olsen, sensing something is fishy, presses the doctor for answers.

Later, over lunch the doctor comes clean when discussing society and his ideas for the future. Taking Olsen into his lab, Salvator reveals a large glass portal to the sea. Salvator speaks into a microphone, apparently summoning something and suddenly the Sea Devil swims into the large glass tank. Olsen can't believe his eyes when the "mythological creature" removes his headgear and is shown to be a good-looking teenager.

Salvator explains that the Sea Devil (Vladimir Korenev) is actually his son Ichthyandr — literally "Fish Man" in Greek — born with a rare lung disease. When the boy was just a baby the doctor cured his condition by replacing his lungs with shark gills. Not only did it save his son's life, but also gave birth to his plan for a perfect society, an underwater republic. Ichthyandr, however, doesn't care about the underwater utopia or Olsen's interest or anything but Gutiere. Is it puppy love or guppy love?

If *Amphibian Man* were just a romance about a half-fish boy and a beautiful girl it would be curious enough, but viewing it in its historical context adds an even stranger aspect. Russian films of the period didn't normally feature pop songs, dance numbers, exotic locations and sentimental love stories. The inclusion of all those elements certainly makes it a bit of a cultural oddity, although it's possible that the film's lush, non-traditional Soviet feel was the perfect stroke of counter programming needed to give it the mass appeal it enjoyed upon release in the U.S.S.R.

Much of the draw of the film lies with the lead actors. Vladimir Korenev and Anastasiya Vertinskaya are both dark-haired beauties, which gives the film considerable visual appeal, but it is their performances that resonate. Unlike many genre pictures where characterization is secondary to special effects, *Amphibian Man* takes the time to create real depth with the main characters.

Ichthyandr is no one-dimensional *Man from Atlantis*. He is not simply a lovesick teen pining for the girl of his dreams, but a man — albeit a half-fish man — capable of deeply melancholic introspection. Take a look at the reviews for American film counterparts to *Amphibian Man* — *The Creature from the Black Lagoon* to name one — and "introspection" isn't a word you'll see very often.

Anastasiya Vertinskaya, already a popular actress at the time *Amphibian Man* was made, adds nice touches that elevate the role from that of love interest to pivotal character. In one fantasy scene she emphasizes the difference between her and Ichthyandr in a subtle but interesting way. Dressed in a silvery suit just like Ichthyandr's, she swims alongside him, but as he glides gracefully through the water, undulating his body like a true water creature, she swims by kicking her legs — like a human. It is a small detail, but it ingeniously illustrates the huge difference between them.

Photographed in Baku, Azerbaijan, the movie boasts high production value, although some of the special effects haven't dated particularly well. The effectiveness of the pivotal shark attack scene is blunted somewhat by some bad matte work, but other underwater scenes are breathtakingly shot. Overall the cinematography fares better on land. One sequence featuring Ichthyandr running through the neon lit city stands out as particularly memorable.

Of course it wouldn't be a vintage Russian film without a philosophical treatise, but once again, breaking with the mold of its contemporaries, *Amphibian Man* soft-pedals the propaganda. Each of the male characters embodies a doctrine, but the messages aren't as cut and dried as they are in other period Russian films. Don Pedro, for instance, could be seen as the personification of evil capitalism, a Mephistophelian who gets what he wants by any means necessary, but in the end even he is revealed to be not such a bad guy; and according to one writer Ichthyandr represents "emotional communism." He's an innocent who doesn't understand why everyone can't share in the bountiful pleasures offered by life. It's close to communist dogma, but with a simplistic, naive edge.

One of the pleasures of *Amphibian Man* is the way in which it plays with your perceptions of what a Soviet film from the period should be, both in terms of propaganda and style. Part *Creature from the Black Lagoon* and part *Beauty and the Beast*, *Amphibian Man* is a charming, multi-dimensional blend of crazy science — gill transplants! — and heart-tugging romance.

Availability: On DVD

THE ASTRONAUT FARMER (2006)

I think Billy Bob Thornton is one of the best actors working today. Too often he falls back on his comfortable grumpy-drunk-guy persona in movies like *Bad News Bears* and *Bad Santa*, but when he breaks free of his tried and true acting tricks the results can be impressive. In a movie from filmdom's only twin co-directing siblings, the Polish brothers, Thornton hands in a moving performance as a man with his head quite literally in the clouds.

"The role of Charlie absolutely resonated with me," Thornton told me in 2007. "I grew up as a dreamer, that's all I did. That's why I made horrible grades in school. This character is no stranger to me. I've been known as an eccentric and gone off and gambled everything to achieve something and failed and succeeded and everything else."

Charlie Farmer (Thornton) is an engaging oddball, an inspirational American folk hero who won't let anything stand between him and his dreams. A former NASA employee, he has left the astronaut program to run his family's farm after the death of his father. An engineer by trade, he runs the cattle farm by day and by night builds a giant rocket ship in his barn. Farmer may have left NASA but his dreams of visiting outer space didn't stop there. Farmer, his wife (another supportive wife role for Virginia Madsen) and children become media darlings when the FBI swoop down on his operation looking for weapons of mass destruction and leak the story to the press.

In one of the movie's high points Thornton delivers a speech about the importance of imagination — how when he was young people told him if he had dreams he could be anything he wanted to be. A lesser actor might have been tempted to milk the emotion out of the scene, but Thornton underplays it and as a result provides one of the movie's most persuasive moments.

"When you read a speech like that in script [you think] 'That's the one, how could I not do that,' but at the same time as an actor that's the kind of speech you have to be careful of because you don't want to overdo it," said Thornton. "There was some talk, not by the Polish brothers, they were all right with me, but from the higher-ups who wanted that speech to be a big rousing, emotional yelling kind of thing. I said, 'Guys, that's not going to happen.' I think the more you can just *say* that kind of stuff . . . just *say* it to people rather than make a point of it, the more effective it is."

The Astronaut Farmer works on several levels. The Polish brothers have stepped out from behind the art house veneer that informed their past work — *Northfolk, Jackpot* and *Twin Falls Idaho* — to make a film that has one foot in the mainstream, but doesn't betray their roots. The movie is beautiful to look at, with a soft glow that feels timeless and nostalgic, but is also rebellious.

When asked "Mr. Farmer, how do we know you aren't constructing a WMD?" by a NASA committee member, Farmer replies, "Sir, if I was building a weapon of mass destruction, you wouldn't be able to find it," with a cutting charm that wouldn't be out of place in *Mr. Smith Goes to Washington.*

"This movie is also a little subversive," says Thornton. "It has got its little knocks against the system. There are actually a couple of heavy statements. If this was a big political movie and you heard those lines those would be like big moments in the movie, and here they kind of go by.

"What's great about the Polish brothers is that even though they're making an emotional drama here they're not exactly normal all the time," Thornton continues. "They add a lot of humor and great moments that maybe wouldn't be in some movies of this nature. A lot of times those movies are quite earnest but this one has got a whimsy about it."

The Astronaut Farmer is a warm family film that breathes new life into the old "follow your dreams" storyline.

Availability: On DVD

"I got everything I own on the line . . . but it's bigger than me."
— MELVIN VAN PEEBLES (PORTRAYED BY SON MARIO VAN PEEBLES) IN *BAADASSSSS!*

BAADASSSSS! (2003)

In 1971 a notorious film by Melvin Van Peebles created a buzz that still reverberates today. The low-budget *Sweet Sweetback's Baadasssss Song* broke box office records at the few theaters brave or smart enough to show it, becoming the number one independent film of the year. The film's financial showing, however, was only part of its success.

For the first time in American cinema an African-American film-maker unleashed a story about a black man who emerged victorious over his white adversaries. In doing so Van Peebles captured the zeitgeist of an entire race of people used to being marginalized on film. It kick-started the blaxploitation genre and inspired a whole generation of filmmakers. It's not a stretch to say that every subsequent African-American film owes a debt to *Sweet Sweetback* and without it we might not have filmmakers such as John Singleton or Spike Lee working in mainstream film today.

Van Peebles' groundbreaking work on *Sweet Sweetback* has been documented several times. The man himself wrote a book about the movie called *Sweet Sweetback's Baadasssss Song: A Guerilla Filmmaking*

Manifesto. The documentary *How to Eat Your Watermelon in White Company (and Enjoy It)* directed by Joe Angio delves into Van Peebles' complex and often challenging personality, and has a 90 percent approval rating on Rottentomatoes.com, but it was another filmmaker and *Sweet Sweetback* cast member who really nailed the difficult birth of this indie film classic.

"I went to my dad to try and option the rights to the book and he said, 'I love you, but I don't want to get screwed on this deal,'" said Mario Van Peebles, son of Melvin and of German actress Maria Marx. "And then he said, 'Just don't make me too damn nice.'"

The beginning moments of *Baadasssss!* find Melvin (Mario Van Peebles, playing his own father) in a pitch session with his producer Howie (Saul Rubinek). His last movie, *Watermelon Man* (in which a bigoted white man gets firsthand knowledge on what it's like to be a black man), starring Godfrey Cambridge, is just about to hit theaters and he's looking for a new project to direct. His agent suggests a comedy called *Fried Chicken Man,* but Van Peebles isn't biting.

He wants to do something else. Something revolutionary. He says his next film won't star "some bougie or clown, like they always do, but a real street brother getting the man's foot out his ass." To his producer's dismay he describes a "ghetto western" in which a black man kills two policemen and gets away with it. "Who's gonna wanna see that?" asks 13-year-old Mario (Khleo Thomas). "Black guys always die at the end."

Realizing no studio would finance this hot button story Melvin walks away from a cushy three-picture deal with Columbia Pictures to enter the shark-infested waters of independent production. With money raised from friends and colleagues he begins production on *Sweet Sweetback's Baadasssss Song* under the pretext that he's making a porno film. If the unions think he's making a dirty movie, he reasons, they'll leave him alone.

Production is fraught with difficulty. Death threats are phoned in and at one point his entire crew gets arrested — "They thought my telephoto lens was a bazooka!" The pressure drives Melvin to the brink.

During post-production his health fails and he nearly goes blind while working in the editing room. Things don't get any easier once the film is complete and Melvin must think outside the box to get distribution and draw an audience for his X-rated picture.

Baadasssss! is a warts-and-all portrayal of the elder Van Peebles that mirrors the wild independent soul of the film it celebrates. Shot digitally for just $1 million, *Baadasssss!* breathes the same air as its predecessor.

"We made it in the same spirit," said Mario, whose film debut came at age 13 in *Sweet Sweetback.* "I think we had one day less to shoot it. Totally independent, you know, ragtag mixed crew. That helped keep me in the role too because I was writing, directing and producing and under all that stress that this cat [Melvin] was under."

There was at least one problem Mario had that Melvin didn't have to deal with. Because he was the film's director, and playing a director in the film-within-the-film, there was often confusion on the set.

"There were definitely times when I would yell 'CUT!' and because I was playing him directing, they would cut! And I was like 'NO, MAN! I meant cut as Melvin, not cut as Mario!'"

Baadasssss! tells an interesting piece of Van Peebles family history, but avoids the pitfalls of other family made biographies. Where many sons may have had the inclination to deify their fathers, particularly one as accomplished as Melvin, Mario treats him fairly, but has clearly taken off the kid gloves. Melvin is portrayed as a tortured soul, arrogant and egotistical, who puts his work before everything, including his family. The result is an inside look at the creative process of a driven man who was at the vanguard of a cultural revolution.

Also fascinating are the film's portrayals of Melvin's battles with almost everyone as he struggled to get the film made and in front of audiences. His final and most publicized skirmish actually helped the movie find its market.

"I wouldn't let [the Film Board] rate the film," Melvin told me in 2002, remembering his battle to get *Sweet Sweetback* a fair rating, "but the rule from the Film Board said if you shot in the United States and you don't go to the United States Film Board, you have to take an automatic X. So, I took the X, but I knew because the jury was all white, and I said, 'That is not a jury of my peers.'

"I made T-shirts, which I made a bundle with. The T-shirts said, 'Rated X By An All-White Jury,' and the logo said that too.

"[Film Board guru] Jack Valenti went ballistic! And I said 'Wait a minute, they're all white aren't they?' 'Yes, but Mel, that doesn't mean anything!' And I said the reason I spelled the title "Badass" as I did, is that the few papers who were sympathetic [and would print the advertisement] could get away with it because it was a misspelling."

As we see in *Baadasssss!* the clever ploy to exploit the X-rating only increased *Sweet Sweetback*'s mystique and audiences flocked to it to see what all the fuss was about, despite the fact that only two theaters in the United States would screen the movie.

"The opening night we made more money than the theater had made in the week before in the opening night," said Melvin, "and they hadn't opened the balcony in 15 years!"

Baadasssss! is an inspiring tribute to Melvin Van Peebles, a man who did it his way, and succeeded not only personally but culturally as well.

"It's like *Seabiscuit* on two feet!" Melvin says.

Availability: On DVD

"... And now, we begin our story with a phrase that is like a time machine for children: Once Upon a Time ..."
— JEAN COCTEAU'S INTRO TO *LA BELLE ET LA BÊTE*

LA BELLE ET LA BÊTE (1946)

Poet Paul Éluard said that to understand Jean Cocteau's version of *La Belle et la Bête*, you must love your dog more than your car. His comment is baffling only if you haven't seen the movie. Once seen it's apparent that *La Belle et la Bête* is so rewarding because it values the organic elements of the film — even the special effects are handmade — and refuses to allow the technical aspects of the film to interfere with the humanity of the story.

Loosely based on the classic Jeanne-Marie Leprince de Beaumont fairy tale, the action in *La Belle et la Bête* begins when a poverty-stricken merchant (Marcel André) pilfers a rose from a grand estate owned by a strange creature (Jean Marais). The Beast strikes a deal with the man. He'll spare the life of the merchant in return for the hand of one of the man's daughters. Reluctantly the merchant offers Belle (Josette Day), a beautiful girl who had been courted by the oafish Avenant (also played by Jean Marais). At first she is repulsed by the Beast, who looks like the love child of the Wolf Man and Mrs. Chewbacca, but over time his tender ways and nightly offers of marriage warm her heart and she learns to love him for his inner beauty.

Cocteau's version strays from the original story with the addition of a subplot involving Avenant's scheme to kill the Beast and make off with his treasures and an unexpected magical personality switcheroo.

It's meant to be a happy ending, but not everyone loved the new coda. When Marlene Dietrich saw an early cut of the film at a private screening, she squeezed Cocteau's hand and said, "Where is my beautiful Beast?"

Other audiences embraced Cocteau's vision. In his diary the poet wrote of a test screening held for the technicians in the Joinville Studio were the film had been made. "The welcome the picture received from that audience of workers was unforgettable," he wrote. "It was my greatest reward. Whatever happens nothing will ever equal the grace of that ceremony organized by a little village of workmen whose trade is the packaging of dreams."

The whole film feels touched by magic, from Henri Alekan's photography, which Cocteau described as having the "soft gleam of hand polished old silver," to the dreamlike delirium of the slow motion and other in-camera special effects to the enchanting fantasy sets that include candle chandeliers held by real human arms and living statues.

Some have criticized *La Belle et la Bête* for its straightforwardness, complaining that the characters are simply drawn, the story one-dimensional. Taking that view, however, misses Cocteau's point. At the beginning of the film he asks for "childlike simplicity," inviting the viewer to connect with their inner child, eschew cynicism and embrace naiveté for the film's 96 minute running time. In 1946 the request was meant as a salve for a post-occupation France that was still dealing with the aftermath of a terrible war. Today, in an increasingly contemptuous world, the message still seems timely and welcome.

Availability: On Criterion DVD

"It's a shame that I didn't marry someone who was my intellectual equal."
— ED AVERY (JAMES MASON) ABOUT
HIS WIFE LOU (BARBARA RUSH) IN *BIGGER THAN LIFE*

BIGGER THAN LIFE (1956)

A year after pulling back the veil on teenage angst in *Rebel Without a Cause*, director Nicholas Ray teamed with James Mason to lay bare the problems of the establishment. Chosen by Jean-Luc Godard as one of the ten greatest American films of all time, *Bigger Than Life* is a forceful drama about an all-American family man pushed over the edge by cortisone addiction.

Based on real-life events as reported in a *New Yorker* article by Berton Rouche, *Bigger Than Life* stars James Mason as Ed Avery, a schoolteacher forced to work a second job at night as a cab dispatcher to make ends meet. He chalks up the occasional sharp pain to overwork, but when he blacks out the diagnosis reveals something much more serious. He is suffering from a rare case of inflammation of the arteries, a condition that could kill him within the year. His only hope is the experimental "wonder drug" cortisone, which could prolong his life.

At first the treatment seems to work. He feels good, energized and self-confident, but soon some troubling psychological side effects emerge. As extreme 'roid rage grips him, he becomes haughty — even going so far as to tell a PTA group that "childhood is a congenital disease" — scornful and abusive, mistreating those around him, with his loving wife Lou (Barbara Rush) and child (Christopher Olsen) taking the brunt of the ill-treatment. Edging closer to the brink of madness, Ed's scorn for his life of "petty domesticity" leads to the idea of sacrificing his son just like Abraham did in the Bible. When Lou reminds him that God halted Abraham, Ed bellows, "God was wrong!"

There's a lot going on here. *Bigger Than Life* predates *American Beauty*'s take on suburban ennui by forty years, attacking the complacency of middle class life and social conformity. At the same time it examines drug abuse, dissects the American male psyche and the breakdown that occurs when people throw accepted social mores out the window. It's a tall order to cram all that into one 95-minute film, but it succeeds because of Ray's carefully focused direction and the humanity that Mason brings to the role.

A lesser actor may have pushed the character of Ed into over-the-top or camp territory but Mason never allows the audience to lose contact with the real man under the chemically induced rage. *Reefer Madness* this ain't. Mason, working with Ray and uncredited screenwriters Gavin Lambert and Clifford Odets, molded the script from a straightforward medical case study into a story that lives and breathes.

Ray and Mason present the changes in Ed gradually. It's a slow burn that first transforms him into a right-wing ideologue who develops an unreasonable moral and mental standard for his family before building to a homicidal crescendo. Mason's intense portrayal of Ed's bubbling cauldron of frustrations and anxieties, all presented in a voice choked with anger, represent his finest performance onscreen.

Ray's visual handling of the film is masterful; he uses both bold colors and atmospheric lighting to perfectly convey the film's changing moods. In one effective scene Ed hovers over his son as the boy does his math homework. Ed's shadow against the wall looks like a hawk ready to swoop down on its prey as the older man harangues his son. Just as strong are the film's sets which bring to life Ed's countenance in architectural form. The home's downstairs — the common areas open to everyone including neighbors and friends — are sparkling examples of 1950s charm while upstairs, hidden from view, are Ed's study and the bedrooms. They are ominous places, dark and secretive, decorated with broken mirrors that reflect Ed's shattered mind.

Bigger Than Life is the grandfather of *American Beauty*, the evil stepdad of *Blue Velvet*, a movie whose radical ideas about the status quo so upset censors in the late '50s that they tightened their grip on films with subversive messages.

Availability: Hard to find

"If this movie doesn't make your skin crawl . . . it's on too tight!"
— ADVERTISING TAGLINE FOR *BLACK CHRISTMAS*

BLACK CHRISTMAS (1974)

Canada is a nation of firsts. Torontonian Don Munro built the first table hockey game here in the early 1930s. Other parts of the country can lay claim to the Jolly Jumper, the celebration of Labour Day, artificial hearts, the Robertson square-head screwdriver, or the mixing of the world's first Bloody Caesar. The country has broken ground in many fields, including film. Florence Lawrence, the first performer to be identified by name onscreen, was born in Hamilton, Ontario, while the first aboriginal actor to portray a Native American on television, Jay Silverheels, hailed from the Six Nations Indian Reserve in Brantford, Ontario.

In a more macabre vein, without a groundbreaking 1974 Canadian horror film there might never have been a Jason Voorhees, Freddy Krueger or Michael Myers. Between them the gruesome threesome have sliced and diced their way through at least two dozen movies, but the mayhem they imposed on promiscuous college girls and teens owes much to one film made in Toronto, a movie *Film Threat* magazine calls "the first modern slasher movie."

Director Bob Clark didn't invent the slasher film with *Black*

Christmas — arguably *Psycho, Peeping Tom* or *Bay of Blood (Reazione a catena)* were the granddaddies of gore — but he did establish the format. Mix and match the fear of an unwelcome visitor to a sorority house brimming with randy college girls, a holiday-turned-violent theme, the anonymous phone call used to terrorize girls, a motiveless killer, a mysterious male stalking young women and a female lead who must conquer her own fear in order to stay alive and you have the plot of dozens of films that were to follow.

Shot in Toronto between February and May 1974 on a budget of roughly $600,000, *Black Christmas* is about an unseen psychotic killer named Billy who makes disturbing, obscenity-laced phone calls to a group of sorority girls. Soon he escalates from one-sided phone sex to dispatching the girls one by one in brutal fashion.

"It was originally called *Stop Me*," says Clark, who was killed in an April 2007 car accident. "I don't think I'm taking unfair credit, but *Black Christmas* was my title, my idea. I love the contrast of the idea of Christmas, the jolliest of all seasons with this dark kind of imagery. Both a horror film and Christmas have tremendous trappings that make a nice juxtaposition."

Apparently others agreed with him. In the next two decades a tsunami of holiday themed horrors — Christmas and otherwise — drifted into theaters: *My Bloody Valentine, New Year's Evil, April Fool's Day* and a Santa's sack of movies featuring death by Christmas tree light.

What sets *Black Christmas* apart from the rest of the Christmas horror pack are the memorable characters. The standout is a pre–Lois Lane Margot Kidder as the sharp-featured brunette Barb, whose alcoholic tendencies foreshadowed the actress's troubled real life. "One of my favorite memories is Margot coming to the set for her famous turtles-screwing-for-three-days scene," said Clark. "She was supposed to be imbibing, and she *was*, to get in character. She was definitely there."

As Barb, Kidder thumbs her nose at any form of authority — be it the thick as a brick Sergeant Nash or the threatening caller — and steals every scene she's in with her reckless energy. When she slurs, "This is a sorority house, not a convent," it is lewd, raunchy and sexy-funny.

Not the typical sorority slasher movie heroine, Argentine-born Olivia Hussey plays as Jess. Hussey brings a quiet strength to Jess that hints at a fountain of inner resolve. It has often been said that slasher films are the most republican of genres because of the punishment meted out on people who go against conservative middle-American values. In other words smoking pot and jumping from bed to bed is bound to earn you a one-way ticket to hell courtesy of some masked madman, while the virgin of the group usually makes it through blood-ied but unbowed. In *Black Christmas* Jess rebels against her boyfriend, planning to have an abortion. Clearly she is no virgin, and yet she is the sole survivor of Billy's rampage.

The boyfriends of Clare and Jess — Chris Hayden (Art Hindle) and Peter Smythe (Keir Dullea) — are studies in opposites. The Halifax-born Hindle plays Chris as earnest and loving (although he does wear a raccoon coat), a stand-up guy who loves his girlfriend even if their rela-tionship is chaste.

Keir Dullea as Peter is a different story. Peter is an eccentric musician who realizes too late that he has traded one passion for another. His love of music overshadowed his feelings for Jess and now she is backing away from him. He is prone to fits of anger, and this hotheaded behavior is the perfect red herring (or McGuffin as Hitchcock used to call them) to make us think he is the killer. It is interesting to imagine how the char-acter might have differed if Clark's first choice for Peter, Malcolm McDowell, had accepted the part.

During shooting Dullea was only available for a week as he had other commitments in Europe. In his short time on the film, he never met Margot Kidder and worked with John Saxon only briefly. "My total experience with working with anybody was Olivia Hussey," he said. Clark shot all of Dullea's scenes first and in editing made it appear as though he was there for the whole time.

Like *Black Christmas*'s other imported movie star, Olivia Hussey,

Keir Dullea's early career showed great promise, but didn't mature into full-blown movie stardom. Two films hinted at his star potential — 1962's *David and Lisa* and *Bunny Lake Is Missing* in 1965 — but it wasn't until he played astronaut Dave Bowman in Kubrick's *2001: A Space Odyssey* in 1968 that his full promise was reached. He failed to really capitalize on the notoriety that movie earned him, leading Noel Coward to famously quip, "Keir Dullea, gone tomorrow."

Uncredited but very effective are the actors who voiced the obscene phone calls. The disembodied voices of unseen evil were supplied by a number of people including Bob Clark, actor Nick Mancuso and several female actors. "[The phone calls are] a compilation of about five actors' voices," says Clark. "I remember what Nick brought it to was an intensity that certainly I had never seen before," said sound designer and composer Carl Zittrer who engineered the calls, mixing in reverb and an array of spooky sounds.

Was *Black Christmas* the inspiration for John Carpenter's seminal slasher flick *Halloween*? It's a question that has sparked a fair amount of debate, so let's break it down. There are similarities that cannot be denied between the two films.

Most obviously both films open with a point of view shot of the killer creeping around the outside of a house at night. Clark uses this shot, and many POV angles to great effect in *Black Christmas*, but he wasn't the first to use the subjective camera to create fear. Clark simply took an old idea and put a new spin on it. He would later say that he hoped to break new ground by "employing some, if not new, certainly reworked and rethought cinematic ideas." Mario Bava used distorted POV in *Blood and Black Lace*, and Hitchcock used it in the shower scene in *Psycho*, just to name a couple famous examples. Clark's innovation in *Black Christmas* was to make the point of view shot his centerpiece, using it to create a mood of terror rather than a secondary complement to the horror already onscreen.

Clark's film is unique in that we never see the killer, he moves in the shadows, a subliminal figure of terror unlike the very visible Michael

Myers in *Halloween*. What they share, however, is motive — neither of them has one. They are striking out at these victims for no reason. Carpenter says he modelled Michael Myers' relentless passion for killing on a film by Michael Crichton. "I must tell you that I cribbed from *Westworld* — Yul Brynner as a robot gunfighter who malfunctions and keeps coming after them. I just took it a step further, but I gave you no explanation." Pre–*Black Christmas* movie homicidal maniacs always had a motive, but we never know why Billy targeted the Pi Kappa Sig house or its inhabitants.

There is one major difference between the two — Billy is literally a raving lunatic, screaming and grunting his way through the film, whereas Michael Myers (and later, Jason Voorhees of the *Friday the 13th* films) is unnaturally silent. It may have just been weird synchronicity that two films about homicidal maniacs open with unusual POV shots and share an ideological bent, but there is no question that *Black Christmas* and *Halloween* are similar.

"I absolve John Carpenter every time," said Clark. "The facts are that I was going to direct a film John wrote a couple of years after *Black Christmas*. He was a big fan of *Black* Christmas . . . and he asked me if I was ever going to do a sequel.

"I said, 'I would make it the following fall and somehow in the interim the killer had been caught and had been institutionalized. I would have him escape one night, and now he is free in the community . . . and he starts stalking them again at the *Black Christmas* sorority house, and I was going to call it *Halloween*.'

"I think he was influenced by it, as were a few others. When you think about what John Carpenter did, [however], wrote a script — really quite different from that idea — directed it, edited it and did the music. It was a terrific piece of work. Maybe the title *Halloween* he should have given me a little of, but I didn't own that either."

Despite the rave reviews, and the prediction of Olivia Hussey's personal psychic that the film would make a bundle, *Black Christmas* didn't fare well at the box office in the U.S.A. To boost admissions, in some markets the movie's name was changed to *A Stranger in the House* to avoid confusion with the flurry of blaxploitation films that were appearing at the time. It was also released as *Silent Night, Evil Night*.

Viewed through today's eyes the movie holds up. It is very stylish, although slower in sections, and with a lower body count than modern horror fans are used to, but it is still capable, more than three decades after its conception, to raise goose bumps. A testament to the film's enduring ability to scare came when NBC cancelled an airing of the film because they felt it was too intense for television audiences. It has also earned the seal of approval from Quentin Tarantino, who cites it as one of his favorite movies.

"It's an interesting film," said Clark, "I thought it was a good, scary, classic horror story, and those have a way of surviving."

Availability: On DVD

"The family that stays together slays together!"
— ADVERTISING TAGLINE FOR *BLOODY MAMA*

BLOODY MAMA (1970)
- - - - - - - - -

Popular culture has kept the rambunctious myth of gangland matriarch Kate "Ma" Barker alive and kicking. She has inspired novels (James Hadley Chase's *No Orchids for Miss Blandish*), songs (the 1977 Boney M single "Ma Baker" and a concept album called *II* by Maylene and the Sons of Disaster), a whole raft of criminal characters on the big and small screen (Ma Jarrett in the 1949 James Cagney movie *White Heat*, Theresa Russell's 1996 film *Public Enemies* and Ma Parker on *Batman*)

RICHARD'S FAVORITE ADVERTISING TAGLINES FOR HORROR FILMS WITH CHRISTMAS THEMES

1. "You've made it through Halloween, now try and survive Christmas!" – *Silent Night, Deadly Night* (1984)
2. "You'd better take care . . . Santa is coming to town!" – *Christmas Evil* (a.k.a. *You Better Watch Out*) (1980)
3. "He's chillin'. . . and killin'. . ." – *Jack Frost* (1996)
4. "His slay bells are ringing!" – *Santa Claws* (1996)
5. "'Twas the night before Christmas . . . and everyone's dead." – *The Christmas Season Massacre* (2001)
6. "Terror is coming home for the holidays." – *Black Christmas* (2006)
7. "They don't work for Santa anymore!" – *Elves* (1990)
8. "He's making a list . . . pray you're not on it." – *Santa's Slay* (2005)
9. "He's icin' & slicin'. . ." – *Jack Frost 2: Revenge of the Mutant Killer Snowman* (2000)
10. "It's beginning to look a lot like – bloodshed!"
    "The sort of Christmas you don't dream of."
    "'Twas the night before Christmas and all through the house, a creature was stirring."
    "A Christmas of another colour, brings a killer on the loose."
    – *Black Christmas* (1974)

and even in the funny pages (Ma Dalton in the *Lucky Luke* comic strip, Ma Beagle and the Beagle Boys characters in Scrooge McDuck), but in real life Ma Barker wasn't the criminal mastermind of popular legend.

According to one Barker clan member, "the old woman couldn't plan breakfast. We'd sit down to plan a bank job [and] she'd go in the other room and listen to *Amos 'n Andy* or hillbilly music on the radio." Luckily there's no rule that says movies have to stick to the facts, otherwise we wouldn't have *Bloody Mama*, Roger Corman's sordidly entertaining, but almost completely fictional account of her life.

Despite the disclaimer "Any similarity to Kate Barker and her sons is intentional," the screenplay is steeped in violent underworld fantasy that was more inspired by the success of *Bonnie and Clyde* than any connection to Barker's reality. Corman, hoping to cash in on the wave of popularity generated by the Warren Beatty/Faye Dunaway outing, quickly slapped together an exploitation film to take advantage of the public's newfound interest in Depression-era hoodlums.

"The words 'exploitation films' have many meanings," Corman told me in 2003. "You could say almost every film ever made is an exploitation film because to me, you are taking the subject and exploiting it. You are investigating it, and on a commercial level, you are generally picking a subject that is of some excitement or of interest. For instance, it might be a horror film, it might be science-fiction film, it might be a murder mystery, it could be a comedy, it could be a musical . . . anything that you could use in the subject to exploit that subject to get an audience."

To this end Corman worked with screenwriter Robert Thom (the pen behind *Wild in the Streets*, *Death Race 2000* and *The Witch Who Came from the Sea*) to craft a story that took the basic facts — Barker was the matriarch of a family of criminal sons — and injected hot button topics like drug addiction, homosexuality, incest and sadism to add spice. The result won't win any awards for accuracy but it makes for one crazy cinematic ride.

The story is fairly simple, mostly made up of a series of vicious vignettes. Corman sets the tone right off the top with a prologue that sees Kate Barker as a child being raped by her brothers. "Blood's thicker than water," says her hillbilly father.

Then things really take a depraved turn.

The story jumps ahead to the Depression years. Barker (Shelley

Winters) has dumped her spineless husband and set off on a brutal crime rampage with her kids — the sadistic Herman (Don Stroud), ex-con Fred (Robert Walden), hophead Lloyd (Robert De Niro) and wallflower Arthur (Clint Kimbrough). They terrorize the countryside, robbing banks, kidnapping millionaires, machine gunning an alligator named Old Joe to death and even stealing a pig!

Machine gun–toting Ma's thirst for villainy is eclipsed only by her taste for kinky sex. She beds her own sons and even seduces Fred's gay jailhouse lover (Bruce Dern). Ma's sexual and criminal spree continues until the bullet-ridden final showdown when the gang faces off with police in a bloody gun battle.

The addition of Shelley Winters in the Tommy gun–toting title role convinced the film's producers, the notoriously tight-fisted American International Pictures, to lavish a longer production schedule than usual on *Bloody Mama*.

"It was a four-week picture," Corman said, "and that was long for me. I don't think I'd done one before that ever required more than a three-week shoot. But I looked at the script and I said, 'This is going to be very tough. We're filming all over the state. We're going to be in the Ozarks, in northern Arkansas, then we're going to be filming around Little Rock and various other places. I really need four weeks.' And they gave them to me."

Four weeks may have been a luxury for Corman, who once shot an entire movie in less than 24 hours, but it's still a pretty tight schedule to pump out a feature film, and it shows in the final product. Anachronisms — everything from television antennas, modern strip malls and bikini tan lines — stand out like sore thumbs in this 1930s piece, but Corman can be forgiven the time-period transgressions because of the great energy he brings to every frame. The movie zips along, the furious pace matched only by the outrageous conduct of this highly dysfunctional family.

The folks on *The Jerry Springer Show* look downright tame compared to this bunch. Corman shines a light on the deviant and desperate behavior of these people, foreshadowing the kind of raw filmmaking favored by a future wave of directors (like Quentin Tarantino) whose powerful depictions of the criminal underbelly delight in pushing the boundaries of good taste. Corman's portrayal of incest and drug addiction was unflinching and, for the time, extreme. "Ma Barker made *The Wild Angels* and *The Trip* look about as menacing as fairy tales," he wrote in his book *How I Made a Hundred Movies in Hollywood and Never Lost a Dime.*

Corman shows a strong hand with his actors. Shelley Winters, the feisty method actor, brings her usual moxie to Ma, appearing to be on overdrive for the entire film. Her opening line at one of the bank robberies is a showstopper. "We're going to play Simon Says, and this," she says, holding up her Tommy gun, "is Simon."

It's entertaining stuff; she's so over-the-top you fear that once she's done chewing the scenery she might burst through the screen into the theater. Later in the film her manic reaction to the death of one of her sons — a churning vortex of jiggling flesh and shrieking — has to be seen to be believed. In his book Corman said that Winters was "certainly unlike any actor I had worked with before."

The rest of the cast are mostly B-movie regulars — Dern, Stroud, Kimbrough and Scatman Crothers — who all hand in journeyman work. But two other actors — one on the way down, the other on the ascent — really shine. Fifties ingenue Diane Varsi (best known for her Oscar-nominated role in *Peyton Place*) as Mona Gibson, the hardened hooker "who can do it better than Ma," takes a role that requires little more than taking her shirt off and gives it some real personality. Any actor who can deliver the line, "You should try my pie crust, little boy. It would melt in your mouth," with any sort of dignity deserves recognition.

Robert De Niro, then an unknown actor with just four credits on his resumé, throws himself into the role of Lloyd, a miserable junkie who resorts to sniffing glue when he can't score any heroin. "When you're working on those model airplanes you get to acting awfully silly," says Ma.

"For his part, he's reversed what he did later as Jake LaMotta in *Raging Bull* and Al Capone in *The Untouchables*," said Winters, who recommended the young actor for the part. "He stopped eating and lost weight as his addiction progressed. We roughly shot in sequence. He consumed vitamins, water, fruit juices and a little bit of nourishment. He lost close to thirty pounds and took on the haggard, sickly look of a junkie."

The extreme weight loss is a bit of a trick, but there's more to his work here than starvation. De Niro spent time with the Arkansas locals, studying the way they spoke and moved to create a well-rounded character and raise Lloyd beyond the hillbilly cliché favored by the other actors. On top of the accent he created a singsongy voice, punctuated with a giggle that gives vocal cadence to Lloyd's naive innocence. The role of Lloyd Barker didn't make De Niro a star, but it is a strong performance that hints at the greatness to come.

In *Bloody Mama* Corman sheds the shackles of good taste and shamelessly plays to the baser elements of the story. It horrified American critics at the time (although was better received in Europe), most of whom still had deep-rooted connections to the safe studio movies and were hopelessly out of step with youth culture. *Bloody Mama* must have seemed like Corman was flipping the bird to them, but Corman didn't make movies for critics, he made them for the people who actually paid to go to the theater. He knew audiences wanted him to push the envelope and once again he was spot-on. Audiences flocked to the story of Ma Barker and the movies it inspired such as *Big Bad Mama, Crazy Mama* and *Boxcar Bertha*.

Bloody Mama is great trashy fun that will appeal to fans of genre and B-movies. "It's still one of my favorite films," says Corman.

Availability: On DVD

Roger Corman Appreciation Society: Richard's Favorite Appearances of the Director on Film, Part One

1. *Apollo 13*: Ron Howard has worked for Roger Corman on
    both sides of the camera. In 1976 the former child star
    headed up the cast in the drive-in classic *Eat My Dust* and
    the following year he wrote, directed and starred in *Grand
    Theft Auto*. "If you do a good job on this picture," Corman told
    him, "you'll never have to work for me again." The film took in a
    bundle at the box office, leading to Howard's career as one of
    Hollywood's most successful directors. He never had to work
    for Corman again, but almost 20 years later Howard worked
    with his mentor, giving him a walk-on part as a congressman
    in *Apollo 13*.

2. *The Godfather, Part II*: Francis Ford Coppola was fresh out of
    film school when he was hired by Corman to create aliens for
    a sci-fi flick called *Battle Beyond the Sun*. He worked his way
    up the rickety Corman ladder, from recording sound on *The
    Young Racers* to eventually writing and directing a quickie
    horror film called *Dementia 13*, which Corman produced.
    Coppola paid tribute to his old boss by casting him as a
    senator in *Godfather, Part II*.

3. *The Howling*: Joe Dante got his start editing trailers for Corman,
    and like so many others, parlayed an entry level job into a
    directorial position. He directed one of the lowest budget
    Corman films ever, *Hollywood Boulevard*, and the *Jaws* rip-off
    Piranha before moving on to big studio films. In the 1981
    werewolf flick *The Howling* Dante poked fun at Corman's
    legendary reputation for cheapness by giving him a cameo as a
    man who checks a pay phone coin return slot for change.

4. *The Silence of the Lambs*: Jonathan Demme began as
    publicist on the film *Von Richtofen and Brown* (The Red

Baron) before writing scripts for *Angels Hard As They Come* (which he pitched as *Rashomon* on motorcycles) and *The Hot Box*. When he couldn't find a distributor for his directorial debut, the self-financed *Caged Heat*, Corman stepped in and agreed to release it. As a thanks Demme often uses Corman in small roles. He has a blink-and-you'll-miss-it appearance in *Philadelphia*, but a juicier role as FBI Director Hayden in *The Silence of the Lambs*.

5. *Cannonball!*: To cash in on the box office success of *Rollerball*, Corman hired Paul Bartel to direct *Death Race 2000*, a curious little film that moved the original's brutal sports story from the roller rink to the race track. Unfortunately, Bartel's vision of the film was more comedic than Corman wanted so much of Bartel's work was left on the cutting room floor, while another director was brought in to shoot violent inserts. Despite their creative differences Bartel continued to work for Corman (although only as an actor), and later cast him as the district attorney in the auto race movie *Cannonball!*

"What's human or inhuman is not for human decision."
– FLORA "SISSY" GOFORTH (ELIZABETH TAYLOR) IN *BOOM!*

BOOM! (1968)

Director John Waters calls *Boom!* the "best failed art film ever," and says he used it as a litmus test on all his first dates. If his potential partners didn't like it then there would be no second date.

I'd guess Waters didn't have a lot of return engagements.

The movie can best be described as an acquired taste, a film so awful it transcends badness and loops around 360 degrees to something approaching greatness. It isn't for everyone, but connoisseurs of great trash art will find something thrilling about *Boom!*

Based on a Tennessee Williams play *The Milk Train Doesn't Stop Here Anymore* and adapted by the playwright, *Boom!* sees Elizabeth Taylor playing Sissy Goforth, a fabulously wealthy boozehound with a long and storied martial history. Her wild years — and six husbands — behind her, Sissy is now living out her dying days on an isolated Mediterranean island, where she spends her time snapping at servants and committing her memoirs to audio tape. Her only friend, a gay neighbor known as the Witch of Capri (Noel Coward in a role written for a woman, and originally offered to Katharine Hepburn), comes to dinner. Otherwise, her life is quite meaningless until the appearance of Chris Flanders (Richard Burton), a penniless poet nicknamed the Angel of Death because of his habit of showing up on rich ladies' doorsteps a day before the undertaker. He shares her last 36 hours before shepherding her off to her great reward.

Nearly everyone who reviewed *Boom!* in 1968 took potshots at the movie and then again for the VHS release in 2000. Not me. I think it is an important movie, the kind of picture that should be studied at film schools as an example of what happens when well intentioned filmmakers go horribly, horribly off the rails.

So what's wrong with *Boom!*?

Much of the blame here must rest directly on the shoulders of director Joseph Losey (who "bragged" that he was the first filmmaker to lose money by pairing up Taylor and Burton). The once solid director of films like *Accident* and *Modesty Blaise* appears to be trying to test the endurance of his audience. Apparently anything he once knew about pacing or editing was thrown out the window somewhere around the time he signed on to make this movie. Mix the painful pacing with some ham-fisted editing and you are left wondering if this film actually had a director.

With its over-the-top histrionics, both in the dialogue and the delivery of the lines — check out Liz's coughing fit on the balcony — *Boom!* feels like a parody of a Tennessee Williams play, rather than the real thing. Liz and Dick drone on for 90 plus minutes, dropping such bon mots as, "Hot sun, cool breeze, white horse on the sea and a big shot of vitamin B in me!" and "You're the heart of a world that has no heart — the heartless world that you live in." The pair ham it up while spouting tongue-twisting dialogue that drips with self importance but has no dramatic logic. Often the characters seem to be talking only because they enjoy the sound of their own voices.

On the upside *Boom!* does feature beautiful scenery, some of the most outrageous costume design of the 1960s — check out Liz's Vegas-inspired kabuki gowns! — and one stunning zoom shot on Taylor's face as she looks out the window of her lonely castle. She was one of the world's great beauties and in this shot, just for a moment you get a hint of the inner life of this woman. It's a rare moment of genuine tension and intrigue in the film, but unfortunately it doesn't last.

Despite *Boom!* being Tennessee William's favorite film adaptation of any of his work — he claimed it was the only one that really captured his style — it fails on virtually every front, except that in its awfulness it has a campy charm, and for the ones who get the joke, great entertainment value.

As John Waters says, "It's the most ludicrous Tennessee Williams film you've ever seen. It's very important to me, it really personifies my tastes."

Availability: Hard to find

"Oh, isn't that wonderful? All the lowlifes in quiet city Boston are dropping dead and you think it's unrelated! Greenly, the day I want the Boston Police to do my thinking for me, I will have a fucking tag on my toe."

– PAUL SMECKER (WILLEM DAFOE) IN *THE BOONDOCK SAINTS*

THE BOONDOCK SAINTS (1999)

The Boondock Saints is notable for two reasons. First, it's a really fun crime drama that nobody saw when it was released and, second, it is witness to the kind of career flame-out by a director not seen in Hollywood since they set fire to the office building in *The Towering Inferno*.

The plot is fairly simple. Set in Boston, but shot mostly on location in Toronto, it's about a pair of brothers, Connor (Sean Patrick Flanery) and Murphy McManus (Norman Reedus), who accidentally rub out two Mafia wise guys during a bar brawl. Instead of doing hard time they are heralded as hometown heroes and the attention turns them into vigilantes who vow to make the streets safe again. Willem Dafoe plays a gay, conflicted FBI agent who must track down and arrest the brothers for murder even though they are making the city a safer place.

Director Troy Duffy, a pre-med dropout who moved to Los Angeles from New Hampshire to give the music biz a go, was inspired to pen the script following an incident in his apartment building. In 1996 Duffy came home one night to find the police wheeling a dead woman out of a drug dealer's apartment across the hall.

"Her leg was hanging over the side, and she had an army boot on," Duffy told journalist Amy Finch. "The heroin guy . . . comes running out of his apartment saying 'That bitch's got my money!' and slams his hand right down her boot. She'd been dead a couple of days."

Despite having no idea about how screenplays are put together he rented a computer and began writing a script, in an attempt to vent his anger and disgust at what he had just witnessed.

"I decided right there that out of sheer frustration, and not being able to afford a psychologist, I was going to write this. Think about it. People watching the news sometimes get so disgusted by what they see. Susan Smith drowning her kids; guys going into McDonald's, lighting up the whole place. You hear things that disgust you so much that even if you're Mother Teresa, there comes a breaking point. One day you're going to watch the news and you're going to say, 'Whoever did that despicable thing should pay with their life.' You think, for maybe just a minute, that whoever did that should die, without any fuckin' jury.

"I [decided I] was going to give everybody that sick fantasy. And tell it as truthfully as I could."

The finished script made the usual rounds in Hollywood, landing on the desk of Miramax bigwig Harvey Weinstein, who outbid all other comers for the property. For a first-timer the deal was huge. Miramax reportedly offered up $300,000 (or $450,000 depending on who you believe), gave Duffy directorial control and gave the go ahead for Duffy's band, The Brood, to do the soundtrack. To top it off Miramax threw in a 50 percent ownership of J. Sloane's, the bar where Duffy had been serving drinks to pay the rent.

There were disputes over casting and generally bad behavior on Duffy's part — "I made a lot of mistakes," he says. "I did not always know what the right thing to do was, I misbehaved, sure." In the ultimate Tinseltown CLM (career limiting move) he ticked off Miramax honcho Harvey Weinstein, who dropped the project before one foot of film rolled.

"I told them I'll jibe with them on every other domain," Duffy says. "If you want to cut my budget, if you want to film half of it in Toronto and half in Boston, I'll jibe with you everywhere except when it comes to casting. So they said, 'Well, Troy, we just can't deal with that.'"

Eventually the film was rescued by indie studio Franchise Films who allowed Duffy to cast *Boondock* the way he saw fit and to use his band on the soundtrack.

The result was a bloody, no-holds-barred crime drama that was dismissed by critics at the time as cheap Tarantino. Onscreen, the bartender-turned-director keeps things moving along at a good clip but offscreen he allowed his ego to get in the way, alienating pretty much everyone involved in the production. The bad reviews, which may have had as much to do with Duffy's bad rep and the movie's troubled production history, hurt the film's chances, but poor distribution doomed it to failure.

Released shortly after the school shootings in Columbine, Colorado, the movie fell victim to theater owners and distributors who were literally gun-shy to promote such a profane movie (the word "fuck" and its offshoots are used a total of 246 times) and one that celebrated violence. As a result *The Boondock Saints* only played in five theaters, grossing 30 grand and disappearing less than three weeks after opening.

Duffy's film, which seemed like a doomed picture found a second life on DVD, becoming a much-rented cult hit. "Blockbuster saved us," Duffy says. "They agreed to take it on exclusively, and from there the rest is history."

For the whole story (and a good companion piece to *Boondock Saints*) check out the documentary *Overnight*, which chronicles Duffy's short rise and free fall.

Availability: On DVD

> "One is always considered mad, if one discovers something that others cannot grasp."
> — DR. ERIC VORNOFF (BELA LUGOSI)

BRIDE OF THE MONSTER (1955)

Edward D. Wood Jr.'s legacy as the Holy Grail of the cinematically challenged is unfair. Writing in the 1980 book *The Golden Turkey Awards* film critics Michael and Harry Medved singled out Wood's movie *Plan 9 from Outer Space* in the Worst Movie Ever Made category while also hanging the title of Worst Director around his neck. Since then his name has been synonymous with failure and ridicule.

To be sure Mr. Wood was no Cecil B. DeMille, but he doesn't deserve the critical sneers leveled at his work. Movies like *Glen or Glenda* and *Jail Bait* were restricted by their über low budgets and appear hopelessly amateurish, littered by ridiculous special effects and melodramatic acting — but they are entertaining and isn't that what it's all about? Many directors have spent a lot more money and not come close to delivering the same kind of giddy fun that *The Sinister Urge* pulsates with.

Take Michael Bay; his movies make loads of money at the box office, but never fail to put me to sleep. Visually his films are spectacular feasts for the eyes. The former commercial director has a knack for making everything look shiny but having great taste doesn't make a great film director any more than great taste makes a Snickers bar a gourmet meal.

The difference between Ed D. Wood Jr. and Michael Bay is simple. Wood's films are inexpertly but lovingly made by someone who is desperate to share his vision. Bay's big glitzy movies feel like cynical money grabs more concerned with the bottom line than personal expression. I'm quite sure that if Bay had to undergo the trials and tribulations Wood had to suffer to get his movies made, he would run to the hills, or maybe just back to his big house in the Hollywood Hills.

Even though his enthusiasm usually trumped his capabilities, Wood was a true artist, a pioneer of the indie spirit, someone who fought tooth and nail to present his vision and — no matter how cockeyed that vision may have been — believed in it and his ability to capture it on film. In time this Hollywood outsider developed a unique do-it-yourself style akin to folk art; his crudely crafted pieces radiate with the passion of the artist.

One of his lesser known films, 1955's *Bride of the Monster*, predates *Plan 9 from Outer Space*, but is cut from the same cloth.

Wood claimed the idea for the film came to him in a dream. "I keep a pencil and pad beside my bed at night because many a dream turns out to be a good plot," he said. "That's where *Bride of the Monster* came from, although it was first called *Bride of the Atom*."

The story is credited to Wood and producer Alex Gordon, who disputes Wood's dream-state inspiration for the film, claiming it was *his* script and he "got Eddie involved to polish" to make it more appealing to its star Bela Lugosi. Whatever the case, it contains all the earmarks of a Wood production, the strange stream-of-consciousness dialogue, bizarre editing, inappropriate use of stock footage and a story that doesn't quite make sense.

Lugosi, in his last speaking role, plays Dr. Eric Vornoff, a mad scientist trying to create a race of atomic supermen. His beefy assistant Lobo is played by Swedish wrestler Tor Johnson, who at 6'3" and 300 pounds was so large that when he was on the road he frequently stole toilet seats from hotels to replace the ones he broke at home. The doctor has been terrorizing the woods around Lake Marsh, kidnapping people to use as guinea pigs in his twisted experiments. He needs a steady supply of victims because the high dose of radiation needed to transform them into mutants usually kills them. (His success rate might have something to do with the equipment he's using. His "high-tech" radiation zapper looks suspiciously like a photographic enlarger hanging from a mike stand and topped with a salad bowl.)

There's a twist when an old colleague of Vornoff's shows up to kidnap him and take him to the U.S.S.R. It seems Vornoff first hatched his plan to raise an army of nuclear giants while he was working for the Russian government. They thought the plan was outlandish and ran the mad scientist out of the country. Now they want him back and he doesn't want to go. When the Russian pulls a gun, Lobo saves his master's life by subduing the agent and feeding him to a giant octopus.

The Russian isn't the only unwelcome visitor. Janet Lawton (Loretta King), a cub reporter, has been snooping around. Worse, she's the girlfriend of Lieutenant Craig (Tony McCoy). Lobo finds her and brings her to Vornoff who prepares to experiment on her. He's interrupted by Craig who has been searching for his lost girlfriend. Once again Lobo uses his muscle to diffuse the situation when he grabs Craig from behind and chains him to a wall.

Vornoff continues his evil experiment on Janet, but something has changed. Lobo has developed a crush on the girl and just as the scientist is about to pull the switch that may well kill Janet, Lobo pounces on him, straps him to the table and zaps him with the lethal juice. Instead of killing the doctor the rays work and he is turned into an atomic superman. The experiment is finally a success! The doctor overpowers Lobo, grabs Janet and makes a break for the woods. With the police in hot pursuit Vornoff must avoid capture, but he really should be more worried about that giant octopus.

Like all of Wood's movies *Bride of the Monster* seems a little disjointed. Continuity is non-existent, the editing is peculiar and the ending is a bizarre non sequitur that involves a massive nuclear explosion. All of these shortcomings can be explained away, however, by Wood's fractured production schedule and budgetary problems — one colleague said that Ed Wood made Roger Corman look like a big spender.

The movie, which should have taken the director no more than 20 days to shoot, actually became a sprawling start-and-stop marathon that dragged on for just over a year. Wood would raise enough cash to shoot 10 or 15 minutes of film, run through that money and shut the production down. Every few weeks he'd move to a new studio leaving behind a trail of burned investors. Finally, a man named Donald McCoy stepped in with enough funds to complete the film. McCoy's money, however, came with two caveats. First, he wanted his son Tony, an actor Wood later called "the worst I ever had," to play one of the leads and, second, he insisted that the movie literally end with a bang. The money man convinced Wood to include the out-of-the-blue nuclear blast ending as a message against the American-Russian nuclear arms race. Wood, desperate to finish the movie, agreed on both counts.

Despite the film's weaknesses the presence of Bela Lugosi elevates the proceedings. In 1931 Lugosi had become a major movie star — it was rumored that after the release of *Dracula* he received more fan mail from females than Clark Gable. Now he was on the skids. Drug addicted, near broke and frail he was working for $750 a day, a sum, Wood pointed out, that was more than he made for *Dracula*. He may have been in poor health, but the 73-year-old came alive when the camera rolled.

Wood utilizes some of the classic Lugosi moves from past movies — the tight hypnotic close-ups of his eyes and the sinister double-jointed finger movements are pure *Dracula* — and takes full advantage of Lugosi's menacing aura. Parts of the performance are, of course, ridiculous. For instance, the platform shoe–wearing body double who battles Lobo clearly isn't Lugosi.

The famous octopus battle scene, Lugosi's final scene in the film, has become the stuff of indie film legend. According to legend Wood "borrowed" the cephalopod (originally seen in the John Wayne film *Wake of the Red Witch*) from the props storage vault at Republic Studios. Trouble was he forgot to liberate the motor that operated the giant beast's tentacles. When it came time to shoot Lugosi was simply lowered down on top of the creature in freezing cold water and told to wave the tentacles in the air, simulating a life-or-death struggle. Lugosi heroically thrashes about with the gigantic beast, but the limitations of a 73-year-old man trying to manipulate the octopus puppet are painfully obvious. "When we got through with the scene, he drank a whole bottle of Jack Daniels just to get warm," said Wood.

Another often cited gaffe, however, is unfounded. It's been widely suggested that Lugosi, saying his lines through a haze of alcohol and drugs, says in one scene that Lobo is as gentle as "a kitchen." Actually, the line is "gentle as a kitten" and that's exactly what he says, though filtered through his heavy Romanian accent.

Lugosi's legacy suffered over the years. His low-rent work with Wood and others tarnished his reputation, but it was a film made after his death that may have left the most lasting and erroneous impression about the man.

Tim Burton's 1994 film *Ed Wood* sees Martin Landau play Lugosi as a bitter, foul-mouthed man with a grudge against Boris Karloff. In the film he calls Karloff a variety of names, including "limey cocksucker." Never happened, according to Forrest J. Ackerman. The founder of the *Famous Monsters of Filmland* magazine and a friend of Lugosi told me in 1995 that "he was a real European gentleman. I never heard him say so much as a hell or a damn and they [*Ed Wood* filmmakers] had him uttering these scatological things about Boris Karloff that he never would have uttered in real life. I don't think he even knew the term 'limey.'"

Though not as well known as Wood's masterpiece *Plan 9 from Outer Space, Bride of the Monster* is equally enjoyable. Michael Bay fans may not get it, but connoisseurs of outsider art certainly will.

See also: *I Woke Up Early the Day I Died.*

Availability: Limited on VHS or as part of the Ed Wood DVD box set

> "I made that armor . . . It's not magic; it's just shiny."
> — **WILHELM GRIMM (MATT DAMON) IN** *THE BROTHERS GRIMM*

THE BROTHERS GRIMM (2005)

Director Terry Gilliam, the only American member of the legendary Monty Python comedy troupe, likes to create new worlds — places in which the real and the unreal coexist comfortably. Rent *Brazil*, *12 Monkeys* or *The Fisher King* and you'll find fact and fantasy bashing heads, each struggling to stake its territory in the story's plot. In *The Brothers Grimm*, Gilliam's first film since the collapse of the 2000 production *The Man Who Killed Don Quixote* (chronicled in the documentary *Lost in La Mancha*), he walks the same path.

"I've always had a problem with fantasy because I actually work in the border line between fantasy and reality," he told me in 2005. "I find so many new films have become so fantastical that you don't really relate to them . . . they're just beautiful events going on in front of you.

"I feel that fantasy to really work has got to spring from reality and the more reality surrounding it, the more the fantasy is magical when it does occur. I try to find that balance. The fact is, on computers you can almost create anything you want, but the trick to me is to use computers and actually ruin the good work the computers do and bring it down to earthly reality."

A fictionalized version of events based on the nineteenth-century German siblings who wrote *Hansel and Gretel* and *Little Red Riding Hood*, *The Brothers Grimm* sees Matt Damon and Heath Ledger as Will and Jake Grimm. They are eighteenth-century ghostbusters, a pair of charlatans who bilk simple country folk out of their money by conducting phony exorcisms of ghosts and demons. Their days as con men come to an abrupt end when they are captured by Napoleon's Army and sentenced to death. Instead of facing a gruesome execution they agree to rid the forest in a nearby town of its evil spirits. Faced with real supernatural forces their brand of ghostbusting is put to the test.

Visually Gilliam is in top form in *The Brothers Grimm*. His vision for the enchanted forest where much of the action takes place is a stunner. It's a dark and scary woodland where anything can happen — little girls disappear, trees come to life, wolves shape-shift and the beautiful but vain queen lives. Gilliam brings this strange and wonderful world to life and it is here that the movie really gels.

"We did spend a lot of time trying to create a forest that was totally believable and yet could be enchanted at the same time," he says. "We basically cut down a lot of forest outside of Prague and shipped the trees into the studio, stuck them in the ground and slowly started building around them. We actually built two forests, there's one inside the sound stage and another forest outside the village which we built. Guy Dyas who designed it is an incredible designer; he did *X-Men 2*. It was about detail and they say either God or the devil is in the details and that was what was important. I'm not sure which was in the detail in this one."

The Brothers Grimm script is a mix-and-match pastiche of classic fables such as *Jack and the Beanstalk, Snow White and the Seven Dwarfs* and *Rapunzel.* While it doesn't always work — Matt Damon's accent comes and goes with the frequency of an airport shuttle bus and why hire someone as beautiful as Monica Bellucci only to cover her with zombie makeup for most of the film — the director's sense of wonder and playfulness does prevail, proving that even second-rate Gilliam is better than most of his contemporaries.

Availability: On DVD

THE BROWN BUNNY (2003)

Eccentric actor/director Vincent Gallo has maintained that he filmed the infamous fellatio scene at the climax of *The Brown Bunny* using remote cameras that he operated himself, with only him and actress/fellator Chloë Sevigny in the room. In 2005, two years after the film was first seen at the Cannes Film Festival actor Jacob Christner came forward, claiming they were his genitals in the scene and not Gallo's.

The movie, which stars Gallo as Bud Clay, a professional motorcycle racer who loses a race on the East Coast and then drives his van cross-country, sparked controversy at the Cannes Film Festival in 2003 when Roger Ebert called it "the worst in the history of Cannes." The critic later admitted that he was, of course, exaggerating — he hadn't seen every movie ever screened in Cannes so he was unqualified to make such a remark.

Ebert's off-the-cuff dismissal of the film started a war of words between the critic and the filmmaker. Gallo responded that Ebert was a "fat pig with the physique of a slave trader." Ebert rephrased a remark of Winston Churchill and responded that "although I am fat, one day I will be thin, but Mr. Gallo will still have been the director of *Brown Bunny*." Gallo then put a "hex" on Ebert's colon, to which the writer countered "even my colonoscopy was more entertaining than his film." The dueling duo later stopped throwing invectives when Ebert revised his opinion of the movie after seeing an edited version.

In this truncated form — Gallo clipped nearly half an hour off the original 132-minute running time — *Brown Bunny* shines as a moving (albeit *slow* moving) bit of personal filmmaking. Acting as star, writer, director and cinematographer Gallo's vision of a man haunted by the memory of his former lover is as deeply seated as possible.

As American road movies go *Brown Bunny* is more Jean-Paul Sartre than Cosby and Hope. There is very little dialogue and much of the film is shot through an increasingly bug-spattered windscreen. It sounds dull, but Gallo taps into the monotonous rhythms of real life to create a gripping portrait of a self-absorbed loner.

It would be easy to see this as a vanity project. Gallo is in almost every frame, but when we see Bud driving (and driving and driving) Gallo often constructs the shot so he is in the corner, with just a hint of his aquiline nose or hair flitting in and out of the picture. Instead of focusing on the actor we see the abandoned, boarded up stores, near-ghost towns and seedy motels that feed his loneliness. Soon we come to understand that his existential crisis cannot be cured by encounters with the random women he meets on the road; his desperation (like his vehicle) is aimed in only one direction, toward Daisy (Chloë Sevigny).

He's not the point of this picture, the journey is.

The film's final scene is the source of much of the controversy sur-rounding the project. By the time Bud ends his journey in Los Angeles, curiosity is piqued as to the nature of his relationship with Daisy. Those looking for easy answers will walk away bewildered when he hooks up with his former flame. After she smokes crack they hug ("Can I touch you? Can I touch you? Can I touch you?" she asks. "I like you," he replies. "Please, can I hug you?" "Okay," he says) and then she performs unsimulated oral sex on him as the camera unblinkingly looks on. Fade to black. It's a shocker, but not exploitive or pornographic. But neither is it romantic. Gallo leaves the scene hanging, forcing viewers to arrive at their own conclusions.

The Brown Bunny was never going to be a mainstream movie, but the controversy surrounding the feud with Ebert and the film's final scene doomed the picture to the box office graveyard. It's a shame because its eccentricities harken back to the plotless road movies of the

'70s that captured the desperate spirit of the open highway. Gallo's courageously non-commercial film is cut from the same cloth as slice-of-life pictures like *Easy Rider* and *Two-Lane Blacktop*. It is a heartfelt and eloquent examination of solitude, longing and loss.

The movie cultivated even more controversy in July 2004 when a billboard depicting the pornographic scene was erected on Sunset Boulevard in Los Angeles. The image was blurred but still graphic enough to cause community outcry and the billboard was taken down only five days later.

Almost a year after the billboard uproar, Christner stirred the pot again with the allegation that he was Gallo's stunt-penis. The body-double says he signed a confidentiality agreement with Gallo and the film's producers, but adds that he doesn't feel he has broken that contract because his own deal was breached when he wasn't paid for letting Sevigny perform fellatio on him in the film.

In a statement released on the Internet, Christner says, "I'm very disappointed. I was assured by the producers that I was going to ride Vincent Gallo's dick all the way to Hollywood but it looks like I've gotten the shaft."

The outspoken Gallo, having made up with Ebert, then set his aim on Christner. "It's odd having so many men obsessed with my penis. If I had a more normal-sized penis, none of this would have ever happened," he told the *Defamer* website. "I have never met Jacob Christner . . . His lie and fantasy is strange though, as there was a woman, Mrs. Christner, who I think had a son named Jacob. Her job was to blow me all day long while I set up the cameras and lights. Mrs. Christner was a great sport, she also helped me rehearse for my newest film, *Mrs. Christner's First Anal*. Strange Jacob would dream of being my body double, knowing what his mom did and all."

Availability: On DVD

> "Let's you and me get acquainted, honey. You may be
> a number to others but not to me."
> **— EVELYN HARPER (HOPE EMERSON) IN *CAGED!***

CAGED! (1950)

The Women in Prison (WIP) genre comes burdened with expectation. The mere mention of the term conjures up images of campy films with psycho wardens who force naive prisoners into kinky sexual situations, voyeuristic shower scenes and slap-and-tickle torture. Sleazoid movies like *Chained Heat* and *Reform School Girls* have upped the titillation factor and boiled the genre down to its basest elements, but it hasn't always been that way. Now regarded as cut-rate B-movie fare, WIP movies began as top-of-the-bill prestige films. The first notable example was *Caged!*, a social commentary picture from Warner Brothers that was nominated for three Academy Awards.

Based on a story by Virginia Kellogg who spent time behind bars to research the piece, *Caged!* begins with the line, "Pile out, you tramps. This is the end of the line." A heavy police truck door swings open to reveal the "new fish," the female convicts being delivered to an unnamed women's correctional facility. We see Marie Allen (Eleanor Parker), a timid 19-year-old sent to prison after a botched robbery attempt with her husband. He was killed while trying to steal $40 and since she was sitting in the car waiting for him she was charged as an accomplice.

During her intake procedure an on-the-ball nurse gives Marie the news that she is "expecting company," probably about two months along with her dead husband's baby. Given number 93850 she's under the watch of Evelyn Harper (the 6′2″, 230-pound Hope Emerson), a sadistic guard so wicked she makes Nurse Ratched look like Florence Nightingale. Harper tries to cozy up to Marie, but once she realizes that the girl has neither money to bribe her with or easy morals, the fiendish matron assigns the young mom-to-be the tough job of scrubbing the floors with toxic lye.

This isn't *Jailhouse Rock*: the clink is a mean, dirty place filled with mean, dirty women. There's a common prostitute named Smoochie (Jan Sterling), "vice queen" Elvira Powell (Lee Patrick) and Kitty Stark (Betty Garde) the butch "booster" (or shoplifter) who has given up on men. "If you stay in here too long," she says, "you don't think about guys at all. You just get out of the habit."

The inmates are a scary bunch (even if some of them look more like starlets rather than hardened cons), but the staff members are even more degenerate. With her imposing frame, stern face and menacing manner, Harper is a classic corrupt prison screw who personifies the brutality of the penal system. Emerson is so effective in the role that at the premiere audiences booed her every time she appeared on screen, and continued to boo and heckle the actress as she left the theater, even though she was pushing her aged mother in a wheelchair.

Marie slowly learns to adapt and in the end finds she must cooperate with convicts to earn parole. By the time she is released she has been tainted by the system and the career criminals she was locked up with. When Warden Benton (Agnes Moorehead) is asked what to do with the Marie Allen file, she looks out her office window at Marie getting into a fancy sedan with some shady looking men and replies, "Keep it active. She'll be back."

Unlike many of the later WIP films *Caged!* isn't an exploitation flick. It aspires to be social commentary, an unembellished look at the horrible prison conditions that could set a young innocent like Marie on the road to a life of crime. When she says, "For that forty bucks I heisted I certainly got myself an education," screenwriters Kellogg and Bernard C. Schoenfeld are hammering home the point that punishment without rehabilitation is pointless and, once sprung from jail, will force inmates to take the easy way out and return to a life of crime. The message is as subtle as a jackhammer, but director John Cromwell (father of actor James Cromwell) uses a steady hand and never allows the movie to get overly preachy.

He infuses every minute of *Caged!* with a sense of dread, creating a Gothic chamber of horrors inside the prison walls that could be used in a "scared straight" program for aspiring thugs. His camera doesn't shy away from the bleak surroundings — the claustrophobia, a tubercular inmate, the solitary confinement — but it is a faraway train whistle that really drives home the horror of confinement. The whistle becomes a symbol of freedom, of escape, and when the melancholy sound fills their jail cells the women fall silent, knowing that most of them will never again be at liberty.

One of the main components of the WIP films is lesbianism and *Caged!* oozes with implied Sapphic sex. Harper's tacit lesbian feelings are pure '50s Hollywood — hinted at but never acted on. Shower scenes, another staple of the genre, are handled gracefully, with no nudity.

Caged! (remade as *House of Women* in 1962) is a grim message movie that for better or worse popularized an entire genre. WIP films — many of which use the word "caged" in the title — have remained in style over the years with many name filmmakers, including Jonathan "*Caged Heat*" Demme and Roger "*The Big Bird Cage*" Corman, cashing in on the trend. Also known as Chicks In Chains or Babes Behind Bars movies, the genre quickly splintered into subgenres, including "private prison" movies like *House of Whipcord* and prisoner of war flicks like *Ilsa: She Wolf of the SS*, but the original stands head and shoulders above most of the films it inspired.

Availability: On DVD

> "Mr. and Mrs. Beetle have too calm a home life. Mr. Beetle is restless
> and makes frequent trips to the city."
> **— TITLE CARD FROM *THE CAMERAMAN'S REVENGE***

THE CAMERAMAN'S REVENGE (A.K.A. MEST' KINEMATOGRAFI HESKOGO OPERATORA) (1912)

The name Ladislas Starevich isn't as well known as *King Kong* animator Willis O'Brien or special effects genius Ray Harryhausen, but without Starevich's groundbreaking work the world of animation would be a much different place. The Polish-born filmmaker pretty much invented the art of stop-motion animation, and left us with one little-seen classic of the silent era.

Starevich (also known as Wladyslaw Starewicz) had dual obsessions. He was a trained biologist with a specialty in insects, but was also fascinated by film and the special effects work of Georges Méliès. Sometime around 1910 while employed as the director of a natural history museum in Lithuania, he combined his scientific and artistic passions by expanding on the "stop trick" or substitution effects of Méliès to create the some of the first full-on stop-motion films.

Starevich's first works were educational in nature, about the lives of dragonflies and stag beetles, starring embalmed insects. He soon branched out, creating revolutionary satiric animated films so technically advanced that one English critic was convinced Starevich had trained live bugs to perform everyday tasks like riding bicycles and walking upright. Almost 100 years later his work still has the same magical effect. Even to eyes accustomed to computer generated images, his stop-motion choreography of the insects, or "puppets" as he called them, is so natural, so fluid that these films still astonish.

His early Russian educational work earned him a medal of appreciation from the tsar, but it is a 1912 classic from the silent era called *The Cameraman's Revenge* that is his masterpiece.

A spoof of the era's melodramas, the story centers on the domestic dysfunction of Mr. and Mrs. Beetle. In a story that predates the adultery filled novels of Jacqueline Susann by 50 years, the couple, seeking solace outside the boundaries of their humdrum marriage, secretly pair off with new playthings. Mrs. Beetle cavorts with a beret-wearing cricket, while Mr. Beetle is fatally attracted by the exotic charms of elegant dragonfly.

The two carry on their affairs, oblivious to the other's indiscretion until the dragonfly's grasshopper boyfriend, the vengeful cameraman of the title, captures one of Mr. Beetle and his mistresses' trysts on film. Caught in the act, Mr. Beetle flees, only to return home to find that everything isn't cricket there. He sees Mrs. Beetle carrying on with her boyfriend and, blinded by the perfume of hypocrisy, flies into a rage.

To cool down they go to the cinema only to discover that the grasshopper is screening his latest film, Mr. Beetle's rendezvous. It gets quite a reaction from the other bugs in the audience — imagine a turn-of-the-century equivalent of the Paris Hilton sex tape. This time it's Mrs. Beetle's turn to get physical. She throws her adulterous husband through the screen, causing the projector to catch fire. The film ends with Mr. and Mrs. Beetle reunited, although in less than ideal circumstances.

The Cameraman's Revenge is 13 minutes of sheer cinematic joy. The melodramatic love-triangle story is so surreal and inventive that it seems fresher than many of the live action films from the same time frame. It is Starevich's attention to detail in the piece, from the natural lighting and real world scale of the sets, to the stunningly graceful way the bugs move, that boggles the mind. The smoothness of movement is beautiful as the dragonfly dances or the grasshopper rides his bicycle. You just might find yourself, like the English critic, wondering if Starevich really did teach bugs to perform for the camera.

The Cameraman's Revenge is a bizarre yet beautiful artifact from one of the pioneers of an art form.

Availability: Online on YouTube

THE CARS THAT ATE PARIS (1974)

\- \- \- \- \- \- \- \- \- \- \- \- \- \-

Approximately 115 people die every day in car crashes in the United States. That's one death every 13 minutes and, according to the World Health Organization, auto accidents claim an estimated 1.2 million people worldwide each year and yet — unless an accident involves small children or a multiple car pileup — they are rarely front page news. Director Peter Weir wondered why.

While driving through France on his way to London, the Australian-born Weir, a young helmer with several short films to his credit, came across Day-Glo-orange jacketed road workers, stop signs in hand. The road was closed, he was told, and he'd have to take a detour. A quick look around didn't reveal any construction or road blockage, but he obliged and took a longer, more roundabout route. As he navigated his way on a twisting secondary road it occurred to him that he hadn't questioned the men, or even asked why he had to leave the main highway.

Later in England he noticed that the British press would salivate over a sleazy story of murder or a crime of passion, usually giving those sensational stories the screaming headlines on the front page, while the far more devastating fact that dozens of people had lost their lives in auto accidents that week was barely acknowledged on the back page of the paper. He reasoned that if you were to plan a murder, make it look like a car accident. They seem to be taken for granted.

A melding of these two experiences gave him the idea for his debut feature film, an absurdist vision of a small apocryphal town called Paris in New South Wales, Australia.

The movie begins with a familiar sight to theater-goers these days . . . a commercial. In it an attractive young couple is on a leisurely drive through the countryside in their Datsun convertible, searching for antiques. They buy a painting at a quaint store, all the while enjoying conspicuously placed Coke and Alpine cigarettes. It's the typical, idyllic scenario often seen in lifestyle ads. There is one major difference, however. At the end of the ad the handsome couple has a car accident and dies horribly in the wreckage. It's a clever and shocking way to set up the audience for the tale to come.

At the end of the ad the camera pulls back to reveal Paris, an isolated outback town nestled in the hills, with brightly painted wrecked vehicles dotting the landscape. It's here the real action begins. The inbred, but enterprising locals have figured out a unique way to eke out a living in this godforsaken place. Lying in wait for passing tourists, they orchestrate car crashes and then sell the salvaged automobile parts and dead motorists' possessions.

Even more far-out than that is the fate of the occasional survivor. If crash victims aren't killed outright by the accident they're taken to town and subjected to bizarre brain experiments by a loopy local surgeon (Kevin Miles). "There's a tremendous challenge out here in the country," he says, "just waiting to be picked up. This is where the exciting work is being done."

One such victim is our hapless hero Arthur Waldo (Terry Camilleri) who stays in Paris after the accident, which claimed his brother George. He's trapped in Paris by the Mayor (John Meillon), a paternal figure, who uses psychological warfare to convince Arthur that he is unable to drive a car. "No one leaves Paris," says the Mayor, who wants Arthur to stay and be his adopted "son."

All hell breaks loose in this strange town when one of the cars belonging to a local youth is burned. The gang of delinquents wants payback and drives their vehicles — including one killer car covered in spikes — through houses and people in a bloody orgy of revenge during the town's Pioneer Days celebration. Arthur, ordered by the Mayor to defend the town and help quell the uprising, repeatedly slams his Coupe into one of the wildly decorated cars, killing one of the teens.

Has he become one of the sadistic townsfolk or has he found a way out of this murderous hell on earth?

Director Weir's debut is a self-assured piece of work that effectively uses the same atmosphere of malicious calm as his next film, and breakout hit, *Picnic at Hanging Rock*. Shot in just 27 days on a tight budget of AUD$240,000, he builds tension throughout the first hour of *The Cars That Ate Paris*, slowly allowing the feeling of unease to grow until the chaotic climax, the melee at Pioneer Days.

The idea of a small community that isn't what it appears is a topic Weir would revisit frequently. In *Witness*, from 1985, an Amish community holds dark secrets; and in 1998's *The Truman Show* the seemingly normal townsfolk were actually actors in a made up world. *The Cars That Ate Paris* set the template for his studies of social corruption.

"To some extent I was thinking about the old politicians' statement of 'the end justifies the means,'" Weir says. "The older members of the town could deal with that. They could suspend their morality, in a sense, during a difficult period, but as a result of their immoral acts, the young people were corrupted, totally. They'd grown up with this kind of violence and were uncontrollable. So I thought this was a rather interesting kind of metaphor under the kind of homage to these horror films."

A box office bomb when it was released in 1974, the film was ignored by audiences in Australia. The few critics who bothered to review it were hostile.

"Curiously, it wasn't attacked for putting across an unflattering image of Australia," says Weir. "I sensed that some of the film's detractors would have liked it to be more vicious. . . . They objected to it essentially on the grounds that it belonged to no genre. They found it impure, jumbled, confused. They couldn't see that perhaps the film was operating inside its own category."

Critical reaction was the same in America, but the movie had changed. Roger Corman, the film's U.S. distributor, re-edited the movie to play up the exploitation aspects of the story, but in doing so stripped the story of its allegorical element, which allowed the picture's anti-consumerism message to be stomped on by the senseless violence. Weir called the re-working a "grotesque monster of a film." It's been suggested that Corman "borrowed" some of the movie's underlying concepts for his 1975 movie *Death Race 2000*.

Movie fans had to wait a long time but in 2004 *The Cars That Ate Paris* was finally re-released on DVD with Weir's original mix of horror, comedy and social commentary intact.

Availability: On DVD

"Where the fuck's my lighter? My brother Wesley gave it to me . . . just before he committed suicide. It's funny. He's the only one who had no sexual interest in me. All my other brothers did. . . ."
— SUSAN SUPERSTAR (EDIE SEDGWICK) IN *CIAO! MANHATTAN*

CIAO! MANHATTAN (1972)
■ ■ ■ ■ ■ ■ ■ ■ ■ ■ ■

Ciao! Manhattan deeply divides those who see it. *The Village Voice*, once the bastion of underground cool, labeled it "the *Citizen Kane* of the drug generation" while Emmy Award–winning filmmaker George Hickenlooper called it "an aberration, a real disgrace." Both positions are bang on — it is beautiful and ugly, crazy and cool, compelling yet disturbing. Viewed as a document of the death of '60s drug culture, it is fascinating stuff, but taken as a chronicle of the life and downward spiral of its star, Edie Sedgwick, it's harrowing viewing.

The filmmakers hadn't intended to make Sedgwick the focus of *Ciao! Manhattan*. Originally they had intended to star Susan Bottomly

— a.k.a. Andy Warhol Superstar International Velvet — a beautiful starlet who had already appeared in Warhol's magnum opus *Chelsea Girls*.

"She was this startling young ingenue whose father was the district attorney of Boston and had convicted the Boston Strangler," said director David Weisman. "We had to . . . get releases from everybody and [because] Susan Bottomly was 17 we needed her father's permission. At the last minute he refused and she was out."

Scrambling to replace their star, Weisman and co-director John Palmer headed down to the Chelsea Hotel "to see if we could roust Edie out of whatever it was she was doing at the moment," remembers Weisman.

Sedgwick had once been the darling of the Warhol universe, an old-money heiress and model whose relatives included a signatory of the Declaration of Independence and the founder of New York's Central Park. She was a gossip columnist's wet dream: beautiful, outrageous and on the scene. Named *Vogue*'s "youthquaker" of 1965 her flame burned bright in New York society. "It's strange, wherever I've been I've been quite notorious," Sedgwick says in the movie, "and quite innocently so, but I've never been anywhere where I haven't been known."

By 1967 though, that light had dimmed. She'd ripped through her entire Sedgwick family trust fund in just a few months, was addicted to drugs, had burned down at least one apartment by falling asleep with candles burning and was reduced to stealing antiques from her grandmother's apartment to get money to buy drugs.

Although she was in rough shape, she still craved attention and readily agreed to do the film. "Sounds fun," she reportedly said. "We'll start shooting in the park tomorrow."

Production of *Ciao! Manhattan* officially began in New York on Easter Sunday 1967. Producer Robert Margouleff says the film started as a "worthwhile project," but "got crazier and crazier" as drug use became endemic on the set. Officially a man named Dr. Robert was the production's astrologer-doctor who, according to Weisman, came equipped with "a horoscope in one hand and a syringe in the other." Unofficially he was Dr. Feelgood, pumping the cast and crew with a toxic mix of vitamins and amphetamines. "The amphetamine haze that surrounded the project at this point was really crippling," said Weisman.

Soon the production was a shamble, ruled by the unpredictable behavior from the cast and crew. In one scene co-star Paul America was filmed pulling up to the Pan Am Building, dropping off Jane Holzer and driving away. He was then supposed to drive around the block and return to make himself available for close-ups. "But he just kept on going," Margouleff told writer Jean Stein. "We didn't hear from Paul again for about eight months until finally David tracked him down in Allegan, Michigan, where he was in jail."

"I was high on some weed I guess," says America in the book *Edie: An American Biography*. "I figured they were taking advantage of me, so I was ready to leave the scene."

In a matter of months most of the cast and all of the money was gone and production ground to a halt. Weisman said he and Palmer struggled to make any story "from hours of beautifully shot but utterly senseless footage" to no avail. Over the next three years the two became obsessed with finishing the project, but the footage wasn't cooperating. It was like a giant jigsaw puzzle with no edge pieces.

Then, in 1970, Weisman and Palmer hit on a new idea to locate Sedgwick and shoot new footage of her looking back at her glamorous days in New York. By this time Sedgwick was living in her home state of California. The beautiful, though damaged gamine of the NYC footage was a ghost, her once fine features dulled by years of drug abuse and hard living. More noticeably she had gotten a boob job (her new, bigger bust explained away in the new footage with one ironic line, "Yeah, I eat better now and do my exercises").

A new cast was assembled, including *And God Created Woman* director Roger Vadim as Sedgwick's shock therapist, Isabel Jewell (a veteran of over 100 films, including *Lost Horizon*, *Gone With the Wind* and *High Sierra*) and actor/director Christian Marquand, best known as the helmer behind the 1968 curio *Candy*. In December 1970 production was rebooted, this time in garish color, at a derelict estate east of Pasadena in Arcadia, California.

The main set was a drained Olympic-size swimming pool, which was draped with black vinyl. Under the plastic roof was Edie's "apartment," filled with memorabilia from her days as New York's leading social butterfly. The place was decorated with giant photos of her formerly gorgeous face, pictures of Andy Warhol, pop art and a round waterbed.

"The pool set," wrote Weisman in the liner notes for the movie's DVD release, "manifested all she had once been, and served as a striking metaphor for how far she had fallen."

"It was the coldest winter they'd had in years in California," Palmer told Jean Stein. "Edie was playing her role — especially down there in the swimming pool — without any top on, to show off those new silicone breasts of hers. She used to put a heating pad on them to warm up the silicone, which, you know, gets cold."

From December until January 1971, they shot the connective footage that would bring the story together. Sedgwick, under the care of a doctor and two nurses and clearly in the throes of drug dependency, rambles almost incoherently about her past in a most raw and naked way. She was playing a character, Susan Superstar, but her fictional alter ego shares striking similarities to the actress's real life. Sedgwick was Susan, the only difference was the name. The pain she displays when talking about sexual abuse, the suicide of her brother and other unsavory details seem too real to have been scripted. Call it a fictional autobiography.

"She was definitely leaving her legacy and Edie Sedgwick was making sure her story got told," said Weisman. "She would say everyday 'It's got to be real. If it's not real there's no movie.'"

The final version of *Ciao! Manhattan*, pieced together by Weisman and Palmer over the next year, introduces Edie as a drug addled, sexually promiscuous heiress seen hitchhiking topless in an early scene. Picked up by a naive long-haired rolling stone named Wes (Wesley Hayes) they return to her family's mansion and meet her mother (Isabel

Jewell) and hippie butler. There he learns of Susan's twisted past glory in New York.

There's no story in the conventional sense. In its place are two rambling narratives, pieced together to form one whole. First the California footage provides a loose framework for Sedgwick to refer to her past life in New York. The second narrative line, involving insane businessmen, models and Warhol regulars like Paul America is shown in black and white flashbacks via the footage shot in 1967.

The change in Sedgwick is remarkable and should act as a cautionary tale of the dangers of drug use. "The contrast between the incredibly sexy gamine she was in 1967 and the slurry wreck she was just four years later is made painfully apparent," wrote filmmaker Brian Frye, "twenty-seven looking forty, with [her] tits flopping all over and slurring like a Bowery bum."

Ciao! Manhattan's portrait of Sedgwick's disintegration has a ghoulish edge, but offers a fascinating up-close-and-personal glimpse of a personality so hungry for attention she would allow herself to be exploited on camera. It's a psychedelic precursor to the entertainment of humiliation made popular by reality shows like *The Surreal Life* that take advantage of faded celebrities eager for another shot at fame.

As for Sedgwick, she is convincing as the drugged-up, delusional former model, handing in a natural and charismatic performance that has as much to do with her state of mind as it does with her acting chops.

She was a self-destructive girl destined for a short life who just wanted to be famous. A palm reader, taken aback by Sedgwick's short lifeline, was comforted by the model who said, "It's okay. I know." For better or worse, Edie Sedgwick, who died at age 28 before the movie was finished, got her wish. She's more famous in death than she was in life. Her story has been told on film (*Factory Girl*), in books (*Edie: An American Biography* among others), off-Broadway (*Andy & Edie*) and even in song (The Cult's "Edie (Ciao Baby)"). But it is *Ciao! Manhattan* that is the definitive and most lasting piece of her legacy.

Availability: On DVD

CONFESSIONS OF A DANGEROUS MIND (2002)

All autobiographies contain elements of fiction. Chalk it up to the vagaries of memory or the writer's need to whitewash or exaggerate personal history; whatever the case, readers go in with the expectation that the autobiography they've picked will be as honest and truthful as possible.

What then, are readers to make of an "unauthorized autobiography"?

In 1984 game show host and impresario Chuck Barris released such a book. It was the world's first unauthorized autobiography and contained the outrageous allegation that the popular host of *The Gong Show*, known as Chuckie Baby, was also a hit man for the CIA with dozens of kills to his credit. Barris says he wrote *Confessions of a Dangerous Mind* in the throes of an existential meltdown. His shows were canceled and he was attacked for dragging television into the gutter with his brand of lowbrow entertainment, or as he put it "polluting the airwaves with mind-numbing puerile entertainment."

"It was the second or third bad time in my life," he told me in 2002. "My programs were cancelled. I made a movie, and it came and went in a weekend. With it went my film career. Everything was just down and I just was disgusted. I checked into the Wyndham [Hotel on Fifty-eighth Street in New York] and I wrote *Confessions of a Dangerous Mind*. Everything was off the eye-chart when I wrote it. It was just purely cathartic. I just sat down there and just poured it all out and into the book. Of course the premise to me was ludicrous. Life is so peculiar. Here I am getting crucified for trying to entertain and I'm getting medals for killing people. That doesn't seem right."

Nine publishers turned the bizarre apologia down before Hyperion Books published it to a resounding thud, both critically and commercially. The book went out of print and was largely forgotten until a script, written by Oscar-winner Charlie Kaufman started making the rounds. Over the years a number of high profile actors, including Mike Myers, Ben Stiller and John Cusack were attached to the project. Finally in 2002 it came close to production with Johnny Depp cast as Barris, George Clooney (also acting as producer) as his CIA contact Jim Bryd and Kevin Smith at the helm.

"Bit by bit it just fell apart," Clooney told me. "We'd be in pre-production and then we'd fall apart. We try again with a different actor, a different director and it would fall apart. So finally we were in pre-production, we were about nine weeks away from shooting and it fell apart again, and I was like, 'Okay, I think I know how to tell the story and I think I can get the film made.'"

With that, Clooney jumped in as director, recast the film and production finally began in December 2001.

The movie keeps the same pseudo-serious tone from the book, placing Barris (Sam Rockwell) directly in the middle of three very different realities — at the helm of a series of very popular network game shows, in love with a free-spirited girl named Penny (Drew Barrymore) and working as a CIA hit man who used his job as a chaperone on *The Dating Game* in Helsinki and West Berlin as a cover to "murder 33 human beings."

Clooney steps out from behind the camera to play Jim Bryd, a G-man in nicely tailored suits who gives Barris his orders while Julia Roberts is Patricia Watson, a sexy super spy who manhandles lines like, "Leave the microfilm in, baby." Clooney pals Matt Damon and Brad Pitt make uncredited cameo appearances as contestants on *The Dating Game*. "Burt Reynolds was on *The Dating Game* and didn't get picked," said Clooney, "and Tom Selleck was on *The Dating Game* and didn't get picked, and I thought it would be funny if those guys came out."

The decision to steer away from the more well known actors who vied for the role and cast Clooney's *Welcome to Collinwood* co-star, the relatively unknown Sam Rockwell as Barris was a good one. Rockwell transcends mere mimicry and really gets under the skin of Barris. His performance looks past the obvious mannerisms — although he nails the classic Barris squint and nervous clapping — to create a fully rounded character. In Rockwell's hands Barris is a complex person. He's a man who has a hard time reconciling what he does for a living — making trash TV — with his own innate sense of dignity. It's this conflict that makes Barris so fascinating a subject. It's a bold and unpredictably dazzling performance.

When casting the role the first-time director felt "you shouldn't have a famous person playing a famous person."

"Well, I'm afraid you might focus on the star as opposed to the character," Clooney told me in 2002, "especially when it's a more obscure one. [Chuck] is sort of an obscure guy and I think that if it was a big star [playing him] would overwhelm the character."

Confessions doesn't take a stand on whether or not Barris actually murdered 33 enemies of the state in the service of his government. "I thought it was important to make a film that worked whether it was true or not," said Clooney.

"If it were true it would be wild, and if it isn't true, what an interesting character that would find the need to tell this story," continued Clooney. "A man who's as successful as he is, needs to tell that story. What was he trying to talk about? And what was he trying to exorcise, from himself that he needed to tell that story? So, I told him, 'I'm done, I'm not going to ask the question, I don't want to hear the answer.'

"I have some opinions on the idea of it, which I don't want to tell you because I actually want people walking out the theater to have their own opinions."

Rockwell claims that he didn't want to know the truth one way or another.

"I didn't want to disprove it because it wouldn't help me as an actor," Rockwell told me in 2002. "I really didn't want to know too much because I didn't want to find out."

For the record, the Central Intelligence Agency denies that Chuck Barris ever worked for them. "Normally, we don't comment on whether people worked here or not, but with something this outrageous and ridiculous, we felt it was necessary to modify that policy in this case," said spokesman Paul Nowack. "It is ridiculous, and it's not true. We could find no record of him ever working here."

Despite good reviews, a bravura performance from Rockwell and the presence of superstars Clooney, Barrymore and Roberts, *Confessions of a Dangerous Mind* didn't fare well at the box office. In its initial release it made only $16 million, about half of what it cost to make.

Availability: On DVD

"The Crime of Dr. Crespi starts where Frankenstein left off!"
— ADVERTISING TAGLINE FOR *THE CRIME OF DR. CRESPI*

THE CRIME OF DR. CRESPI (1935)

In front of the camera Erich von Stroheim was known to the public as "The Man You Love to Hate." Behind it he might have been known as "The Man the Studios Love to Hate" because of his haughty attitude and disregard for the Tinseltown power structure.

In a Hollywood career that spanned 40 years the Austrian-born director and actor saw his stock rise and fall many times. He first made a name for himself during World War 1 playing cruel aristocratic German villains. In one film he actually throws a crying baby out a window! The stereotype earned him the title "The Man You Love to Hate."

In the silent era he was also a much sought after director until his arrogance (he made a nine-hour movie called *Greed*), budgetary follies (he was the first director to spend over $1 million on a film) and attention to detail (his scripts were often as long as the novels he was adapting) made him unemployable by the big studios. Unable to find important work behind the camera, he was forced to concentrate on performing.

Despite his hatred for acting — he couldn't remember his lines and didn't like taking orders — he was a striking screen presence. His well-crafted pompous screen persona was put to good use in Jean Renoir's *La Grande illusion* and Billy Wilder's *Sunset Boulevard*, for which he was nominated for the Academy Award for Best Supporting Actor, but it is a little-seen 1935 film that captures von Stroheim at his ominous best.

In *The Crime of Dr. Crespi*, loosely based on Edgar Allan Poe's "The Premature Burial," von Stroheim plays the embittered titular character, a chain-smoking doctor consumed by thoughts of revenge against Stephen Ross (John Bohn), the current husband of Crespi's former flame Estelle (Harriet Russell). He'd give everything to be her every-thing again, and hatches a twisted plan to win her back.

The mad doctor gets the chance at vengeance when Ross comes down with a mysterious disease that only Dr. Crespi's surgical skills can remedy. Unfortunately the operation is not a success and Ross dies shortly after the procedure . . . or does he? In fact Crespi has secretly administered a powerful drug that placed his patient in suspended ani-mation which apes the signs of death. His lifeless body belies the fact that he, horrifyingly, has all his faculties about him. Knowing that the drug will wear off after a few days Crespi rushes things along, forgoing an autopsy or embalming and makes arrangements to have the sentient man buried alive! Before the funeral Crespi visits Ross at the morgue to gloat over his fate; when the casket is lowered into the grave Crespi's insane revenge plot is complete.

It isn't until Crespi's colleagues, Dr. Arnold (Paul Guilfoyle) and Dr. Thomas (Dwight Frye), become suspicious of the alleged death and have the body exhumed that the lovesick doctor is exposed as a mur-derer.

The Crime of Dr. Crespi makes the best of its poverty row production standards, resourcefully using lighting effects to create a unique visual style that is part Universal Horror and part film noir. It's a memorable looking film. As was often the case with these low budget thrillers, there's little in the way of a musical score, just some stock music that undoubtedly cost the film's producers little or nothing. No matter, the movie makes an impression because of the twisted story and even more twisted performance from von Stroheim.

The former director's presence elevates what could have been a run-of-the-mill, bottom-of-the-bill shocker. His characterization of the eccentric doctor is outrageous, a completely unsympathetic bad guy. He portrays mood swings that range from calm and controlled to full-out ballistic. In the latter mode his voice becomes a shrill staccato, a vocal representation of his fractured state of mind.

Director John Auer emphasizes Crespi's mania with the use of extreme close-ups. The up-close-and-personal shots reveal Crespi's craziness in riveting detail. The camera work creates an atmosphere of dread and doom that maximizes the story's thrills and chills. The supporting actors are fine; they're journeymen actors who could be relied on to hand in decent performances while working quickly and for little money. The standout of the secondary cast is Dwight Frye, the character actor who was usually typecast in oddball riffs on his famous roles from *Dracula* and *Frankenstein*. In *Crespi* he is allowed to, for once, strut his stuff as the hero and sink his teeth into something other than the lunatic roles he usually played. He even gets to flirt with a pretty nurse, something that his most famous alter ego, Fritz the vicious hunchbacked lab assistant in James Whale's *Frankenstein*, would never do.

The Crime of Dr. Crespi was likely made as a throwaway, a movie for "the shirtsleeve audience" and not the critics, but it transcends its humble origins by way of inventive direction and an unforgettable central performance from "The Man You Love to Hate."

Availability: Out of Print VHS

Richard's Favorite Casting Stories

1. Charles Bronson won his first screen role in Henry Hathaway's 1951 film *You're in the Navy Now* not because of his acting skill, but because of his amazing ability to belch on cue.

2. When Shelley Winters was invited to audition for a supporting role in a 1990 film, she sat down at the casting director's desk, pulled out her two Best Supporting Actress Oscars from a bag and asked, "Do you still want me to read for this part?"

3. In 1979 the night before Mel Gibson was supposed to audition for a film directed by George Miller he got involved in a brawl with three other men. Bloodied and beaten Gibson showed up for an audition the next day with stitches in his head, a broken nose and a disconnected jaw. His battered face was perfect for the part he was trying out for, and director Miller gave the bruised actor the title role in the road-warrior flick *Mad Max*.

4. *Premiere* asked musician Brian Vander Ark how he had landed the role of bassist Ricki Bell in the Mark Wahlberg film *Rock Star*. "There's a great story where William H. Macy, when he wanted the role in *Fargo*, called up Joel Coen and said if he didn't get the part, he'd kill Joel Coen's dog [much as his character in the film might have done]," Vander Ark said. "So when the director [Stephen Herek] called me to tell me he liked the song I wrote ["Colorful"], I told him that if he didn't give me the part, I too would kill Joel Coen's dog. And it worked out."

5. In 1934, while casting the part of Mark Antony in Cecil B. DeMille's *Cleopatra*, producer Benjamin Glazer arranged for the strikingly handsome Henry Wilcoxon to audition. On the

day of the tryout the actor was taken into an office where DeMille was working with his costume designer, Natalie Visart. The director looked the actor over before turning to Visart. "Well, Nat, what do you think of him?" he asked. "My God, C.B.," Visart replied, glancing up, "what a head for a helmet!" That began a long and fruitful association with director Cecil B. DeMille, which saw Wilcoxon (who later turned producer) become the director's most trusted ally.

6. "I was shopping in a grocery store," the Hawaiian-born actress Tia Carrere said, "and a producer's mother and father approached me and said their son was doing a movie in Hawaii and I would be perfect for the female lead in it. I had never had any sort of acting ambitions or training. . . . I read for the casting director. I had no idea what I was doing . . . I pretended I was a shy local Hawaiian girl falling in love with a Caucasian Casanova and got the female lead in a movie called *Aloha Summer*." Carrere was just 17 when she was discovered.

7. When Quentin Tarantino was casting *Pulp Fiction* he had some trouble finding the right actress for the role of Mia Wallace, the big-time thug's wife with a big-time coke habit. "I knew her backward and forward, but I had no idea what she looked like," he said. "Every actress from Isabella Rossellini to Alfre Woodard, Holly Hunter and Meg Ryan read for the part." He says he knew he had to cast Uma Thurman in the role when "I had dinner with another actress and felt like I was cheating on Uma."

8. Stella Adler–trained method actor Benicio Del Toro wasn't happy with his first audition for the role of the thuggish Dario in the James Bond movie *Licence to Kill* and begged the casting director for another try that same day. On the second go around he says that Bond franchise owner and producer Cubby Broccoli sat in on the read-through, but fell asleep

almost immediately. Coming to after Del Toro's audition he asked, "How tall are you?" Receiving the reply "6 foot 2," he gave a curt "Good" and gave the part of the youngest Bond villain ever to the 22-year-old Del Toro.

9. When Joan Crawford was asked whether she had ever used the casting couch to win a role she said, "Well, it sure beat the hard, cold floor!" Rumor has it that Crawford wasn't shy about aggressively going after the parts she wanted. To land the lead role in 1928's *Our Dancing Daughters* Crawford allegedly stripped in front of the film's producer to convince him to give her the lead. When the man told her that he wasn't in charge of the casting, the director was, Crawford promptly visited the director, repeated her performance – and got the role that made her a star. Apparently 25 years later she did the same thing to land the role of Jenny Stewart in the romance *Torch Song*.

10. Frances McDormand met her future husband, director Joel Coen, at an audition for *Blood Simple*, but she almost blew the audition by not returning back for the call-back later that same day. Usually struggling actors will move heaven and earth to make a call-back, but McDormand had a previous engagement – she had to watch TV. "My boyfriend at the time had his first five lines on a soap opera," she said, "and I felt committed to watching it with him." The Coens rescheduled her second audition and later she was offered the part of Abby in the film.

DAY OF WRATH (VREDENS DAG) (1943)

By the mid-1920s Carl Theodor Dreyer was hailed as the finest director to ever emerge from Denmark. His first true masterpiece, 1928's *The Passion of Joan of Arc*, was based on the actual transcripts of Joan's trial. It blended realism and expressionism in a way never before seen onscreen. Critics raved but audiences stayed away.

The failure of that movie and his next one, *Vampyr*, coupled with his irascible attitude and fanatical perfectionism made him unemployable in Denmark's burgeoning film business and he didn't step behind a camera again for 10 years. In 1942, after a decade of working as a journalist, he returned to film, making a short educational movie on unwed mothers. *Mødrehjælpen* (*Good Mothers*) was a subject close to his heart as he was the illegitimate son of a housekeeper who died during a frantic self-performed abortion. He delivered the film on time, on budget and was rewarded with the money to make his next feature, *Day of Wrath* (*Vredens Dag*).

Adapted from Hans Wiers-Jenssens' novel and filmed during the Nazi occupation of Denmark, the movie is a period piece that deals with the contemporary themes of social and religious repression. Set in 1623, 100 years after the Protestant Reformation, the country is in the grip of religious fanaticism. Witch trials are frequent and any strange or aberrant behavior is cause for denunciation.

In one village Herlofs Marthe (Anna Svierkier), an old lady accused of sorcery, has been sentenced to burn at the stake. In a last ditch effort to save her own life she begs Anne (Lisbeth Movin), the young wife of the aging Reverend Absalon Pederssøn (Thorkild Roose), to intervene.

Many years before, Anne's mother had been likewise accused of witchcraft but had escaped a fiery death when Pederssøn testified on her behalf.

Despite Herlofs Marthe's threats to reveal that his testimony was false and a calculated act designed to win Anne's affection, the clergyman remains taciturn save for the offer to pray for her soul. After being tortured the old lady is burned alive. As the flames engulf her writhing body she curses Pederssøn, vowing he will die for what he has done to her.

Pederssøn ignores the old hag's curse, chalking it up to the crazed last words of a troubled person bound for "the other place," but soon his life is changed forever.

Anne, feeling trapped in a loveless marriage to the pious old man, sets into motion a roller coaster of events when she falls in love with Pederssøn's son, Martin (Preben Lerdorff Rye), and admits to him that she wishes her husband would die. Her affair and death wish will have repercussions that will call into question the effectiveness of Herlofs Marthe's curse.

In a career that spanned 60 years, Dreyer made a total of 14 films — only five with sound. Stylistically *Day of Wrath* marked a turning point for the director, establishing the tone for all of his sound works. He uses stark black and white cinematography to highlight his beautifully composed but pared down shots. The simple elegance of Dreyer's work clearly influenced others, with Ingmar Bergman an obvious acolyte who seems to have borrowed heavily from *Day of Wrath* for his film *The Seventh Seal.*

Dreyer's habit of running long uninterrupted takes and slow tracking shots, however, was more than simply a stylistic choice.

Many of *Day of Wrath*'s scenes extend into uncomfortably voyeuristic territory, as though the director is using his unblinking camera to pry every last drop of emotion from his actors. Dreyer had a technique of shooting long, continuous takes — often multiple times to break his actors down, draining them of the impulse to overact or even act at all. His goal was total naturalism and in *Day of Wrath* he achieves it.

Particularly effective in this regard is Lisbeth Movin's intensely poignant take on Anne. She gives a compellingly real performance that brims with the longing for real love and freedom, tinged with both sadness and sexuality. It's a complex character, given real life by Movin in a performance that, despite starring in three dozen more films over the next 40 plus years, would come to define and dominate her work. Her stunning final scene in the film should be mandatory viewing in acting schools for anyone with a habit of overacting.

With its austere *mise en scène* and uncluttered, raw performances, *Day of Wrath* is an uncompromising portrait of intolerance and repression; heavy going, but well worth the effort.

Availability: Hard to find

My Favorite Movie You've Never Seen

"*Ajantrik* [also known as *The Unmechanical* or *Pathetic Fallacy*, directed by Ritwik Ghatak (1958)]. What I love is how Ritwik Ghatak has managed to capture the ambiguity and inconsistencies in his characters. Not only does it make the characters authentic, but makes for a fascinating story."

— Deepa Mehta, the Oscar-nominated director of *Water*

DEAR FRANKIE (2004)

Dear Frankie is a four hankie movie. It is a tearjerker about Lizzie, played by Emily Mortimer, who has fled from her abusive husband, and is raising her deaf son, Frankie (Jack McElhone, who appeared with Mortimer in 2003's *Young Adam*). Instead of telling Frankie the terrible truth about his father, Lizzie tells the boy that his dad is away at sea on a freighter named the *Accra*. Frankie writes to his old man, and his mother, lovingly, but probably misguidedly, intercepts the letters and answers them herself.

First tearjerker moment of many: Lizzie says Frankie's letters are important to her "because it's the only way I can hear his voice."

Everything is going well until the day that a ship named the *Accra* actually docks in Glasgow. Frankie assumes his father is on-board, so to keep up the reassuring lie she's told her son, Lizzie decides to find a man who will pretend, temporarily, to be Frankie's father. He comes in the tall, dark and handsome form of Gerard Butler, no longer hiding his rugged good looks behind a mask as he did in *Phantom of the Opera*. He is the fatherly stranger who brings comfort to both mother and son.

There are some lovely moments in this quiet little film that could have easily strayed into melodrama or sickly sweet sentiment, but are actually played with a welcome bit of edge. When the Stranger asks about Frankie's deafness, Lizzie tells him, "Frankie wasn't born deaf. That was a gift from his dad." It is those sad details, mixed with tenderness, wisdom and insight that give the movie its life and its edge. Disney this ain't. There is emotional truth on display here that feels authentic.

Director Shona Auerbach, in her feature debut, gives us not only emotional truth, but physical as well. There are no soft focus or glamour shots to be found in *Dear Frankie*. Auerbach's Scotland doesn't fit the mold of most romantic movies. It's a hardscrabble place where people have to struggle to make ends meet and her photography reflects that ethos.

Ditto with the characters. These are damaged people who are just trying to make out as best they can, turning a bad situation into something that is, at least, tolerable. Lizzie is not the typical lovesick mother we've seen a thousand times in lesser movies, but a complex, unpredictable character who is trying to give her son a better life than she has had. Butler, who wasn't yet the object of desire he would become after *300*, hands in a good, kindhearted performance, but it is Emily Mortimer (*Lovely & Amazing* and *Lars and the Real Girl*) as the struggling single mother who shines brightest.

Dear Frankie is a better movie than its synopsis would suggest, emotionally precarious and fulfilling.

Availability: On DVD

"I'm an English teacher, not fucking Tomb Raider."
— BETH (ALEX REID) IN *THE DESCENT*

THE DESCENT (2005)
▬ ▬ ▬ ▬ ▬ ▬ ▬ ▬

The Descent is scary. Run home to your Momma scary. Scream like a little girl scary. Close your eyes and think of something else scary. "Hold me, I'm scared" scary.

It's the story of a group of thrill-seeking female friends who meet a couple of times a year to climb mountains, base jump and leap out of planes. When we first meet them they are all happy, smiling broadly while whitewater rafting. This being a horror movie you just know that soon those smiles will be wiped off their cheery faces.

Sure enough, not even five minutes in things take a turn when tragedy strikes one of this feisty bunch. The group works through the heartbreak in the only way they know how — by taking another huge risk. This time they decide to jump in a big hole. They go spelunking in the Appalachians (although aside from a few establishing shots on location the movie was shot entirely in Scotland and at the U.K.'s Pinewood Studios).

The yawning underground cave becomes the perfect setting for a horror film. The darkness, shadows (and some mysterious shadowy figures) and claustrophobic atmosphere play off basic primal fears — fear of the dark, fear of small, enclosed spaces, fear of not being in control. As the women go further down into the cave their situation becomes dire and the tension builds for the viewer. They find evidence of another, failed expedition from a hundred years previous along with some strange cave paintings. These unsettling discoveries put a wedge between the women, who each interpret the life-saving importance of the artifacts differently. This fracture leads to a breakdown in friendship that ultimately may doom the spelunkers.

There are also pale, slimy subterranean monsters, hungry for human flesh, but the real horror here is psychological as director Neil Marshall skillfully turns up the heat, making the audience feel for this cast of unknowns as their resolve is pushed to the limit. An alternate name for this movie could have been *No Way Out*; the mounting feeling of hopelessness as our heroes shimmy through endless tiny cracks and crevasses in a fruitless bid for escape propels the action. Two miles underground there isn't any sunshine and the movie reflects that, getting darker the farther down they travel. The cinematography takes advantage of the gloom, using the shadows from the cavers' flashlights and flares to create eerie, unforgettable images.

Also effective is the use of sound. In the silence of their underground crypt the noises of dripping water, heavy breathing and bodies scraping against rock are amplified, becoming the soundtrack to the terror felt by the women as one by one they meet grisly ends. It's bleak and violent and gets bleaker and more violent as the movie goes on.

The Descent has plenty of gory moments but it isn't the blood and guts that terrify. It is the impossible situation, the unrelenting air of menace that really plays on the viewer's fears.

Availability: On DVD

"I'm an artist. When you tell people that they usually say, 'What's your medium?' I usually say, 'extra large.'"
— JEAN-MICHEL BASQUIAT IN *DOWNTOWN 81*

DOWNTOWN 81 (1981)

- - - - - - - -

Downtown 81 chronicles the New York City that Rudy Giuliani didn't want you to see. Shot in 1980–81 in Manhattan by fashion photographer Edo Bertoglio, it's a time capsule of the Big Apple's vibrant underground arts scene, complete with all the grit and grime that made New York great before Giuliani swept it all away in his attempt to sanitize the city and increase tourism. Not exactly a documentary and not really a narrative, *Downtown 81* (originally known as *New York Beat Movie*) is a hybrid of fact and fiction, placing a make-believe story in a very real city with real people playing themselves.

"The script was more or less inspired by Jean-Michel [Basquiat]," screenwriter Glenn O'Brien told me in 2007. "We wanted a wandering character to tie all the elements together. Edo liked Danny Rosen, a young musician who plays Jean-Michel's friend in the limo/Rock Lounge scene. I thought Jean-Michel had more charisma and that he was going to be an important artist. I wrote a more general treatment, but when I sat down to write the script it was for Jean-Michel."

Basquiat was a struggling 19-year-old musician and artist long before the Disney Store moved into Times Square. When we first meet him he's checked himself out of the hospital and hitched a ride to his apartment with a beautiful model in a convertible who wants "to take care of him for the rest of his life."

As the woman drives off he discovers that he's been locked out for failure to pay $500 rent. Talking his way into the apartment, he convinces the angry landlord (former Yardbirds and Rolling Stones manager Giorgio Giomelsky) that he has money tucked away inside. It's a lie of course. Instead he offers the proprietor a painting in exchange for his rent and gets thrown out into the street.

The balance of the movie follows Basquiat as he tromps around the garbage-strewn Lower East Side looking for the model, someone to buy his painting and a place to crash. He rings up one sale from an eccentric old lady, but she insists on paying with a check, and he only wants cold hard cash.

From there on in *Downtown 81* takes the form of a mini-road picture. The camera follows his trip through Manhattan as he hangs out with proto-rapper Fab Five Freddy, takes in a fashion show and checks out No Wavers DNA at their rehearsal space, a rowdy Kid Creole and the Coconuts at the Peppermint Lounge and avant-rock violinist Walter Steding playing in the elevator of the Mudd Club.

Finally a gravelly voiced bag lady (Blondie's Debbie Harry) in a dark alley begs him for a kiss goodnight. She says she is a fairy princess under an evil spell, and if he kisses her the curse will be broken and she'll grant his every wish. They smooch but nothing happens. "That was such a great kiss I really thought you were a princess," he says ruefully.

"Well, watch this baby," she says as a cloud of smoke erupts around her. She emerges as a rather stoned looking princess and grants him his wish; a bag full of money. "Most people don't know how to make a wish, or what to wish for," he says. "I wish they did."

Downtown 81 disappeared for almost 20 years. Although principal photography was completed in 1981, the production was abandoned after producers ran into financial problems during post-production. The whole project was considered a lost cause until 1998 when the film was reassembled from various work prints by producer and fashion stylist Maripol Fauque (she designed Madonna's look for *Like a Virgin* among many others). Restoration included cleaning up the image and soundtrack, which had been severely damaged and blowing the picture up from 16 mm to 35 mm. The film's producers rounded up many of the original cast to re-dub their lines, although Basquiat, who died of a heroin overdose in 1988 at age 27, was voiced by slam poet Saul Williams.

"We actually tried lip-readers, but they were useless," said O'Brien of the job of recreating 20-year-old dialogue. "They told us crazy things. Eventually I think we got very close to everything. Tim Wright actually remembered the lines he improved at Vanguard Studio.

"At some points there seem to have been slight changes in dialogue and a bit of improvisation because several times we were stumped because lines didn't match up, like in the 'Felons' scene. I supervised the recording of the dialogue and that was very labor intensive."

Ironically the delay in release may have worked in the film's favor. Released in 1981 it would have been, at best, a snapshot of a subculture and would have likely been swept under the table in comparison to the more slickly produced videos appearing on MTV at the time. Twenty years on, however, the film takes on social significance as a document of a long gone moment in time when New York's intermingling art and music scenes pulsated with excitement and new ideas. As fascinating is the footage of Basquiat, the movie's charismatic star. It's remarkable to see this now legendary figure frozen in time in the years before he was discovered by Andy Warhol and took the art world by storm with his collage-style painting.

"I have seen the film so many times, but I am still amused to see my old friends, several of whom are no longer around," O'Brien said. "Actually most who are still around are in pretty good shape. I would have loved to see Jean-Michel, Cookie [Mueller who played the second go-go dancer], Bradley [Field who played the studio manager], et cetera get old.

"Also it's interesting to see how different audiences react, especially where they laugh. I also find it interesting how DNA still manages to drive people out of the theater."

Like other films that were completely of their time, such as Ulli Lommel's *Blank Generation*, *Downtown 81* is an artifact, a film with a particular sensibility that could only have been made at the time it was made.

Availability: On DVD

"General Feraud has made occasional attempts to kill me. That does not give him the right to claim my acquaintance."
— **ARMAND D'HUBERT (KEITH CARRADINE) IN *THE DUELLISTS***

THE DUELLISTS (1977)
■ ■ ■ ■ ■ ■ ■ ■ ■

Alien, with its intensely dark approach to science fiction and unforgettable "chest-burster" scene, is the movie that put director Ridley Scott on the map, but it wasn't his first feature film. Two years before he journeyed to outer space he traveled back in time to the Napoleonic era to bring one of Joseph Conrad's novellas to vivid life. *The Duellists* earned him a Best First Work Award at Cannes, but failed to establish him as an A-list director.

Based on Conrad's account of a true story, the movie begins with Stacy Keach's narration setting the time and place as Strasbourg in the "the year Napoleon Bonaparte became ruler of France." Harvey Keitel is the ferocious Gabriel Feraud, a lieutenant in the 7th Hussars with a proclivity for dueling. One character describes Feraud's love of sword fighting, saying, "You make fighting a duel sound like a pastime in the Garden of Eden!" When Feraud mercilessly lances a young man who insults Bonaparte his arrest is ordered. A genteel, reserved young lieutenant Armand D'Hubert (Keith Carradine) is dispatched to find him and place him under house arrest.

When the two meet, Feraud, incensed that D'Hubert would try to arrest him for defending Napoleon's honor, predictably challenges the younger man to a duel. D'Hubert quickly incapacitates Feraud, slicing his arm open and worse, wounding his pride. Both men are placed under house arrest for dueling, but when war breaks out they are freed to go to battle.

The story follows the two main characters for the next 15 years as they participate in the trek of Napoleon's Grande Army through Europe. While war ravages the continent, a personal battle is fought between the two soldiers as Feraud cannot forgive D'Hubert for humiliating him. He describes the younger man as a "boudoir soldier" and "staff lackey," and cannot wait to run him through. Assigned to separate companies they meet only sporadically, but when they do, violence ensues with Feraud demanding duels and D'Hubert the unwilling opponent. "I am going to be killed responsibly," he says, "on horseback, as a compliment to the cavalry" — not, he implies, at the end of Feraud's sword.

They fight a series of six duels, paralleling Napoleon's major battles of the period. In one meeting in Russia in 1812 on a wartorn battlefield the pair face off in an honor match, pausing only long enough to bond together — both are exceptionally good, brave soldiers after all — to mutually dispatch some Cossack intruders before resuming their duel.

The pigtailed Feraud, obsessed for the better part of two decades with collecting on his dept of honor, allows hatred to consume him, while D'Hubert takes a calmer approach even though the neurotic dueling costs him dearly in terms of his personal relationship since his love, Laura, leaves when she can no longer take the constant tension. No matter how he tries to extricate himself from the situation he keeps getting drawn back in.

When the two adversaries return to France, there is a regime change and Feraud is arrested for treason. By then, however, the fixation on dueling has become a *folie à deux* and D'Hubert intervenes to spare his antagonist's life so that he may live to duel another day.

Made on a budget of only $900,000, it had first been pitched to Hallmark who passed, thinking the $700,000 price tag a bit rich for their blood. Scott stretched every dollar, a trick he learned as a commercial director with over 3,000 ads to his credit. He shot on existing locations — no buildings were built for the film — using tricky editing and lots of dry ice to mask any anachronisms and had the crew stand in as extras, anything to save a few dollars.

The result is a sumptuous-looking film that benefits from Scott's artistic eye for composition. He takes pains to ensure that each of the six duels is distinct and staged differently, and pays close attention to the details. Costumes and props are beautifully represented, framed by a visual style that recalls the eighteenth-century look of another period piece, Stanley Kubrick's *Barry Lyndon*. It's an interesting step in the genesis of Scott's visual flair from commercial director to the Ansel Adams of the big screen.

Also interesting is how *The Duellists* thematically echoes much of Scott's future work. Intense conflict is often at the heart of Scott's films — think *Alien, Blade Runner, Thelma & Louise, Gladiator, Black Hawk Down* and *Kingdom of Heaven* — a topic very much explored here. Feraud and D'Hubert's duels are the result of an antiquated gentleman's honor code and Feraud's obsessive behavior, but Scott uses them as an allegory for the futility of war, using a personal battle to comment on the much broader subject of discord.

The Duellists may not have vaulted Scott to the forefront of international directors but it did act as a calling card, earning him enough attention to land the helmer's job on *Alien* and establish a tone which would inform his later and better known work.

Availability: On DVD

"See the naked young Franciscans whipped with cactus. See the bandit leader disemboweled. See the priest ride into the sunset with a midget and her newborn baby. What it all means isn't exactly clear, but you won't forget it."
— ADVERTISING TAGLINE FOR *EL TOPO*

EL TOPO (1970)

In December 1970 Holocaust survivor and avant-garde film curator Jonas Mekas organized a three-day festival devoted to experimental films at the Elgin, a dilapidated 600-seat theater on Eighth Avenue near Nineteenth Street in New York City. The biggest draw over the three nights were the films of John Lennon and Yoko Ono, which attracted full houses and enthusiastic audiences. Eager to take advantage of the hundreds of young people descending on their theater, Elgin management tacked on an added feature, Alejandro Jodorowsky's surreal *El Topo*, as a midnight show because, as they said in ads, it was "a film too heavy to be shown any other way."

With virtually no coverage from the "straight press" the movie caught on, playing to capacity audiences comprised mostly of hippies who watched the film night after night through a cloud of self-generated smoke. They were, according to Vincent Canby "repeaters who come back to turn on and to be turned on." When asked if he wanted viewers to be stoned while watching the film, Jodorowsky said, "Yes, yes, yes, yes. I demand them to be."

It was a counterculture phenomenon that gave birth to the midnight movie. Soon theaters all over New York and elsewhere were playing movies like *Pink Flamingos, Eraserhead, Freaks* and *The Harder They Come* for audiences eager for entertainment once everyone else was tucked safely in their beds.

El Topo's run was extended until June 1971 when John Lennon, who had seen the film at least three times at the Elgin, convinced Beatles manager Allen Klein to purchase the rights to the movie for his company ABKCO and give it a wide release. The official national release never materialized as trouble brewed between the eccentric filmmaker and the headstrong Klein.

The film was pulled from distribution, hidden away in the ABKCO vault for 30 years before earning a re-release on DVD in 2007. In a 1990 interview Jodorowsky said Klein told Roger Ebert, "*El Topo* is like wine, all the time it gets better. I am waiting until you die, and then I am going to have a fortune."

This great "lost" classic hasn't lost any of its punch in its time away. It is still as confounding, bizarre and hallucinatory today as it was when Jodorowsky first unleashed it on an unsuspecting public. It's violent, ("more phony gore than maybe 20 years of *The Wild Bunch*," wrote one reviewer in 1971), preachy, incoherent but strangely compelling and entertaining. No synopsis could possibly do *El Topo*'s loopy story justice, but you should know what you're in for before you rent, so here goes. . . .

The film is split into two halves. In the first section El Topo (Jodorowsky), a mysterious, bearded man in black, is seen on horseback with his naked son (the director's real-life son Brontis). The pair stumbles across a freshly raped and pillaged village, with corpses littering the landscape. Enraged, El Topo vows he will track down those responsible for the carnage. In short order he hunts down and dispatches the banditos, leaves his son with a group of monks, abandoning him for a young beautiful woman named Mara, Mara Lorenzio in her only film role. "She's never seen the movie," said Jodorowsky years later. "Once I received a postcard from her that simply said, 'I'm not dead.' This is all I know about her." El Topo then embarks on a quest to obtain sacred enlightenment.

To achieve this Zenlike state he first must battle the four master gunmen of the desert and absorb their mystical knowledge. By cheating he prevails over each master, but once the mission is complete Mara and an enigmatic woman in black riddle El Topo with bullets, leaving him for the vultures. The women disappear and El Topo is rescued from a grisly fate by a group of deformed men, women and children who drag his battered body to their secret mountain cavern.

And that's just the first part. Sound strange? You ain't seen the half of it.

Part two. Awakening years later and now sporting a peroxide afro, El Topo has become a saintly figure, worshipped by the misshapen and inbred citizens of the mountain lair. Spiritually alive, El Topo promises the cavern people that he will help them take back their place in the local town from which they were banished years ago.

Shaving his head and wearing a long white robe, El Topo and a spirited little person (Jacqueline Luis) go to the town and perform an acrobatic clown act to raise money to bore a hole in the side of the mountain, through which the cave dwellers can escape.

The town, they discover, is a brutal place run by a sadistic sheriff and a strange religious cult, where Russian roulette is a favorite pastime. When little Luis discovers she is pregnant, El Topo takes her to a church to do the right thing and marry her, only to discover that the priest is . . . the son he abandoned years ago.

This bizarre trio reluctantly works together to complete the tunnel. Once finished the newly liberated mountain people walk, crawl and limp into town to an uncertain future.

Drenched in symbolism and blood, lots of blood, *El Topo* is an exploitation film with the sheen of an art house movie. Jodorowsky takes the sacred cows of avant-garde and art house and minces them into meatloaf, assaulting the conventions of narrative and visual art, while at the same time loading the movie up with sexual and visceral thrills *à la* Roger Corman. It's an intoxicating, if not a little disorienting mix.

The Chilean born Jodorowsky, a former student of legendary mime Marcel Marceau, was no stranger to controversy. His first film, *Fando and Lis*, was denounced as "corrosive and corrupting" by the Mexican government and put him on the wrong end of death threats following its premiere in 1968. With the release of *El Topo* the director continued to court controversy when he told a reporter that in the name of authenticity, during a scene where El Topo sexually assaults Mara, he actually beat and raped his female co-star.

"When I wanted to do the rape scene, I explained to [Mara] that I was going to hit her and rape her," the director said in a December 1970 interview. "There was no emotional relationship between us, because I had put a clause in all the women's contracts stating that they would not make love with the director. We had never talked to each other. I knew nothing about her. We went to the desert with two other people: the photographer and a technician. No one else. I said, 'I'm not going to rehearse. There will be only one take because it will be impossible to repeat. Roll the cameras only when I signal you to.'

"Then I told her, 'Pain does not hurt. Hit me.' And she hit me. I said, 'Harder.' And she started to hit me very hard, hard enough to break a rib . . . I ached for a week. After she had hit me long enough and hard enough to tire her, I said, 'Now it's my turn. Roll the cameras.' And I really . . . I really . . . I really raped her. And she screamed.

"Then she told me that she had been raped before. You see, for me the character is frigid until El Topo rapes her. And she has an orgasm. That's why I show a stone phallus in that scene . . . which spouts water.

"She has an orgasm. She accepts the male sex.

"And that's what happened to Mara in reality. She really had that problem. Fantastic scene. A very, very strong scene."

The bizarre nature of the film coupled with comments like that strongly divided critics in 1970. Steven Fuller, writing in *Changes*, called the film a masterpiece, others compared it to Federico Fellini's *Satyricon*, while the *Los Angeles Free Press* labeled it "the greatest film ever made."

Not everyone was as effusive. The *Boston Globe*'s Ty Burr derided the movie, calling it "gutbucket Luis Buñuel," while the *Los Angeles Times* called it "a dreary, protracted exercise in sadomasochism."

For his part, Jodorowsky seemed unfazed by the criticism, leaving it up to the individual to decide for themselves. "If you are great, *El Topo* is a great picture," he said. "If you are limited, *El Topo* is limited."

Availability: On DVD

My Favorite Movie You've Never Seen

"*Hot Tomorrows* (1977) is a wildly eccentric feature by Martin Brest (director of *Beverly Hills Cop* and *Scent of a Woman*). Made when he was a student at the AFI, it's like *Seventh Seal* on acid. Maybe I just imagined seeing dead people dancing in a Busby Berkeley style musical number . . . but I don't think so!"
— Ron Mann, Gemini Award–winning director of *Comic Book Confidential* and *Grass*

EVIL ROY SLADE (1972)

Cobbled together from odds and ends of three unaired television pilots for a spoof western called *Sheriff Who?* — so named because every week there would be a new sheriff killed by outlaw Evil Roy Slade — and ignored when it first aired on television on February 18, 1972, *Evil Roy Slade* was rediscovered on vHs. It has since become something of a cult classic.

Created by Garry Marshall and Jerry Belson, Roy Slade (an acronym for Sneaking, Lying, Arrogance, Dirtiness and Evil) is a bandit so despicable that when he was just an orphaned baby, left stranded in the desert, no one would adopt him — not even the wolves. He raised himself, and even had to change his own diapers. That kind of upbringing is rough on a child and as an adult Slade (played by John Astin of *The Addams Family*) is the meanest man in the Wild West.

The theme song warbles that he "made fun of old people . . . scared little children just to see them run." When confronted with an ambush of little people lawmen Slade tells his gang to "aim for their tiny little hearts."

He's bad alright, but he falls for Betsy Palmer (Pamela Austin) during a bank robbery — "You've got a good head on those shoulders," he tells her, "and a good body under those shoulders." She's a sweet schoolteacher who tries to "cure him of meanness." It's a bit of an uphill battle for Roy who has nastiness bred in his bones. "I tried it honey, but I just can't do it. This straight life ain't for me," he says at one point. "It's too boring! My idea of a nine-to-five job is nine men robbing five men!"

There are a few others who'd like to see Evil Roy give up his life of crime, including Nelson L. Stool (Mickey Rooney), the president of Western Express, and Bing Bell (Dick Shawn), a former marshal with a penchant for bedazzled cowboy hats and a way with a song. Bell has come out of retirement to track Roy down.

In the end Roy is almost undone by the very things that have always been the cornerstones of his life — betrayal and deceit.

Evil Roy Slade isn't here because it's a great example of filmmaking. It isn't. It is a competently made television movie, helmed by Jerry Paris, a director-for-hire with literally dozens of sitcoms and TV movies to his credit. It isn't here because of its *mise en scène*, or interesting character arcs. No, it's here for one simple reason. It's really funny.

Packed to the rafters with sight gags and one-liners, *Evil Roy Slade* never lets up and could easily give the better known comic westerns *Blazing Saddles* and *Cat Ballou* a run for their money. Marshall and Belson never met a joke too stupid, a situation too outrageous that they wouldn't try and milk some humor out of.

When Roy rides a miniature horse through the desert, it's funny. When he arrives home on the horse, hours late and says, "Sorry I'm late, honey, but I kinda dragged my heels getting here," it's outrageous. It's the stupidest joke ever, but it works, and if you don't like that one, just wait a minute, and there will be at least five more gags coming at you hard and fast.

The joke to running time ratio probably outpaces *Airplane!*, although there are far fewer double entendres here than in a Jim Abrahams and David Zucker comedy (in spite of Nelson L. Stool's private train having "Number 2" written on the side).

Astin plays Slade as a riff on his Gomez Addams character — calm and cool on the outside, but completely psychotic on the inside. His way with a one-liner, usually accompanied by bulging eyes — sells even the skimpiest of material and he is joined by a supporting cast of hams, including Milton Berle, Edie Adams, Dom DeLuise, Henry Gibson, Ed Begley Jr. and Penny Marshall, who wring every bit of humor out of this script.

Evil Roy Slade has the same anarchic flow as the better received work of Mel Brooks or Abrahams and Zucker, but with a G-rating that makes it appropriate for kids and a cutting, inventive edge that'll keep the parents interested.

Availability: On DVD

"We're going to see things no one has ever seen before. Just think about it."
— CORA PETERSON (RAQUEL WELCH) IN *FANTASTIC VOYAGE*

FANTASTIC VOYAGE (1966)

Sci-fi fans can be forgiven for assuming that *Fantastic Voyage*'s story originated in the fertile mind of author Isaac Asimov. The novel was released six months before the movie debuted in theaters and the book, which has sold over two million copies, trumpets Asimov's name on the cover in type almost as big as the title. In fact, the legendary author of *I, Robot* and *Building Blocks of the Universe* was brought in to pen the novelization of the film, a tie-in that would be used to stir up interest in the movie.

Well before Azimov's book, however, there was a loose treatment that became the basis for screenwriter Harry Kleiner's script about a team of miniaturized scientists who travel inside the body of a comatose colleague. Kleiner took an unusual approach to the job, setting aside the actual writing until he had gone back to school. He reasoned that for the film to be effective he'd need a working knowledge of the medical and scientific aspects of anatomy. Enrolling at UCLA, he took an intensive three-week refresher course that gave him a working knowledge of the human body. He simultaneously wrote the script and a much longer reference guide, which, according to the movie's press book, would be the filmmaker's "road map for developing the film's unique and breathtaking look inside the world of the human body."

Kleiner crafted a story about scientist Jan Benes (Jean Del Val) a prominent scientist who, while working behind the Iron Curtain, discovered the secret of atomic miniaturization. The CIA helps him defect to the West, which naturally ticks off "the other side" who know how to miniaturize objects, but just can't stabilize the process enough to make it practical. You see the discovery isn't perfect — the shrinking method only works for 60 minutes — but further study has revealed a possible solution.

Benes has figured out the key to the process, but before he can implement this innovation an attempted assassination leaves him comatose with a dangerous blood clot in his brain. He's the only one who knows how the new process works so it is imperative that he be saved. Trouble is, the clot cannot be removed through surgery. Having exhausted traditional medical treatments a team of bionauts, Charles Grant (Stephen Boyd), pilot Captain Bill Owens (William Redfield), Dr. Michaels (Donald Pleasence), surgeon Dr. Peter Duval (Arthur Kennedy) and his assistant Cora Peterson (Raquel Welch) board a submarine, the *Proteus*, which is then miniaturized to one micrometer in length and injected into Benes.

Their fantastic voyage has begun, but time is at a premium as they only have one hour to locate and neutralize the clot. As they wind their way through Benes's heart, inner ear and the alveoli of the lungs to replenish their supply of oxygen they meet many obstacles. When it's discovered that the surgical laser crucial to the rescue operation has been damaged it seems there might be a double agent on-board. By the time they reach the clot they have only six minutes to operate and exit the body.

Fantastic Voyage is very much a film of its time. The mid-'60s were a technology crazed era, when the president talked of going to the moon and much of what once seemed to be science fiction appeared to be becoming science fact. Science was very much a part of popular culture; in fact *Star Trek*, the best known sci-fi series of the decade, premiered on NBC the day after *Fantastic Voyage* opened in New York. It was a hopeful time when people believed that technology could do anything.

Coupling the movie's crazy science with a Cold War theme and the idea of miniaturizing people to repair a former Soviet scientist's brain hits the zeitgeist nail right on the head. Add some attractive actors, some amazing (for the time) special effects and you've got something singular. Or so it would seem.

"Unfortunately the picture didn't do as well [at the box office] as it could have done," said director Richard Fleischer in a 1989 interview. "The people who were trying to sell it didn't really know how to handle it. They had simply never seen a movie like it before. The ads didn't let the audience know that it was an intelligent science fiction film. Instead, the public probably had the impression that it was some sort of monster movie. Meanwhile I was trying to impress the audience with the majesty of the human body."

Fantastic Voyage seems a little dated today, but in 1966 it was the most expensive science fiction film to date, featuring elaborate sets: The Miniaturization Center set alone took 50 builders 50 days to construct, for a total of 16,000 hours; scientifically accurate recreations of the internal pathways of the human body; and a giant lung (complete with nicotine stains!) made of fiberglass, poured latex and cement that measured 340,000 cubic feet.

Its look is retro-cool, with a visual interpretation of outer space that's more lava lamp than hydrogen plasma, but those mind-boggling visuals are secondary to another aspect of the production that drew in a lot of teenage boys. No, it's not the educational side of the movie, although that was one of the film's selling points. It's Raquel Welch, who got her big break playing Cora, the spirited medical laser technician and the only woman aboard the *Proteus*.

By 1966 Welch had appeared on many television shows, mostly in uncredited roles, but by the end of the year the one-two punch of *One Million Years B.C.*, in which she played the fur-bikini clad cave woman Loana, and *Fantastic Voyage*'s epic scene of swimming in the blood stream in a form-fitting wetsuit cemented her status as an international sex symbol.

While some reviewers noted that the bulk of Welch's "characterization is in her wetsuit," she doesn't really fare worse than anyone else in the cast, who simply play this pseudo science in the most straight-ahead way possible. Each cast member is required to spout scientific mumbo-jumbo about navigating through reticular fibers and endolymphatic ducts and each do so in a most deadpan way while Jacques Cousteau–ing it through Benes's body.

The science, so carefully researched by Kleiner, doesn't really hold up to scrutiny. The anatomy is spot on but there are logical flaws that don't make scientific sense. Spoiler alert! After the crew makes their escape the *Proteus* and the saboteur's body remain inside. Both have been altered — the submarine destroyed, the saboteur eaten by a white blood cell — but atoms from them are still inside Benes. Why wouldn't those atoms expand and kill their host body?

It's this error that won the film the Piltdown Mandible Award at the 1966 Harvard Lampoon Movie Worsts Awards. The Academy of Motion Picture Arts and Sciences wasn't as bothered by the lapse and gave the film two Oscars, one for Special Visual Effects and another for Art Direction.

For his part Asimov wrestled with the story's scientific slip-up, correcting it by having the debris of the sub leave the body through a tear duct in the tie-in book and adding his own expertise to several other sequences, including the scene where the crew siphons off air from Benes's lung. Asimov surmised that there would be no scientific basis for this procedure as the crew was miniaturized and the air would consist of regular sized molecules. He solved the problem by giving the crew a miniaturization device on-board the ship.

Despite its leaps of logic and inaccuracies, *Fantastic Voyage* is a great time capsule from an era when anything seemed possible, whether it was miniaturization, the end of the Cold War or even Raquel Welch as a scientist.

Availability: On DVD

Richard's Favorite Mad Movie Science

1. "This is the warning device. It's so sensitive that before an earthquake happens, before it's either seen or heard, this device senses it. Obviously, we call it a 'sensor.'"
   – *Around the World Under the Sea* (1966)

2. "Well, radiation causes photosynthesis – that is, the growing process – to continue night and day. The radioisotopes act as a – sort of an artificial sun; a sun that never sets!"
   – *Beginning of the End* (1957)

3. "Plan 9? Ah, yes. Plan 9 deals with the resurrection of the dead. Long distance electrodes shot into the pineal and pituitary gland of the recently dead." – *Plan 9 from Outer Space* (1959)

4. "Commander, I have found that people are always jumping to wild conclusions concerning atomic reaction. Science fact and science fiction are not the same. Not in the least!"
   – *The Monster That Challenged the World* (1957)

5. "No! Now I know the reason for my failures. It was the kind of skin graft I used, taken from girls who were dead, so the cells were dead cells. That's why I always failed. That's what was wrong, and from now on I must use grafts from living women only, and then my crimes will be complete." – *The Awful Dr. Orloff* (1962)

6. "Within the next few minutes we expect to make world-shattering history! The dual-powered *Lunar Eagle* will take off with a liquid fuel method, and outside the Earth's atmosphere will convert to atomic power. When the moon's orbit is reached, by retro-power the first landing on the moon will be attempted! If all goes as planned, touchdown on lunar soil will be 27 hours from X minus zero!" – *12 to the Moon* (1960)

7. "That bird is extraterrestrial! It comes from outer space – from some godforsaken anti-matter galaxy millions and millions of light years from the Earth. No other explanation is possible." – *The Giant Claw* (1957)

8. "What a fool I've been! I've allowed the duo-thermal impulsator to be attached only to the body! Let's see what Grandfather's notation says . . . You see? The duo-thermal impulsator must also be attached to a living brain, to transmit living vibrations to the artificial brain!" – *Jesse James Meets Frankenstein's Daughter* (1966)

9. "At the risk of being simplistic, what you're looking at is a quasi-neural matrix of synthetic RNA molecules." – *The Demon Seed* (1977)

10. "Where the land masses split the oceans will be sucked in, and the colossal pressure generated by the steam will rip the Earth apart – and destroy it." – *Crack in the World* (1965)

Tommy (Ray Barlow): "Look, I don't know what the hell
your point is, but . . ."
Varla (Tura Satana): "The point is of no return and
you've reached it!"
— DIALOGUE FROM *FASTER, PUSSYCAT! KILL! KILL!*

FASTER, PUSSYCAT! KILL! KILL! (1965)

Nineteen sixty-five was a big year in pop culture history. Bob Dylan, Fender guitar in hand, was booed by folk purists for going electric. Both *Days of Our Lives* and *A Charlie Brown Christmas* debuted on network television. Richard Hickock and Perry Smith, the *In Cold Blood* killers, were executed in April of that year, and a turbo-charged movie starring three women so well-endowed their bra sizes were off the alphabetical map shocked audiences with its outrageous ultra-violent story.

Russ Meyer was one of Hollywood's most idiosyncratic filmmakers. A string of soft-core movies with titles like *Skyscrapers and Brassieres, Wild Gals of the Naked West* and *The Immoral Mr. Teas* (the first cutie nudie film to rake in over $1 million at the box office) established him as the leading auteur of smut. An experienced World War II combat cameraman, Meyer had an unerring eye, which most often he focused on abnormally endowed women. "I always had a tremendous interest in big tits," said the director, who once toyed with the idea of calling a movie *The Bra of God*.

Early financial success meant that he was able to self-produce his films, free from the constraints that come attached when you use someone else's cash. As a result his body of work is a singular vision, a "swinging tribute to unrestrained female anatomy." It pushed the limits of onscreen nudity, with added dollops of violence and sex for good measure. Taboos were shattered, audiences were titillated and Meyer made money.

The porn king's unbroken run of box office hits came to a screeching halt with the release of 1965's unusually titled *Faster, Pussycat! Kill! Kill!* "It just died, laid an egg," said Meyer. "No one cared."

Meyer envisioned *Faster, Pussycat!* as a change from his usual sexploitation fare. "I had men kicking the shit out of women," he said, "so I thought, 'Why don't we do one where the women kick the shit out of the men?'" To this end he hired John E. "Jack" Moran to flesh out his idea.

Moran, a hard drinking part-time liquor store clerk, came up with the story of three curvy, mascara-sodden go-go dancers with a passion for violence. Fueled by booze, he wrote the script in just four days, churning out dialogue that according to critic (and former Meyer screenwriter) Roger Ebert, "seems phoned in from another universe."

The movie begins when our three supercharged women, Varla (Tura Satana), Rosie (the singularly named Quebec-born Haji) and Billie (Lori Williams), challenge all-American boy Tommy (Ray Barlow) and his sniveling girlfriend Linda (Susan Bernard, the first Jewish playmate for *Playboy*) to a "chicken-race" in the desert.

Following the race — won by running him off the track — the mean-spirited Varla taunts Tommy until they come to blows. She quickly incapacitates him with karate chops before breaking his spine with a sickening crack. (In reality it was a Foley artist splitting a walnut to produce the sound.) Leaving his body for the vultures, the balloon-chested trio kidnaps Linda.

At a nearby gas station the girls see the muscle-bound Vegetable (Dennis Busch), and his disabled father, the Dirty Old Man (Stuart Lancaster). A loose-lipped gas station attendant lets it slip to the leather-clad vixens that the old man has a fortune stashed on his property. They hatch a plan. Billie is interested in the hunky Vegetable — "Two of everything, and some left over," she moans — while Varla has her eye on stealing the man's money.

They discover he lives in a rundown farmhouse with his two sons, the aptly named Vegetable and the "normal" one, Kirk (Paul Trinka). Using the innocent Linda as bait they ingratiate themselves to the old man. Over lunch they tell him a cock-and-bull story about how they are returning the unstable Linda (whom they have drugged with sleeping pills) home to her rich parents.

It turns out they have stumbled into a very strange situation. The Dirty Old Man is a depraved dude who relies on his slow-witted son to supply him with willing young women. Both have issues, and suffer hysterics when the regional freight train runs by their house.

"Sound your warning," says the old man, teeth gnashing as the train passes, "send your warning. Huff and puff and belch your smoke, and kill and maim and run off unpunished!" What follows is a twisted tale of seduction, rape, double-crosses and murder that sees the movie end in a frenzy of outrageous action.

The words and scenario may have come from Moran's booze-addled brain, but the realization of the movie is pure Russ Meyer. Every scene is more lurid and fantastic than the last, leading up to the film's loopy conclusion. His razor-sharp editing style, crazy action and outrageous visuals have the visceral power of a drop kick to the head. Meyer's phobia of showing his actors blinking onscreen required him to use a rapid fire cutting technique that revs the pace of the movie up to Indy 500 standards. It's fast and furious, beautifully rendered in "glorious black and blue" by cinematographer Walter Schenk.

Another major component of the look of the film is its three go-go booted leads, Tura Satana, Haji and Lori Williams. Hand-picked by Meyer, the trio of buxom beauties at the center of the movie were chosen for their physical attributes as much as their acting ability.

Despite having some movie experience in beach party and Elvis movies, 18-year-old Lori Williams almost wasn't cast as Billie because Meyer didn't think she was well endowed enough. A little padding and some revealing outfits took care of Meyer's initial problem with Williams, but when she tried to actually act in the film, Meyer had to put his foot down.

"I would have lines lying atop the Porsche," she said. "Nobody does that. I fought Russ on that. I had studied serious acting. Why don't I just talk? He said, 'You don't understand, this is a cartoon. This is camp, exaggerate it, be corny.' And he was right."

Haji, a burlesque dancer who worked with Meyer several times is well cast as the crackerjack Rosie. Her ample 38D-23-37 more than fulfilled Meyer's standards, even if her accent, not quite Italian, not exactly Spanish either, is a little uneven.

At center stage is Tura Satana and her gravity-defying cleavage. A tough burlesque dancer who had once dated Elvis and also tutored Carol Burnett in the fine art of striptease, Satana is *Faster, Pussycat*'s secret weapon. As Varla she's evil, seductive and just a little crazy.

It's impossible to imagine the movie without her, but she almost didn't bother to audition because of Meyer's reputation as a soft porn director. Only after her agent assured her the movie wasn't going to feature nudity — it comes as close to the line as possible without revealing anything — did she agree to go.

"Russ asked me, 'How would you play the lead in this script?'" she said, recalling the audition. "So I read a couple of scenes and I said, 'I could play her two ways. I could play her very soft and feminine or I could play her as a very ballsy woman.'" After reading it both ways Meyer elected to go with the extreme version that we see in the film, which film critic Richard Corliss called "the scariest" performance in the Meyer canon. The fierce performance won over Quentin Tarantino, who told *Entertainment Weekly* that he'd give up five years of his life to work with Tura Satana.

Unlike Meyer's previous films the women remain clothed throughout. That doesn't mean that he eschews cheesecake altogether — there's cleavage galore and plenty of gratuitous shots of the gals putting on their bras and showering — but he's uncharacteristically prudish when it comes to showing any skin. It's as if he believed that showing them naked would strip away their power, reducing them to objects. Or perhaps the powerful women simply refused to doff their clothes. Either way, Meyer blamed the lack of success of the film in its original release on the lack of naked flesh. "People complained when I didn't show Tura Satana's big tits naked," he said.

In the years since its initial release *Faster, Pussycat! Kill! Kill!* has become one of Meyer's most influential, but less seen films. Embraced by both punk and camp culture, the film's tentacles have spread throughout popular culture to the point where more people have probably seen projects inspired by the movie than the film itself.

Hairspray director John Waters cites it as an influence, claiming that he and Divine based the character Dawn Davenport in *Female Trouble* on Satana. Paying tribute, Waters calls *Faster, Pussycat!* "beyond a doubt, the best movie ever made. It is possibly better than any film that will be made in the future."

The rebellious spirit of the film seems to have struck a chord with musicians, many of whom reference the film in their work.

White Zombie used samples from the film on the album *La Sexorcisto: Devil Music, Vol. 1*, while the Cramps covered "Faster Pussycat" on the album *Smell of Female*. The "All These Things That I Have Done" video from the Killers is clearly influenced by the look of *Faster, Pussycat!*, and Rob Zombie used clips from the film in his video "Dead Girl Superstar." The flick has inspired two band names — Faster Pussycat and the Los Angeles based rap-metal band Tura Satana — plus at least one porno, *Faster Pussycat Fuck! Fuck!*

Tura Satana offers up her own reason why she thinks the film strikes a chord with the people who see it. "I think that the message that the film sends is a message to women in general," she says. "It is that women can be feminine and yet still be strong. They no longer have to feel that they are the weaker sex. We might not have the same strength that the males do, but we can learn to use the strengths that we have to make ourselves heard and felt throughout the world."

Limited availability on DVD

"Ladies and gentleman, by way of introduction, this is a film about trickery . . . fraud . . . about lies. Tell it by the fireside or in a marketplace or in a movie, almost any story is almost certainly some kind of lie, but not this time. This is a promise. For the next hour, everything you hear from us is really true and based on solid fact."
— **ORSON WELLES IN THE INTRO TO** *F FOR FAKE*

F FOR FAKE (1974)

Has there ever been a sadder waste of talent in Hollywood than Orson Welles, the boy genius who took the theater world by storm and conquered radio before heading west to make movies? After being beaten down by William Randolph Hearst's campaign to ruin him and his movie *Citizen Kane* combined with his own arrogance, Welles wiled away his Hollywood years just like any other hack actor, taking gigs to pay the bills. Still, occasional flashes of brilliance would shine through. *F for Fake*, his last completed film, proves that for Welles, while the mute button may have been on much of the time, there was no off switch for his genius.

F for Fake can't rightly be described as a documentary, it's too stream-of-consciousness for that. Welles called it an "essay film"; blurring the line between fact and fiction he pays tribute to the world of charlatans, scoundrels and con men using a blend of documentary footage and staged scenes. Serving as onscreen host and narrator Welles focuses on "two world leaders in fakery": internationally famous art forger Elmyr de Hory and his biographer Clifford Irving.

The Hungarian-born de Hory, the subject of Irving's book *Fake!*, was a con man extraordinaire who fooled experts with his finely crafted fakes of Picasso and Modigliani paintings. The master forger was driven to a life of fakery when the art establishment rejected his own, more personal paintings. To poke a stick in the eye of the art world, he started manufacturing the fakes, sometimes at a rate of one or two a day to show up the experts who declared his forgeries to be authentic. "If they are hanged long enough in the museum they become real," he says of his paintings, adding, "I don't feel bad for Modigliani, I feel good for me."

Irving wasn't simply de Hory's biographer. He created a scandal of his own in 1972 when he bilked publishers McGraw-Hill out of three-quarters of a million dollars, claiming he could deliver a first person biography of reclusive millionaire Howard Hughes. Trouble was, Irving had never met Hughes and had no access to him.

Welles, who calls himself a charlatan early on, weaves the two stories together with personal asides on his own history with fakery — terrifying the nation with his legendary *War of the Worlds* broadcast, talking his way into the Gate Theater in Dublin as a teen — all the while performing onscreen magic tricks for a group of kids. But close-up magic isn't the only sleight of hand going on here.

Welles uses his considerable skill as a filmmaker to piece these random strips of celluloid together into montages that beguile the eye and play tricks with reality. His masterful editing creates rhythms within the film as he plays with the idea of what is real and what is not by cutting back and forth between reality and the film being edited on a Movieola. The clever technique lets the viewer in on the creation of the film and how some details are manipulated to create the story the filmmaker wishes to tell and how truth can suffer as a result. It's simultaneously a celebration of the creative process and an exposé of how that process can be used to bend the truth.

F for Fake is elliptical, providing more questions than answers, but that is the value of it. When Welles says, "It's pretty but is it art? How is it valued? The value depends on opinion, opinion depends on the expert, a faker like Elmyr makes fool of the experts, so who's the expert? Who's the faker?" he is challenging the viewer to reassess their own assumptions about art.

It's challenging, interesting stuff presented by a man who spent his life trading in the unreal world of celebrity but, through his art, always strove to find the truth.

Availability: On DVD

"I'm not the vocalist . . . I'm the singer."
— STOKER (NODDY HOLDER) IN *FLAME*

FLAME (1975)
■ ■ ■ ■ ■ ■

In 1974 Slade were the biggest band in the United Kingdom. Their energetic brand of glam rock moved more singles in the U.K. than any other group of the 1970s, with a series of 12 Top Five singles (five of which entered the charts at Number One) from 1971 to 1974 dominating the British charts in a way unheard of since the reign of the Beatles.

Although Quiet Riot had a U.S. hit with their cover of the band's "Cum on Feel the Noize" in 1983, Slade's success never touched North American shores — but their influence helped shaped some of the biggest U.S. bands of the 1970s. Kiss bassist Gene Simmons called them the band's biggest influence ("There would probably never have been us without them," he said) while Joey Ramone said he wanted to create some of the intensity of the band for himself, so he formed the Ramones and "a couple of years later I was at CBGBS doing my best [imitation of singer] Noddy Holder."

Slade proper broke up in 1991 with the departure of Holder, but the band's legacy lives on through constant greatest hits repackagings of their chart-busting string of singles and a little-seen 1974 film called *Flame.*

"We didn't want to do *A Hard Day's Night* sort of slapstick, speeded-up film thing," says Holder, "because we thought that would be too obvious for Slade."

The original scenario for *Flame* was a goofy idea in line with previous films starring bands like the Monkees (*Head*) and the Beatles (*Help!*). It was a sci-fi spoof called *Quite a Mess*, based on the extremely successful Hammer Film *The Quatermass Experiment*. That idea was vetoed by guitarist Dave Hill who declined to take part when he realized his character was killed off in the first 15 minutes by a nasty triffid. Instead the band decided to work with screenwriter Andrew Birkin (brother of Jane) and first-time director Richard Loncraine and do something no popular group had ever done before — make a downbeat gritty film, a dark look at life on the road.

"Each scene in the film is actually a true story from different bands we knew or heard stories about," Holder told *Classic Rock* in 2007. "In fact, I don't think there's anything fictional in it as such, it was just that the names were changed to protect the innocent."

When we first meet the members of the fictional Flame — guitarist Barry (Dave Hill with a name that pays tribute to *Peter Pan* author J. M. Barrie), bassist Paul (Jim Lea, who nicked his name from Paul McCartney), drummer Charlie (Don Powell, borrowing the name of Rolling Stones drummer Charlie Watts) and Stoker (Noddy Holder, lifting the name of *Dracula* author Bram Stoker) — it's 1966 and they are all unsuccessfully gigging on the pub circuit. Stoker fronts the Undertakers and in a scene inspired by proto goth rocker Screamin' Lord Sutch, tries to make a dramatic stage entrance by bursting out of a coffin. Unfortunately his future bandmates have sabotaged the stunt by padlocking the casket shut and ruining the show.

Despite this inauspicious meeting the four musicians bond and form Flame, a rowdy club act that gets signed to a major label run by the ruthless Robert Seymour (Tom Conti) and his sidekick Tony Devlin (Kenneth Colley, best known as Admiral Piett from *Star Wars Episodes V and VI*). The first sign of trouble comes when bassist Paul asks

Seymour if he likes the band's music. "My personal preference really doesn't come into it," he says. "Let me put it this way, I don't smoke cigarettes but I manage to sell a few." To Seymour the band is simply a commodity to be bought and sold, nothing more.

Soon they discover that life in the big leagues isn't what they expected as Seymour subjects the band to ridiculous publicity stunts and doesn't always have their best interests in mind. Their lives and careers are further complicated when an ex-manager (Johnny Shannon) materializes and tries to win the band's contract back with threats and violence.

Flame works well on several levels. There's comedy in the ridiculous (but true) *Spinal Tap*–like situations the band finds itself in, but the funny bits never overshadow the movie's main thrust — the tainted view of the music industry.

Slade were one of the premier glam rock bands of their generation, but *Flame* is anything but glamorous. It's a warts-and-all look not only at the music business, but at the working class life of the band members. Shot in just six weeks on location in Nottingham and Sheffield, the movie places the action against a gray-toned backdrop of 1970s working class England — depressing terraced estate housing, polluted canals and grimy factories.

None of the band members will ever be mistaken for professional actors — "Jimmy took it seriously; Don's very witty; Dave doesn't come out of it too well," said Holder of his bandmates' work in the film — but the performances are natural and Holder has a great deal of charisma as the raucous singer. It's this lack of polish that gives the film much of its charm. The guys are essentially playing themselves and their Midland accents are at times almost impenetrable, so much so that for the U.S. release some prints came subtitled. Listen carefully and on at least one occasion the band members refer to Stoker by his real name, Noddy.

Casual music fans can enjoy the film's atmosphere and storytelling, while musicologists will take something more from it. "It was funny at the premiere," Holder says. "The fans downstairs were laughing in certain places, but the business people upstairs were all laughing in totally different places because they knew who the stories were really about."

Despite all its high points and a rockin' soundtrack, *Flame* never had a chance at the box office. A victim of the band's diminishing popularity and fans' reluctance to embrace the movie's dreary tone, it became cinematic roadkill immediately upon release. It's a shame because while *Flame* may be the bleakest rock and roll film ever made by a Top 40 rock band, it's also one of the best, falling somewhere between *Don't Look Back* and *This Is Spinal Tap* as a rock and roll cautionary tale.

Availability: On DVD

"The game is tailored specifically to each participant. Think of it as a great vacation, except you don't go to it, it comes to you."
— CONSUMER RECREATION SERVICES CUSTOMER RELATIONS AGENT JIM FEINGOLD (JAMES REBHORN) IN *THE GAME*

THE GAME (1997)

Imagine Frank Capra on downers. *The Game* is director David Fincher's twisted take on *It's a Wonderful Life*, an alternate look at a man's life that goes from bad to worse.

Michael Douglas is Nicholas Van Orton, an emotionally frigid but outrageously wealthy man. In his case money has definitely not bought happiness. He's a piece of work, the master of his domain, alone in his huge mansion, save for his put-upon housekeeper. A snarky attitude and biting wit has alienated everyone around him — when his brother asks if he thinks of him anymore, Nicholas replies, "Not since family week at rehab" — and as his 48th birthday approaches (Douglas was 53 at the time) a dark shroud surrounds him.

The upcoming anniversary is a private milestone, laden with heavy personal baggage. When Nicholas was just a boy he saw his dad kill himself on his 48th birthday. His father's unexpected suicide scarred him and now on the cusp of his own 48th, old feelings from the day of his father's death are breaking through his carefully constructed, emotionally sterile facade.

After spending his birthday alone, watching CNN and eating a hamburger off a silver tray, Nicholas is visited by his estranged younger brother Conrad (Sean Penn), who gives him an unusual present, something for the yuppie who has everything. "Make your life . . . fun," he says as he gives him an invitation to The Game.

Details on The Game are sketchy. Nicholas knows it is run by a mysterious company called Consumer Recreation Services, who claim that it will "provide whatever is lacking" in his life and that it will be "a profound life experience." Enigmatic customer relations rep Jim Feingold (James Rebhorn) likens it to "an experimental Book of the Month Club," but doesn't provide much in the way of particulars. Despite the lack of solid information on The Game — a set of rules might be nice — Nicholas signs on.

"Initials . . . initials . . . and sign here," says Feingold with a Mephistophelian giggle. "In blood. Just kidding!"

Soon his life is turned upside down as his carefully constructed existence comes apart at the seams. "I'm being toyed with by a bunch of depraved children," says Nicholas as simple things start to backfire — a pen leaks, a toilet overflows — but as The Game goes on, the stakes start to rise and things get downright surreal as CNN's Daniel Schorr mocks him through the television.

Soon the very fabric of his being is torn apart and for the first time in his adult days he must experience powerlessness, poverty and rejection. Physical danger seems around every corner as he gets trapped inside a cab sinking into the bay and left for dead in Mexico.

The Game, it turns out, is a real life role-playing game, a Dungeons & Dragons for adults in which the point of The Game is to figure out the point of The Game.

Here the story really starts to get oblique — complete with an ending that would make *Sixth Sense* director M. Night "Twist Master" Shyamalan green with envy — with multiple sleights of hand blurring the line between what is real and what isn't in Nicholas's trip to the *Twilight Zone*. To uncover any more of the labyrinthine plot details would reveal too much.

The Game has a twist ending that will throw you for a loop the first time you see it. Does it hold up on repeated viewings? The answer is yes (are the machinations of *The Usual Suspects* any less effective now that you know how it ends?) for a few reasons.

The Game is a well-paced story that occasionally may stretch the boundaries of credulity, but never fails to bend the rules of how thrillers work. There's nothing predictable about the progression of the story, and the turns thrown at Nicholas by The Game not only keep him off balance, but also keep the viewer guessing.

Fincher — who made this film between two of his more successful movies, *Se7en* and *Fight Club*, and went on to *Panic Room* and *Zodiac* — keeps the pedal to the metal and rarely gives the viewer time to think. Good thing too, because *The Game*'s jigsaw puzzle plot requires a good dollop of suspended disbelief.

Critic James Berardinelli compared it to the kind of movie that suspense master Alfred Hitchcock used to call "refrigerator films." That is, movies that seem well crafted and hold together while you're watching them, but make less sense later when you give them a second thought while "standing in front of the refrigerator." *The Game* definitely isn't a film that holds up to close scrutiny plot-wise, but the living nightmare created by the movie is such an intense roller-coaster ride, such a great examination of paranoia, that all is forgiven.

Next is the central performance of Michael Douglas. Nicholas is the kind of character that provided the bedrock of Douglas's mid-1980sonward career, the highly strung man at the end of his tether. Think of this role as the love child of two of his previous characters, *Wall Street*'s Gordon Gekko and William "D-Fens" Foster of *Falling Down*, a high-flyer in for a very big dose of ego-adjustment.

On an unexpected note, *The Game* is much funnier than you would think. David Fincher's films aren't known for their humor, but Douglas brings a dry wit to the role that helps to humanize a character that otherwise may be too much of a cliché to identify with. For example, when Nicholas loses a shoe while climbing a fire-escape ladder, he says, "There goes a thousand dollars."

"Your shoes cost a thousand dollars?" his companion says.

"That one did."

It's a funny exchange, made funnier by the situation and Douglas's pinpoint comic timing. In an interview with *Uncut* Douglas says he felt it was important to introduce humor to the story.

"I thought we needed . . . some comedic relief versus David's fear of comedic release. We used to joke about what I called my Jerry Lewis routine . . . to try some double-takes to get some humor into it. This was 'a game.' We'd established how serious the guy was. I felt instinctively we [also] needed some outbursts from this guy."

Layered with equal measures of icy detachment and rage, it's Douglas's best performance from his late-'90s period, rivaled only by his BAFTA-winning role in 2000's *Wonder Boys*. He hits all of Nicholas's facets perfectly.

Also very much on display is Fincher's elegantly provocative film-making. Dark and brooding, he still manages to inject playfulness into the look and feel of the movie. His direction is sleek, purposeful and effectively glides through most of the plot's deficiencies. Fincher himself places the movie in a special category apart from most of his other work.

"A movie is made for an audience and a film is made for both the audience and the filmmakers," he told *The Guardian*. "I think that *The Game* is a movie and I think *Fight Club*'s a film."

He goes on to call *The Game* and *Panic Room* (his 2002 "woman-trapped-in-a-house" movie) "footnote movies, guilty pleasure movies. Thrillers," adding, "they're not particularly important."

Whatever the director's take on *The Game*, it remains an exciting, confounding and deftly appealing way to spend 128 minutes.

Availability: On DVD

"Marriage is like a mousetrap — easy to get in but hard to get out. And the husband is the piece of cheese."
— **UNCLE MATT (LEON ERROL) IN *THE GIRL FROM MEXICO***

THE GIRL FROM MEXICO (1939)

The Latin Lucille Ball, Lupe Velez, born in 1908 to a prostitute mother in San Luis de Potosi, Mexico, was best known for her series of "Mexican Spitfire" films. In 1939 she first played Carmelita Lindsay, a fiery Mexican entertainer in a low-budget slapstick comedy titled *The Girl from Mexico*, which proved very popular with audiences. It was so successful, in fact, that RKO spun off a franchise featuring Velez. She played Carmelita seven more times in movies made between 1940 and 1943, with titles like *Mexican Spitfire's Baby* and *Mexican Spitfire Sees a Ghost*, which was released as the main half of a double bill, coupled with Orson Welles classic *The Magnificent Ambersons* as the added feature, a fate usually reserved for B-pictures.

As is so often the case, the first cut is the deepest. For my money, the best of the "Mexican Spitfire" films is the original, *The Girl from Mexico*.

The story begins in Mexico with American advertising executive

Dennis Lindsay (the Brandon, Manitoba–born Donald Woods) searching for talent to headline a New York nightclub. His eyes light up when he meets sizzling cabaret performer and titular star Carmelita (Velez). She's perfect, beautiful and talented, but once back in the Big Apple the crackerjack singer proves to be more of a handful than the staid Dennis bargained for.

One night Carmelita and Dennis's Uncle Matt (former Ziegfeld comic Leon Errol) cause trouble and generate headlines when she disrupts a boxing match by crawling into the ring. She's a hot tamale, alright. Dennis is not pleased with her outrageous behavior but even though she's a pain in the ass, she's a beautiful one, and Dennis soon finds himself in love with her.

There's just one problem (it wouldn't be a screwball comedy without a romantic complication). He's engaged to be married to Elizabeth Price (Linda Hayes, mother of Cathy Lee Crosby). Not one to let a trifle like a fiancée stand between her and her man, Carmelita actively pursues Dennis, with the full approval of Uncle Matt but to the horror of his shrewish wife Aunt Della (Elisabeth Risdon).

After lots of witty repartee, mistaken identities and farcical situations, to Uncle Matt's delight the couple end up in one another's arms.

Although *The Girl from Mexico* is what critic Andrew Sarris called "a sex comedy without the sex" it pops with sexual tension, particularly from the firecracker Velez, who perfected her onscreen persona in this film — sexy and sassy with a dash of slapstick.

For the next four years she and Leon Errol (the role of the Spitfire's husband was played by several different actors over the course of the franchise) would pump out variations on *The Girl from Mexico* with diminishing returns.

Her strong points were always on display — the broken-English malapropisms, her hair-trigger temper and deftness with physical comedy — but the quality of the scripts wasn't there. The snappy dialogue of the first movie was reduced to screaming fits and nagging in subsequent editions, and while the chemistry between Velez and Errol was undeniable, the rubber-legged actor's portrayal of the lovable lout Uncle Matt grew wearisome. The last of the series, *Mexican Spitfire's Blessed Event*, came (and quickly went) in 1943.

By then Velez's career was waning. Audiences had grown tired of her Latin Lucille Ball routine, and her former contemporaries, Douglas Fairbanks, Mary Pickford and Stan Laurel and Oliver Hardy, were, for the most part, relegated to the Hollywood history books. Velez too was finding it harder to find work, and her personal life — a stormy marriage to Johnny "Tarzan" Weissmuller and a failed romance with Gary Cooper — was getting more attention than her acting roles. Her charms were legendary in Hollywood circles. "Lupe had a unique ability to rotate her left breast," said Errol Flynn. "Not only that, she could counter-rotate it, a feat so supple and beautiful to observe that you couldn't believe your eyes."

On December 13, 1944, downhearted over her failed romance with songwriter Harold Raymond and pregnant with his child, Velez committed suicide with an overdose of Seconal.

Velez wanted to die as she had lived — glamorously. She carefully planned everything — she wore a beautiful silk nightgown, applied fresh makeup and arranged herself in a demure pose in a room filled with flowers and scented candles. She knew photographers would take her picture in death, and that picture would make front cover news the next day. Everything had to be perfect.

Unfortunately, Velez didn't plan on her overdose of pills reacting badly with her last meal.

In his book *Hollywood Babylon* writer Kenneth Anger perpetrates the unsavoury (and likely, untrue) legend of the sad conclusion to the story. "When Juanita the chambermaid had opened the bedroom door at nine, the morning after the suicide, no Lupe was in sight. The bed was empty. The aroma of scented candles, the fragrance of tuberoses, almost but not quite masked a stench recalling that left by Skid Row derelicts. Juanita traced the vomit trail from the bed, followed the spotty track over to the orchid-tiled bathroom. There she found her mistress,

Señorita Velez, head jammed down in the toilet bowl, drowned. The huge dose of Secanol had not been fatal in the expected fashion. It had mixed rech-erously with the Spitfire's Mexi-Spice Last Supper."

Apparently Velez's career wasn't the only thing in the toilet.

In December 1965 artist and experimental filmmaker Andy Warhol paid tribute to "Whoopee Lupe," directing Edie Sedgwick in the title role of *Lupe* which was based on the life (and death) of the actress.

Lupe Velez was only 36 years old when she took her own life.

Availability: Hard to find

GODSPEED YOU! BLACK EMPEROR (1976)

In '60s- and '70s-era movies like *Angel Unchained*, *Beat Girl* and *Bucket of Blood*, bikers, beatniks and hippies rode roughshod over traditional American film as beacons of a quickly fading past and emerging youth culture. Like many North American exploitation filmmakers Japanese directors often found rich material in the new freedoms being enjoyed by their country's rebellious teens. Post-war Japanese radical filmmakers like Nagisa Oshima and Seijun Suzuki emulated their American counterparts, making films that accentuated the quickly growing divide between that country's war-ravaged adults and teenagers.

One of the most famous, but little seen films of this period is *Godspeed You! Black Emperor* (*Goddo supiido yuu! Burakku emparaa*), an eccentric documentary about the exploits of Japanese B?s?zoku —

"violent running tribe" — or biker gang, the Black Emperors. The film is at best a cult item, hard to find and rarely shown in theaters. If the name rings a bell for you, it is likely because an avant-garde post-rock band of the same name based in Montreal provided some of the music for *28 Days Later* and have released several critically acclaimed albums, including *Lift Your Skinny Fists Like Antennas To Heaven.*

The first documentary by director Mitsuo Yanagimachi gets inside the comings and goings of the eight-year-old Black Emperor gang, all men in their early 20s, all too young to have been directly touched by the horrors of the World War II. They're a new breed — proudly declaring their outsider status as grifters, dropouts and idlers — that have left behind many of the old ways of their country while embracing cultural outlaw touchstones from the West. They spray graffiti on city walls, tattoo themselves with swastikas and modify their bikes to be faster and louder. The Emperors aren't the desperado one-percenters (the real bad asses, said to make up one-percent of people who ride choppers) of their American counterparts but some biker traditions from the West are evident, although watered down in form. Punishment beatings are common, but they are open-handed affairs where slaps take the place of closed fists.

So they're wild and mild — fundraising drives, an almost total ban on drug use and their strict hierarchical club structure aren't exactly ripped from the nonconformist's handbook — but there's no denying their passion to break away from the norm.

Yanagimachi presents the story as a pastiche of images bound together by the exploits of the club. His camera has intimate access to the members, their meetings and their private conversations. In the days of reality television this kind of thing has become the norm, but Yanagimachi shows skill in not allowing his camera to get in the way of the action. Watching the gang members in action you get the feeling that they are not performing for the camera, that this is true cinema-vérité.

While *Godspeed* has no main narrative focus, Yanagimachi spends most of his time with Decko, a Black Emperor grandee about to make a court appearance to answer to the charge of vandalizing a taxi. The director digs deep, peeling away the layers of Decko's bravado until the truth is revealed — he's a scared young guy who doesn't want to go to jail, who begs his mother to come to court with him.

It's an intimate portrait of a young man in crisis and provides the movie's backbone and most dramatic moments. The rest of the film is a much looser look at the culture of the B?s?zoku. Less pointed toward one character and more focused on the overall essence of the culture, it includes beautiful black and white photography of the gang's night motorcycle runs.

Are the B s zoku a social ill, a gateway to the yazuka (Japanese organized crime groups) or simply an extreme youth social club? *Godspeed You! Black Emperor* doesn't offer any answers; instead it does something that many modern documentaries don't do — it allows viewers to make up their own minds.

Availability: Hard to find

"I can't stand being in this house. In the first place, it makes me terribly nervous. I'm scared to death of doors, locks, people roaming around in the background, under the trees, in the bushes, I'm absolutely terrified."
– EDITH "LITTLE EDIE" BOUVIER BEALE IN *GREY GARDENS*

GREY GARDENS (1975)

Documentary filmmakers never know where the story is going to take them. A case in point is the making of *Grey Gardens*, a 1975 film by David and Albert Maysles.

When the doc-making brothers — best known for directing *Gimme Shelter,* their vérité take on the doomed Rolling Stones Altamont Speedway free concert — were asked by Jacqueline Bouvier Kennedy Onassis and Lee Radziwell to make a film about their childhoods, the brothers thought they would spend the next couple of years working with the former first lady and her glamorous sister.

The Maysles began pre-production on the proposed film by interviewing members of the extended Bouvier family, including two reclusive cousins who lived in a decaying 28-room mansion in East Hampton, New York, called Grey Gardens, so named because of the color of the cement garden walls. Although surrounded by the summer homes of the wealthy on the left and right, their once grand house was now better suited to the Addams Family than members of an American royal family, with overgrown gardens, cats and raccoons aplenty and constant demands from health inspectors to clean the place up.

After two months of work the brothers realized they didn't want to make a film about the famous sisters; there was a much better story in the eccentric cousins.

Jackie O. was out and the 80-year-old Edith Bouvier Beale and her daughter Little Edie were in. The filmmakers spent two months documenting the lives of the oddball cousins, using portable cameras to unobtrusively film their daily routines in the dilapidated house. Occasionally we hear an off camera question or catch a glimpse of a crew member, but for the most part it is a two-woman show.

Over the course of the years that the women lived together they developed a unique way of life. The Maysles capture the bizarre behavior of the women — from Little Edie's habit of wearing skirts upside down, to their tendency of talking over one another, to their fondness for bursting into song. It's all very strange but *Grey Gardens* is not just a voyeuristic freak show. The Maysles are able to cut through the outlandish behavior and reveal the deeper relationship between mother and daughter, which is what gives this film its humanity and makes *Grey Gardens* required viewing.

What emerges is a touching portrait of mother and daughter, two people linked so tightly, their dependence on one another has formed what the Maysles call a "closed system," or fused personality. They don't need the outside world to survive and don't look to anyone but one another for approval. The pair coexisted for so long without much contact with the outside world that they are completely guileless in their interaction with the camera. Whether they're starved for attention or just have no barriers, they openly welcome the documentarians into their world and in doing so share with the viewer the compelling melancholic saga that their lives had become.

Some have criticized the Maysles for taking advantage of these women, for co-opting their story for profit. Is it exploitative? I don't think so, and neither did Edie. According to Albert Maysles, "When we finished the film we brought the film and projector to Grey Gardens, and afterward Edie paused for a moment and then turned toward me, and in a very loud voice she shouted, 'The Maysles have created a classic!'" Apparently Big Edie agreed. On her deathbed when she was asked if she had anything to say about her life she said, "It's all in the film."

The Beales are long in the graves — Edith died in 1977, Little Edie in 2002 — but they haven't been forgotten. In 2006 Albert Maysles released previously unseen footage from the *Grey Gardens* shoot for a Criterion DVD release, and assembled a new film, *The Beales of Grey Gardens*, which received a limited theatrical release. That same year a musical based on the documentary opened on Broadway, earning Tony Awards for its stars Christine Ebersole and Mary Louise Wilson. At the time of this writing a feature film based on the Maysles doc is planned with Drew Barrymore and Jessica Lange slated to play the leads.

Availability: On DVD

"Devour the moose!"
— COACH BILL RESLER IN *THE HEART OF THE GAME*

THE HEART OF THE GAME (2005)

The Heart of the Game is a documentary that focuses on Darnellia Russell, a young Seattle woman who led her high school basketball team to a state championship. Imagine the best parts of *Hoosiers* and *He Got Game* infused with the passion of *Hoop Dreams* and you get the idea.

Filmmaker Ward Serrill initially planned to shoot the Roosevelt Roughriders for one season to create a documentary about the unorthodox coaching style of Bill Resler, a cherubic man who turned the team into champions.

"I used to be, as strange as it seems," director Ward told writer Stacey Chapman, "a CPA and I went to visit a friend. At my friend's house was this fellow Bill Resler. Bill immediately sat down and started telling me basketball stories. Forty-five minutes later I was still yucking it up with him and I said to myself, 'I think I came across a world class character.' Later, when I followed him into the gym here are these girls smashing and crashing and flying into each other and laughing and having the best time I have ever seen in a gym anywhere."

Ward ended up staying seven years, shifting the focus from Resler to Darnellia Russell, a talented, but troubled teen who became the team's star player.

The first half of the film is an entertaining, but standard sporting movie set-up. We meet the players and get to know the passionate Resler, a round-faced man who looks more like Santa Claus than a basketball coach. Resler is the star of the film's first half, eloquently speaking about the players and the recounting their triumphs. His approach is unorthodox. He uses animal metaphors to help the girls understand the killer instinct he is looking for, likening the players to a pack of wolves. "Devour the moose!" he yells during the game, kicking his wolf pack metaphor up a notch. His "Draw blood!" technique seems to unleash the inner beast in these teenage girls, and they become a formidable team.

It isn't until we meet Darnellia that the movie becomes something special. She has an intuitive physical ability on the court, but it is her off-court struggles that provide the heart of the movie. When her personal life interferes with her basketball — and the possibility of getting a scholarship — the film becomes more than just a chronicle of a team of winners, it deepens to include social comment.

Like all good sports movies *The Heart of the Game* isn't actually about sports. It is about the strength of the human spirit, the ability of the underdog to overcome obstacles and picking oneself up after falling. These are all clichés, and it is easy to be cynical about a movie that so blatantly wears them on its sleeve, but often clichés are clichés because they're true. *Heart of the Game* rings true and, like the title suggests, has a lot of heart.

Availability: On DVD

HEARTS OF THE WEST (1975)

Set in the 1930s, *Hearts of the West* is a low-key satire with Jeff Bridges as Lewis Tater — "Taylor?" "No . . . Tater" — an Iowa farm boy who aspires to be the next Zane Grey. After he signs up for a correspondence course on how to be a cowboy he gets a hankerin' to head West and pay a visit to the school in Nevada where he hopes to soak up some local flavor and "hang around the campus." To his surprise the "college" doesn't exist, it's just a post office box run by two shady characters played by Anthony James and Richard B. Shull.

Disappointed, he checks into a hotel to plot his next move. He doesn't want to go back to Iowa, but he can't really stay on the little patch of desert in Nevada either. Later that night while he's trying to sleep one of the con men breaks into his hotel room and tries to kill him. Lewis escapes into the desert in the con man's car, which soon runs out of gas. Lewis abandons the automobile, takes a box from the trunk and sets out on foot.

Luckily he's found the following morning by a posse of men on horseback. They're movie cowboys, rough and tumble guys eking out a Depression-era living cranking out oaters for fly-by-night operations like Tumbleweed Productions.

Lewis is disappointed that they're not "real" cowboys.

"Well, sure we're cowboys," says Howard Pike (Andy Griffith). "What do you suppose we are? Weasels? Look at that guy's face, right there. Show him your profile, Wally. Now don't that look like a western type to you? That right there is a cowboy's face."

"Reeks character," says Wally (Raymond Guth) turning to show his profile, "That's what they told me . . . *reeks.*"

They bring Lewis to the Wild West of Hollywood and Vine — Los Angeles — and hook him up with a dishwashing job at the Rio Café. Lewis is happy busting suds at the restaurant, but to make extra cash he finds work as a saddle tramp extra in a movie with despotic, but untalented director Burt Kessler (Alan Arkin). His scene-stealing overacting almost gets him canned on the first day, but his good nature and willingness to do a dangerous stunt — the classic jump from a building onto the back of a horse — at no extra charge gains the favor of the cheap director who decides to make Lewis the star of his next B-movie.

"Those damn cowboys!" says Kessler. "I always said they were great, didn't I? I always said you can't beat 'em."

"You always said you couldn't trust 'em . . ." says his cameraman (Dave Morick).

"Well, you misunderstood me," Burt Kessler retorts, stomping off.

Meanwhile Lewis finishes his first novel, *Hearts of the West*. Reading much like the cheesy scripts Kessler specializes in bringing to the screen, it's ripe with purple prose: "Lightening shadows stole across the harsh desert sands while the kid unholstered his deadly Colt."

Things seem to be going great guns — he even falls in love with a pretty script girl (Blythe Danner) — until a friend tries to pass off Lewis's writing as his own and his film career is interrupted by the con men on the hunt for the box he took from their car.

Hearts of the West looks like an old-time western, but has a very modern deconstructionist attitude about the Hollywood dream factory that inspired it. It's a comedy, but not the guffaw-out-loud kind. The satire in *Hearts of the West* is pointed, exploring Hollywood's self-importance, dishonesty and materialism, but is also gentle. It may not inspire laughing fits, but for much of the running time you'll find yourself with a satisfied smile plastered on your face.

Centered on Bridges's terrific performance as the easygoing dim bulb Lewis, director Howard Zieff — the former commercial director who made the "No Matter What Shape (Your Stomach's In)" and the "spicy meatball" ads for Alka-Seltzer — wisely allows the tone of the movie to take its lead from its star. Bridges is so likeable, so agreeable that it's impossible not to be won over by his charisma and talent and it is that magnetism that elevates *Hearts of the West* from average to excellent.

Availability: Out of Print VHS

"I trust their greed. They will do anything if they are saddled with gold."
– GENERAL MAKABE (TOSHIRÔ MIFUNE),
REGARDING THE TWO PEASANTS IN *THE HIDDEN FORTRESS*

THE HIDDEN FORTRESS (1958)

One of the highest grossing Japanese films of its day, *The Hidden Fortress* (*Kakushi-toride no san-akunin*) is considered to be one of Akira Kurosawa's minor masterpieces. Perhaps because it is a comedy it doesn't command the respect of *Rashômon* or *The Seven Samurai*, but the effortless way it mixes comedy, action and drama with beautiful widescreen cinematography should place it in the upper tier of the Japanese maestro's works.

Here's the pitch: Set in medieval Japan, the story sees General Rokurota Makabe (Toshiro Mifune), a defeated warlord, smuggle Princess Yuki (Misa Uehara) out of enemy territory and back to the safety of her homeland. On the road home, they encounter two bumbling peasants, Tahei (Minoru Chiaki) and Matakishi (Kamatari Fujiwara). In a bold move for the time, Kurosawa breaks with tradition by telling the story from the vantage point of the two peasants rather than the heroic characters. With the princess disguised as a mute farmhand — her upper-class accent would give her away — and a fortune in gold in tow, this unlikely band travel the countryside, trying unsuccess-fully to avoid trouble and enemy soldiers.

If the basic outline sounds vaguely familiar to you, don't be shocked. The influence of *The Hidden Fortress* on more popular films has far out-stripped the number of people who have actually seen it. George Lucas cites it as one of the inspirations for the original *Star Wars*, basing C-3PO and R2-D2 on Tahei and Matakishi and Princess Leia on the spirited Yuki. That's what he admits to; others have also noted striking similar-ities to *The Hidden Fortress* in *The Phantom Menace*. Certainly he's not alone in using the film as inspiration. Many Asian action movies have based their stories on a heroic male lead guarding a mouthy princess, and celebrated animator Hayao Miyazaki says he lifted bits of the film for his most famous work, *Princess Mononoke*.

Spending some time with *The Hidden Fortress* reveals why it has influenced so many filmmakers. Although Kurosawa deliberately designed the "jidai-geki" (period-set picture) film to be accessible as a way to pay back Toho Studios for their support of his commercially riskier art house films, it is as well crafted and entertaining as any of his more famous works.

Over the course of its 139-minute running time the director makes spectacular use of the frame, utilizing wide-screen cinematography for the first time in his career. (Better known as CinemaScope the process is referred to here as "Toho Scope.") He fills every inch of the screen with beautifully composed shots. For sheer power of image, check out the adrenaline-pumping horseback chase that precedes the spear duel; it'll make your eyeballs dance.

It's a visually stunning movie, but it's the way Kurosawa balances the humor, action and dramatic scenes in the film that really elevates *The Hidden Fortress*. Comedic relief is supplied by the faint-hearted Tahei and Matakishi, the film's Greek chorus who bumble their way through the storyline, mostly trying not to get killed. Using wild facial expres-sions and lots of physical bits-of-business — check out their pantomime for the supposedly deaf princess for one over-the-top example — they dominate the first half of the movie with their antics.

Their slapstick is in stark contrast to the code of honor displayed by the General, who is the very model of stoicism and bravery. Because the character is underwritten — he is only required to be heroic — charismatic Kurosawa regular Toshiro Mifune, the John Wayne of Japanese films, uses his natural command of the screen to give General Makabe a regal air that a lesser actor simply could not pull off.

Misa Uehara, in her first screen role, embodies the elegance, nobility, strength and arrogance that made Yuki a role model for so many princess characters in later films.

Kurosawa expertly juggles all these disparate elements, throwing in intricately staged action scenes on top of it all, to create a magnificent film that once seen, won't be forgotten.

Availability: On DVD

"Elizabeth, I just had the craziest dream. You know,
if you saw it in the movies, you'd never believe it."
— ATHANAEL (JACK BENNY) IN *THE HORN BLOWS AT MIDNIGHT*

THE HORN BLOWS AT MIDNIGHT (1945)
— — — — — — — — — — — — — —

Although Jack Benny was one of the pre-eminent stars of early television and radio, the box office failure of one 1945 film ended his big screen career. "This was neither an A-picture nor a B-picture," he joked. "There is no known alphabetical letter under which you can classify *The Horn Blows at Midnight.*"

In this elaborately staged fantasy film directed by Hollywood legend

Raoul Walsh, Benny plays a mild-mannered musician who dozes off during a Paradise Coffee (It's the Coffee that Makes You Sleep!) commercial. While sawing logs he dreams that he is Athanael, a horn playing angel in a celestial orchestra who, at the request of the alluring Elizabeth (Alexis Smith), is introduced to The Chief (Guy Kibbee) who has a job for him.

In the big man's lavish office Athanael is told that the Front Office isn't happy with the way things are going on Earth. Dismissing the planet as an expendable "six day job," they have decided to destroy it. Athanael is instructed to go to New York City and announce the apocalypse by blowing his trumpet at midnight on Judgment Day.

He meets resistance for his mission from two twitchy fallen angels, Osidro (Allyn Joslyn) and Doremus (John Alexander), who are indulging in Earth's, well, earthly pleasures too much to allow Athanael to signal the end of their bacchanal. They enlist the help of suave jewel thief Archie Dexter (Reginald Gardiner) to steal Athanael's trumpet and delay the end of the world. When they successfully keep Athanael from fulfilling his mission, his passport to Heaven is revoked and he is unable to return to Paradise.

Elizabeth convinces The Chief to give Athanael one last chance, and to make sure he doesn't blow it this time she comes to Earth to help him. Unfortunately things aren't going well on the ground. A destitute Athanael has traded his trumpet for a meal, triggering a series of events that climaxes with a crazy scene featuring all the leads hanging, daisy-chained, from a skyscraper, each grabbing the previous person's feet and hanging on for dear life. At the end of the chain is Athanael, who is dunked into a oversized prop jug pouring a cup of coffee on a billboard.

Jack Benny was a huge success on television and radio but never set the box office on fire. In *Horn* he brings a perfectly calibrated, innocently bewildered feel to the role of Athanael, but his trademarked cheapness and slow-burn style of comedy are replaced with simple, but effectively staged slapstick routines (being chased around a hotel room and eating outrageous food at a restaurant) which seemed out of place to audiences more comfortable with his familiar radio persona. Despite impeccable comic timing his image was so ingrained in the public consciousness that he was forever typecast. It killed his movie career; *The Horn Blows at Midnight* was the last film to feature him in a leading role.

The Horn Blows at Midnight is a good example of the religion-based fantasy film, popular in the early to mid-'40s. These movies typically featured visions of Heaven, hell and the citizens thereof, coupled with ordinary people forced to make big moral decisions. Unlike Alexander Hall's *Here Comes Mr. Jordan*, Ernst Lubitsch's *Heaven Can Wait* or Archie Mayo's *Angel on My Shoulder*, *The Horn Blows at Midnight* sank without a trace, likely because, although it is a comedy, it has a much different tone than the others. Rather than offer solace to an audience tired of war and strife in the world, *Horn* takes the unusual step of asking the punters to cheer on a fallen angel so he can trigger the end of the world. It's a funny movie, but for viewers who had just lived through the horrors of World War II and read about the use of A-bombs over Nagasaki and Hiroshima, the storyline might have been a bit too close to home.

Availability: Out of Print vHs

John Cassavetes, the maverick director of *A Child Is Waiting*. "When I started making films, I wanted to make Frank Capra pictures," he said. "But I've never been able to make anything but these crazy, tough pictures. You are what you are." (Photo credit: The Hollywood Collection)

A still from the opening credit sequence for *A Child Is Waiting*. The movie's advertising tagline read: "Burt Lancaster & Judy Garland take an untouched theme — and make it touching and unforgettable!" (Photo credit: The Hollywood Collection)

Kirk Douglas as hard-nosed reporter Charles "Chuck" Tatum in *Ace in the Hole*. The film lost a ton of money and, in an attempt to salvage their investment, the studio re-released it under the name *The Big Carnival* without director Billy Wilder's permission.

(Photo credit: The Hollywood Collection)

Laurence Fishburne and Keke Palmer star in *Akeelah and the Bee*, the first film to be produced by Starbucks Coffee. (Photo courtesy: Maple Pictures)

Keke Palmer as a South Los Angeles girl who attempts to win a national spelling bee in *Akeelah and the Bee*. (Photo courtesy: Maple Pictures)

Javier (J.R. Villarreal) and Akeelah (Keke Palmer) at the spelling bee in *Akeelah and the Bee*.
(Photo courtesy: Maple Pictures)

Willem Dafoe as FBI agent Paul Smecker, a role originally offered to Kevin Spacey, in *The Boondock Saints*. (Photo courtesy: Maple Pictures)

The Brothers Grimm, Jacob (Heath Ledger) and Wilhelm (Matt Damon). "Eliminating Evil Since 1812!" (Photo courtesy: Miramax Film Corp.)

Jacob (Heath Ledger) and Wilhelm (Matt Damon) in Terry Gilliam's *The Brothers Grimm*. The actors were originally cast in the opposite roles, but after discussions with the director were allowed to change parts. (Photo courtesy: Miramax Film Corp.)

Confessions of a Dangerous Mind director and co-star George Clooney with lead actor Sam Rockwell. Rockwell plays game show host and alleged hit man Chuck Barris, a role originally offered to Mike Myers, Ben Stiller and Johnny Depp. (Photo courtesy: Miramax Film Corp.)

Confessions of a Dangerous Mind star Sam Rockwell with the real-life Chuck Barris. Barris says he wrote the book the movie is based on while "in the throes of an existential meltdown." (Photo courtesy: Miramax Film Corp.)

George Clooney directs Drew Barrymore and Sam Rockwell on the set of *Confessions of a Dangerous Mind*. (Photo courtesy: Miramax Film Corp.)

George Clooney directs *Confessions of a Dangerous Mind*. "Directing is really exciting," he says, "but in the end, it's more fun to be the painter than the paint." (Photo courtesy: Miramax Film Corp.)

Shauna Macdonald in a scene from *The Descent*. "I'm genuinely scared of the dark and I don't like being in enclosed spaces and I don't particularly like being on my own in a house."
(Photo courtesy: Maple Pictures)

Shauna Macdonald as spelunker Sarah in a bloody scene from *The Descent*. "They drag you through the mud in the morning and spray you with blood," she said. "Everything soaks through your clothes and into your skin and it dyes you for 12 hours. When we went out at night it would be hilarious, because we would just keep finding dirt in each other's ears and under our nails." (Photo courtesy: Maple Pictures)

The Descent director Neil Marshall decided to not cast stunt people or dancers as the creepy "crawlers," instead choosing to go with professional actors who could bring some individual character to the creatures. (Photo courtesy: Maple Pictures)

A scene from Alejandro Jodorowsky's surreal *El Topo*. When asked if he wanted viewers to be stoned while watching the film, Jodorowsky said, "Yes, yes, yes, yes. I demand them to be." (Photo credit: The Hollywood Collection)

Lupe Velez, known as The Latin Lucille Ball, was best known for her series of "Mexican Spitfire" films. (Photo credit: The Hollywood Collection)

Alexis Smith and Jack Benny in *The Horn Blows at Midnight*. "This was neither an A picture nor a B picture," Benny joked about the movie's box office failure. "There is no known alphabetical letter under which you can classify *The Horn Blows at Midnight*." (Photo credit: The Hollywood Collection)

A scene from Charles Burnett's *Killer of Sheep*, a movie made as the director's Master of Fine Arts thesis film at UCLA. (Photo courtesy: Milestone Film & Video)

Henry G. Sanders in a scene from *Killer of Sheep*. Director Charles Burnett cast Sanders in the film after a chance encounter in an elevator. The director liked the man's "unusual face" and asked him to do a screen test. (Photo courtesy: Milestone Film & Video)

Kaycee Moore and Henry G. Sanders slow dance to Dinah Washington's version of "This Bitter Earth" in a poignant scene from *Killer of Sheep*. (Photo courtesy: Milestone Film & Video)

Martin director George A. Romero, whose original cut of the film was two hours and forty-five minutes. His original cut has been lost and the film now clocks in at a more economical 94 minutes.
(Photo credit: Mr. Chaos Collection)

The Monster Squad gang from left to right, the Gillman (Tom Woodruff Jr.), Frankenstein's Monster (Tom Noonan), Dracula (Duncan Regehr), the Mummy (Michael Reid MacKay), the Wolf Man (Carl Thibault) and in front, André Gower as Sean. (Photo courtesy: Maple Pictures)

Frankenstein's Monster (Tom Noonan) in a classic scene from *The Monster Squad*. "I think Tom Noonan brought just the right amount of conviction and gentleness and sadness to Frankenstein's Monster," said director Fred Dekker. (Photo courtesy: Maple Pictures)

The Monster Squad's Dracula (Duncan Regehr). "Duncan Regehr was a terrific Dracula," said director Fred Dekker. "He had just the right combination of nobility and evil and animal rage and all the stuff that are the hallmarks of that character." (Photo courtesy: Maple Pictures)

When Joan Collins made *Seven Thieves* she was better known for her stormy personal life than her on-screen acting chops. (Photo credit: The Hollywood Collection)

John Barrymore as Oscar Jaffe, the pompous Broadway director, in 1934's *Twentieth Century*. Legend has it when the actor asked director Howard Hawks why he should play the role, Hawks replied, "It's the story of the biggest ham on earth and you're the biggest ham I know." (Photo credit: The Hollywood Collection)

"That television set isn't a hallucination; it's a Twonky!" says Coach Trout (Billy Lynn), in Arch Oboler's *The Twonky*. (Photo credit: The Hollywood Collection)

IDLEWILD (2006)

When André Benjamin and Antwan Patton, better known as André 3000 and Big Boi of the Atlanta-based hip-hop group OutKast, decided to branch out into film they didn't look to MTV for ideas. Instead, creating a frenetic fusion of old and new, they cherry-picked inspiration from a variety of sources: *Moulin Rouge,* hip-hop culture, Warner's cartoons, *Six Feet Under* and gangster movies of the 1930s.

"I think it was a great choice because you got to leave this world and go to another world," said Benjamin. "I've always been a fan of 1930s style. It was probably one of the best eras, especially for a man's dress. Just showing up on the set, putting on your wardrobe, listening to the music, every day leaving the set and playing Cab Calloway, or watching *Stormy Weather* and *Casablanca* . . . It was a different time.

"I had to actually learn how to walk differently and sit differently because in the '30s, they didn't slouch. They sat up straight. Your chest is poked out. You exude that class. It's different now. Now, it's chill and everybody is laid back, and then, on Sunday, you may dress up. Back then, it was the opposite. You'd dress up every day and then on Sunday, you'd chill out. It was a blessing, for me. That's the best thing about making movies, to get that experience and to live out certain fantasies and do things you wouldn't have done."

Idlewild, named for the Georgia town in which the action takes place, is both rooted in the past and very forward-looking. Hip-hop collides with jazz, dancers mix the jitterbug with breakdancing and the star of this 1930s road show is a rapper. Think of it as a remix of *The Cotton Club.*

Set against the backdrop of a 1930s southern speakeasy, Benjamin and Patton play Percival and Rooster, friends since childhood, despite the differences in their personalities. Percival is the shy son of a mortician who plays piano at the speakeasy. Rooster on the other hand is the flamboyantly dressed star of the show who flirts with all the women in the movie except his wife. When a Mob boss is slain by his underling (a terrific Terrence Howard) Rooster must take over the speakeasy and learn to do business with the violent and unreasonable gangster who now controls the flow of booze into the club. Meanwhile Percival falls for a beautiful new singer in the club, and comes out of his shell just in time for the violent and bloody finale.

Idlewild manages to skirt around my usual problem with musicals — the silliness of people bursting into song at the drop of a hat — by setting most of the musical numbers in a Prohibition era speakeasy ironically called The Church. Here we get the movie's strengths: spectacularly choreographed dance numbers mixing dance styles old and new, cool retro-modern sounding music from OutKast, Macy Gray and newcomer Paula Patton and a rich and interesting visual pallet.

"As far as the extra added values in the movie, we call it that funk," said Benjamin. "That's the funk you bring to the movie. We are film fans. Bryan [hip-hop video director Barber] would say, 'Have you seen *Amelie*? Did you see how they tricked this?' So we knew what kind of game we were playing here. We knew what type of film we wanted to make. It can't be so straight and narrow all the time. It has to be magical in some kind of way, at least for this film."

There's lots of eye and ear candy to distract us from the movie's flaws. Benjamin and Patton are sturdy performers, but their acting chops pale by comparison to their co-star Terrence Howard, who owns the screen each time he steps into frame.

The script doesn't do either of the neophyte actors any favors — it must have been tough for Benjamin to sing a love song to a corpse in his big screen debut — and is a bit too hallucinatory for its own good (what would you expect from a former music video director?), but

Idlewild's energy, beauty and verve more than make up for its short-comings.

Availability: On DVD

"He smashed up his desk, gave up a wife, three mistresses and went back to the simple life. Then his troubles really started!"
– ADVERTISING TAGLINE FOR *I'LL NEVER FORGET WHAT'S 'ISNAME*

I'LL NEVER FORGET WHAT'S 'ISNAME (1967)

Brandy-faced actor Oliver Reed once said, "I like the effect drink has on me. What's the point of staying sober?" After his career took off in the 1960s, Reed appeared in over 100 films, but he found greater fame as a hollow-legged hellraiser.

Reed's piss artist exploits ranged from practical jokes (like when he spiked snooker ace Alex Higgins's whisky with Chanel perfume) to the silly (like the time he arrived at Galway airport in Ireland lying drunk on a baggage conveyor or stripped during dinner and jumped into a huge tank containing goldfish) to the downright outrageous. He was once forced to leave the set of a television talk show after arriving drunk and attempting to kiss feminist writer Kate Millett. Then there are the countless anecdotes such as Reed and 36 friends drinking, in one evening, 60 gallons of beer, 32 bottles of Scotch, 17 bottles of gin, four crates of wine and one bottle of Babycham.

His boozehound lifestyle cost him many roles. Touted to replace Sean Connery as James Bond, his reputation for craziness scared Bond gatekeeper Albert R. Broccoli off. "With Reed we would have had a far greater problem to destroy his image and re-mold him as James Bond," he wrote. "We just didn't have the time or money to do that." Later it was rumored that Reed turned down roles in both *Jaws* and *The Sting*, but that was denied by one studio bigwig who said, "Reed didn't turn us down. We turned him down. We like our stars to have respect — Oliver Reed didn't respect anyone and he showed it."

His drinking didn't interfere with his career in Europe, however, where he was probably Britain's biggest mid-1970s movie star, making a career of playing angry young (and sometimes not so young) men. One of his greatest, and least seen takes on the disillusioned soul was 1967's *I'll Never Forget What's 'Isname.*

In his third outing with director Michael Winner (the first two, *The System* a.k.a. *The Girl Getters* and *The Jokers* are quick-witted, fast paced Swingin' '60s London flicks), Reed plays 32-year-old Andrew Quint, an advertising wunderkind at a huge firm run by the powerful and Machiavellian Jonathan Lute (Orson Welles). Quint is rich, talented, has a perfect family — a wife and little daughter — and three mistresses, but he's also dreadfully unhappy.

In a classic "take this job and shove it" moment he turns up at his high-rise office dressed to the nines in a business suit. The only thing out of place is a gleaming axe slung over his shoulder. In lieu of a resignation letter he smashes his hardwood desk into kindling. His career in advertising literally in pieces, he grins a mysterious grin and sets off to find a simpler way of life.

He lands at *Gadfly*, a well-regarded but almost bankrupt literary magazine run by a lascivious old friend from school named Gerald (Harry Andrews). The cigar-chomping Lute, who can't fathom Quint's rejection of his high-flying ad job for a soul-satisfying but low paying position, is hell-bent to lure his former employee back to the fold. To that end he buys *Gadfly*, thereby making Quint his employee all over again. In order to win his freedom Quint reluctantly agrees to make a commercial for a new Japanese 8 mm movie camera for the Lute Agency.

The ad resembles Fellini on acid. The former ad whiz deliberately tries to sabotage his waning career by creating a clip so off the wall he's sure no one will air it. Filled with images of Nazi mass graves, atomic bomb explosions, cruel portrayals of his exes and Marianne Faithfull roaring, "You fucking bastard!" the ad is guaranteed to offend everyone who sees it. It's sure to end his unwanted advertising career and get Lute off his back. Except his plan backfires. In a *Producers*-esque plot twist the commercial becomes a smash and even earns the agency an award. Will Quint ever be able to regain his integrity and be at peace with himself?

In its closing moments the film gives us a dark, unvarnished look at the social culture of Britain in the 1960s. Winner makes good use of quirky editing, handheld camera work and loads of great Swingin' '60s iconography — cool London locations and groovy mini-skirted birds — to communicate pointed observations on Western social values. Winner is razor sharp in his take on corporate culture and the high price of success, but the film's light ironic tone softens the harsh subject matter. Its playful nature is the spoonful of sugar that helps the medicine go down.

Although clearly a product of the '60s, *I'll Never Forget What's 'Isname* doesn't seem dated. Perhaps it's because the moral quandaries of business are still a relevant topic, but I'd suggest it's also an upshot of two lead performances that are completely believable and compelling.

Orson Welles as the manipulative Lute was rarely better than he is here. In 1967 he was still a few years away from squandering his talent doing commercials and voiceovers for cartoons. He was still a commanding figure, the kind of guy who could have been voted "Most Likely to Sell His Soul to the Devil" in high school. His presence is imposing, imbuing Lute with the majesty of a man used to getting what he wants. When Quint tells him, "I'm going to get an honest job," his answer is not only condescending, but frightening. "Silly boy," he says, "there's no such thing." Welles delivers the line with ease and it sums up his entire character. He's a corrupt man with no moral boundaries who'll do whatever it takes to get ahead.

As good as Welles is, it is Reed that leaves an indelible impression. His opening scene with the axe is a grabber, both in its theatricality and Reed's handling of the action. He's credible as an ad exec, but there is a dynamic darkness that lies behind his eyes, a rabble-rousing spirit that his finely tailored Carnaby Street suit can't mask. Reed's underlying real life proclivity for trouble gives Quint an unpredictable quality that makes the character sparkle. The raw power on display here is Reed at the height of cool before alcohol and hard living blurred his toughly handsome good looks.

The film's loose morality concerning sex (Quint has mistresses galore and there's an implied oral sex scene) and language (it is one of the first films to use the word "fuck") prompted the Catholic Legion of Decency in the United States to condemn the movie. This, coupled with the film's very English take on the class system and the Motion Picture Association of America's refusal to give the film its seal of approval, probably cooled the film's chances of boffo box office in North America. The film quickly faded and was largely forgotten until its re-release on video in 2000.

Thirty years after making *I'll Never Forget What's 'Isname*, the years of elbow bending finally caught up with the larger-than-life Reed during the filming of *Gladiator* in 1999. He died suddenly of a heart attack in St. Julian's, Malta, reportedly after drinking three bottles of rum and beating five sailors at arm wrestling. His death came while he was in the middle of shooting the Roman epic, and his remaining scenes were produced using electronically simulated images.

"I'm not a villain, I've never hurt anyone," he said before his death. "I'm just a tawdry character who explodes now and again."

Availability: Out of Print VHS

THE INTRUDER (1962)

The Intruder is director Roger Corman's greatest achievement on film, but also his biggest regret. The legendary moviemaker believed in the script's message of integration so much he took a second mortgage on his house to bankroll the production. When the movie stiffed at the box office Corman tried to salvage his investment by tacking the more incendiary *I Hate Your Guts!* title on the film for re-release but even that didn't help. Audiences still stayed away in droves. "[*The Intruder*] was, and remains to this day," said Corman, "the greatest disappointment of my career."

Based on a novel by *Twilight Zone* scribe Charles Beaumont, *The Intruder* features a pre–*Star Trek* William Shatner as Adam Cramer, a hate-monger so rotten he makes the KKK look like a high school glee club. Dressed head to toe in white and passing himself as a social worker, Cramer is actually a provocateur sent by the "Patrick Henry Society" of Washington, D.C., to Caxton, Missouri, a small southern town, to glad-hand and promote segregation. Desegregation in schools had recently passed into law and in the film 10 African-American students are scheduled to enroll at a formerly all-white school in the area. Cramer's job is to make sure that doesn't happen.

Cramer befriends town bigwig (and bigot) Verne Shipman (Robert Emhardt) and slyly brings to the surface the underlying racism the locals usually keep to themselves. When he asks Shipman what his stand on segregation is, the reply is chilling. "That's a stupid question young man," he says, "I'm a southerner."

Behind closed doors Cramer stirs things up further, using his considerable charisma to seduce several of the town's married ladies and underage girls. This, and not his vile politics, will prove to be his undoing.

After Cramer makes a fiery speech for the local yokels, racial violence erupts — crosses are burned on the black side of town and an explosion in an all-black church kills a preacher. In the aftermath of the bombing Cramer is held responsible and taken to jail.

The locals, who have now come to see Cramer as a hero, aren't pleased and arrange bail. Only one man in town seems to be on the side of right, newspaperman Tom McDaniel, who is beaten to a pulp for ushering the black kids to school — while his own daughter falsely accuses one of the African-American students of rape. Following those accusations the young man is almost lynched in the schoolyard.

The Intruder is based on a real event that saw a rabble-rouser establish a neo-fascist party in a small Tennessee town. He agitated the hoi polloi so profoundly the National Guard had to be brought in to keep the peace.

In a search for authenticity Corman decided to shoot in the South, choosing the town of Sikestown, Missouri. He hoped that by shooting in the mid-South he could avoid the hardcore racial attitudes of Alabama or Mississippi, but only he and star Shatner had the full script. Everyone else had a doctored version in the event it fell into the wrong hands. Corman would coach the actors on the spot, teaching them their real lines just before the cameras rolled. At first the strategy worked, but as word got out about the true nature of their film, death threats started coming in and the production was forced to move — three times.

The local setting may have endangered the cast and crew, but it lends an authentic feel to the film. The small budget of just $80,000 forced Corman to embrace a gritty documentary look for the footage, which furthers the impact of the material. It feels like the real South and not a studio backlot.

To further establish a sense of place Corman utilized the townsfolk of whatever town he shot in, and while not all their acting is Hollywood quality, there is a naturalism to their performances that lends a vibrant air of realism to their scenes. In exploiting the real racist attitudes of the non-actors — the N-word rolls off their tongues a little too naturally to be anything but authentic — Corman doesn't pull any punches in his depiction of mid-century southern life.

Heading up the cast is Shatner as white supremacist Adam Cramer. Still four years away from finding fame as Captain Kirk, in *The Intruder* Shatner reigns in his proclivity for overacting and delivers the best performance of his career. His Cramer is a complex character who, while charismatic and slick, is also the embodiment of hate and cowardice. He's a snake oil salesman in a bright white suit who feeds off the intense emotions he is able to stir up in the local citizenry. It's an edgy, impassioned performance that holds off on the histrionics until they can be effectively used in the speech scene to whip the crowd into a hate-filled frenzy.

Legend has it that Corman wasn't impressed with Shatner's take on the character and blamed him for the movie's financial failure. Years later Shatner joked that Corman's new title for the re-release of the film, *I Hate Your Guts!* was probably aimed at him.

The Intruder was Corman's 33rd film as a director and the first picture he ever made that lost money. Although it won awards at film festivals all over the world its poor box office convinced Corman to shy away from movies with an explicit societal message. From that point on he stayed entrenched in the world of genre films, but began weaving light social commentary into the fabric of his stories.

"After *The Intruder*," he writes in his book *How I Made a Hundred Movies in Hollywood and Never Lost a Dime*, "I was obviously not particularly eager to take risks and set myself up to take another beating."

The Intruder echoes many of the themes of its better known cousin *To Kill a Mockingbird* — the disdain of vigilante violence, the possible lynching of an innocent man for rape — and is an ahead-of-its-time drama that is still powerful today.

Availability: Out of print DVD

Roger Corman Appreciation Society: Richard's Favorite Appearances of the Director on Film, Part Two

1. *The Fast and the Furious*: Years before Vin Diesel and Paul Walker were even a glint in their parents' eyes Corman co-wrote and produced the original 1955 version of *The Fast and the Furious* and puts in an appearance as a roadblock state trooper.

2. *Body Bags*: In 1993 horror mavens Tobe Hooper and John Carpenter collaborated on a horror anthology film for television called *Body Bags*. Several old-timers like John Agar and Robert Carradine make appearances, as well as noted horror directors Wes Craven, Sam Raimi and, of course, Roger Corman. Hooper cast Corman as Dr. Bregman alongside Mark Hamill in a story about an eye transplant gone horribly wrong.

3. *Scream 3*: Wes Craven cast Corman in *Scream 3* as an uneasy executive at Sunrise Studios who wants the production of *Stab 3* shut down, citing the connection between film and real life violence.

4. *Lords of the Deep*: Mary Ann Fisher is best known as the producer of quickie exploitation flicks with titles like *Spacejacketed* and *Stray Bullet*. In 1989 she helmed a low-budget retooling of *The Abyss* called *Lords of the Deep* that featured Corman as the head of the evil Martel Corporation.

5. *The Day the World Ended*: Like Alfred Hitchcock, Roger Corman turns up in dozens of cameo roles in his own films. Often, to save money he would take a walk-on rather than pay someone else to do it. Sharp-eyed viewers will spot him as everything from Louise's fiancé in *The Day the World Ended*, seen only in a framed photograph, to a Greek soldier in *Atlas*, to an office worker in *Naked Paradise*.

I WOKE UP EARLY THE DAY I DIED (1998)

It's not uncommon for scripts to kick around for years before getting made. Quentin Tarantino, for example, persistently pitched his screenplays for *True Romance, Natural Born Killers* and *Reservoir Dogs* for four years before hitting pay dirt. *Total Recall* was optioned for $1,000 16 years before Arnold signed on and it became a hit. But few scripts have had as strange a trip to the screen as *I Woke Up Early the Day I Died*.

Edward D. Wood Jr., the storied director of *Plan 9 from Outer Space*, worked on the script for *I Woke Up Early the Day I Died* for 10 years, and despite having big-name actors Aldo Ray and John Carradine signed on found it impossible to find backing. He was so passionate about the project that once, when he was evicted from a house by marshals who gave him just minutes to vacate the premises and only one suitcase in which to pack his belongings, he chose the script over his other personal items. "One thing he did take was one of the last scripts he wrote," said his wife Kathy, "one he really loved, *I Woke Up Early the Day I Died*. And this one angora sweater that he loved so much."

In 1978 when Wood died at age 53 the script became the property of his wife, who refused to sell it unless it was made the way Ed intended it to be seen. Her husband had in mind an uncompromising avant-garde film with no dialogue, just sound effects, screams and songs. It wasn't until Kathy Wood met Italian director Aris Iliopulos that she found someone who would honor the script just as Wood wrote it.

The resulting picture contains many of the usual Wood obsessions — death, graveyards, the bizarre and even burlesque — and was met with the same kind of reviews that greeted most of Wood's work. "Sitting through this film is like Chinese water torture," said *Mr.*

Showbiz.com while James Berardinelli of *Reel Views* suggested that the movie would cut short Iliopulos's directorial career. The reviews were scorching, and legal problems prevented the film from receiving a theatrical release, but seen for what it is (if you can find the rare German DVD), a no-holds-barred tribute to an often maligned film-maker, the movie reveals many charms.

Billy Zane heads an all-star cast as a demented thief who, dressed as a nurse, escapes from a mental home by injecting a hospital worker with poison. On the outside he steals some suitable clothes — although he seems reluctant to part with the white pumps that were part of the RN wardrobe — and gets down to the business of being bad. He robs a bank, killing a loan officer who gave him a rough time. Now on the run from the police he hides in a cemetery where he stows the loot in a coffin while a strange funeral takes place nearby. When a bagpiper (Ron Perlman) starts to bleat, we learn that loud, aggressive noises cause Zane's character, the Thief, brain pain and make him pass out. When he wakes up the money is gone and he becomes convinced that one of the mourners stole his cash. The search for his money turns into a murderous quest to track down and kill each of the mourners.

This is one seriously strange movie but a couple of things save it from simply being a cinematic curiosity. Zane kicks out the jams in the lead role. In a career that is no stranger to over-the-top performances his Thief stands alone. It's a manic performance that combines slapstick with melancholy, completely silent save for some grunts and groans. He hands in a feverish physical delivery that is unique on his resumé. Never before or since has he pranced down a flight of stairs with such weird grace.

Surprising and amusing cameos are made by the rest of the all-star cast: Karen Black, Nicollette Sheridan, Eartha Kitt, Rick Schroder, Andrew McCarthy, John Ritter, Will Patton, Christina Ricci, Jonathan Taylor Thomas, Sandra Bernhard, Max Perlich, Ron Perlman and even Ed's widow Kathy Wood. Of particular note is Tippi Hedren as a deaf woman who opens a can of whoop-ass on Thief before he tosses her into the Pacific as music from *Psycho* plays on the soundtrack.

Stylistically, Iliopulos steers the film into ground somewhere between an Ed Wood picture and the kitschy surrealist philosophy of John Waters. He plays up the laughs more than Wood would have — one of the joys of Wood's work is its deadpan seriousness — but he is faithful to the spirit of the script. He pays tribute to Wood by not only incorporating many of the director's trademarks into *I Woke Up Early the Day I Died*, like wonky editing, loads of stock footage and cheap props, but also by showing Wood's original script notes on screen *à la Pop Up Video*.

It's a unique film, with a startling and unusual look, but it is the soundtrack that really grabs. Sometimes called a silent film, it is anything but. There's no dialogue, but there is an extremely busy soundtrack, rich with music and sound effects that help propel the story. Iliopulos weaves together an aural landscape using found sounds like screams and shrieks, Zane's grunts, a mix of pop and rock songs, (Eartha Kitt sings a ballad; Darcy Clay's country-fried punk rock tune "Jesus I Was Evil" appears), and an effective score by Larry Groupe to set the mood. His work in the sound department really creates the emotional backbone of the movie and is the film's crowning achievement.

I Woke Up Early the Day I Died isn't for everyone (the hallucinogenic visuals and relentless aural assault might be too much for the casual viewer) but even if you don't like it, I'll guarantee you won't be able to forget it.

Availability: Hard to find

"Danny's senses registered everything sharp and clear
with the painful intensity of junk sickness."
– WILLIAM S. BURROUGHS'S NARRATION IN *THE JUNKY'S CHRISTMAS*

THE JUNKY'S CHRISTMAS (1993)

If you're a fan of Christmas claymation but feel Rudolph and Frosty lack street credibility, a little-known animated movie about Danny the Car Wiper might be just the thing to make your Yuletide bleak. *The Junky's Christmas* is based on a short story from the 1989 William S. Burroughs book *Interzone*, a miscellany of his writings from the 1950s.

The film's opening image is black and white footage of the legendary beat writer warming himself by a crackling fire, bathed in the twinkling lights of a glowing Christmas tree. Wizened by age and drug abuse, his bony fingers gingerly pluck a book from a stack on the mantel. Cracking open a copy of *Interzone* he begins to read.

"It was Christmas Day and Danny the Car Wiper hit the street," he says as the image fades to a claymation view of the New York City skyline, "junk sick and broke after 72 hours in a precinct cell."

The voice is unmistakable, a cigarette-tinged rasp that sounds a bit like crusty old Mr. Potter from *It's a Wonderful Life*. Burroughs gives a straightforward reading of junky Danny's search for a pusher open for business on Christmas Day. He leads us through the deserted streets of mid-century Manhattan to a Dr. Feelgood who gives Danny just enough dope to keep him from the D.T.s. Along the way Danny meets an old friend in worse shape than he is, attempts to steal a present from the back seat of an unattended car, finds a severed leg in an old suitcase and then resells the case for money to get a room in a flophouse.

Alone in his dingy "six dollar a week room" he carefully prepares his fix, methodically dissolving the drug in water and carefully sucking the mixture into a syringe. Before he has a chance to feed his veins fate intervenes and Danny unexpectedly learns about the Christmas ideal of giving without receiving anything in return.

The Junky's Christmas takes all the trappings of Christmas claymation, turns them on their head and then sticks a needle in their arm. The style of the piece recalls the familiar feeling of *Rudolph the Red-Nosed Reindeer* and *Santa Claus Is Coming to Town*, but filters all the sentiment and holly jollies out of the piece. The brief redemptive uplift at the end is a small payoff given the brilliantly detailed portrait of drug isolation that precedes it.

The animation is wonderfully detailed and beautifully cinematic. A 1950s New York is lovingly crafted out of clay, shot with sweeping camera movements that bring to mind the mobile lens work of George Miller and drained of color to lend an air of noir to the proceedings.

Vividly animated characters with expressive faces convey the desperate world that Danny lives in, and while they're anything but cute, the animators wisely avoided creating grotesque caricatures of the citizens of the streets. Instead we're given clay figures with heart and soul, but also with troubles and addictions. It's tough enough to pull off realistic social illness on film at the best of times, let alone when the medium you've chosen is clay, but directors Nick Donkin and Melodie McDaniel grace *The Junky's Christmas* with believable figures.

The Junky's Christmas is a nightmarish tale that could only have sprung from the experience of William S. Burroughs. His presence, as narrator and in the live action sequences bookending the movie, lends an air of street cred to the story. It's worth the price of the rental to see him carve the Christmas turkey at the end of the film — with a switchblade.

Availability: On DVD

> "You are not a child anymore. Soon you will be a goddamn man. Now start learning what life is about now, son."
> **— STAN (HENRY GAYLE SANDERS) TO HIS SON (JACK DRUMMOND) IN *KILLER OF SHEEP***

KILLER OF SHEEP (1977)

It's been called one of the most striking debuts in movie history and proclaimed a treasure by the Library of Congress, but for 30 years it was almost impossible to see. Shot on a shoestring budget of $10,000 over the span of a year on weekends in and around the Los Angeles neighborhood of Watts, *Killer of Sheep* was submitted as a Master of Fine Arts thesis film at the School of Film at the University of California in 1977 by director Charles Burnett who would later go on to make more than 20 films, TV movies and documentaries, including *America Becoming* and *Namibia: The Struggle for Liberation.*

From there it went on to win a critic's award at the Berlin Film Festival, make the National Society of Film Critics 100 Essential Films of All Time list and become an acknowledged landmark in African-American film. All that hoopla without the benefit of a theatrical release. The movie was screened occasionally at film festivals and in schools, but rights issues with the music on the soundtrack prevented it from earning a wide release until 2007 when it was restored and issued on DVD by Milestone.

Shot in a neo-realist style, *Killer of Sheep*'s protagonist is Stan (Henry Gayle Sanders), a pensive African-American man beaten down by poverty and his backbreaking job at a slaughterhouse. Plagued by insomnia brought on by money worries Stan is slowly losing his grip as existential despair envelops him. This sorry state is the loose framework from which *Killer of Sheep* hangs its action.

There isn't an easily defined story, but rather a series of events that stem from Stan's insomnia and the effect it has on those around him. Like life, *Killer of Sheep* is a series of random moments that add up to a whole. "I just wanted to do regular stories," said Burnett. To achieve that he fills the movie with the minutia of real life: Stan's wife's (Kaycee Moore) frustration at the growing distance between them; two friends who try to recruit him into a criminal plan; a liquor store owner who comes on to him sexually and a failed attempt to buy an engine to fix up an old car. All unrelated incidents, connected only by Stan and his diminished and increasingly isolated, unsmiling state.

Hopeless as it may seem, there are also lighter episodes in Stan's life. Burnett allows quietly joyful moments to play out — a hug from his daughter, a dance with his wife. Burnett blunts the rough edges of the movie with these gentle moments, but doesn't offer solutions to Stan's plight. He was in a bad way when the movie began and will likely be in a bad way long after the end credits have rolled. "This is real life," the film seems to say, "deal with it."

Burnett definitely comes from the "show-me-don't-tell-me" school of filmmaking and uses images and music the way most filmmakers use dialogue. Many scenes are wordless, or almost so, and are effective because he allows the action to speak for itself. A slow dance between Stan and his wife choreographed to Dinah Washington's version of "This Bitter Earth" speaks volumes about their relationship, even though not a word is spoken. It's beautifully poetic and real, transcendent and yet grounded.

Killer of Sheep is a profound film, one that eschews the traditional narrative form to fully and unapologetically examine a life lived in poverty. Burnett's focus stays on the human toll of a life lived under severe restraints, both financial and personal, and as a result remains as powerful today as it was when it was first filmed in the mid-'70s.

Availability: On DVD

> "You like money. You've got a great big dollar sign there where most women have a heart."
> — JOHNNY CLAY (STERLING HAYDEN) IN *THE KILLING*

THE KILLING (1956)

Jim Thompson, the boozy author of blood-splattered crime stories such as *The Getaway* and *The Grifters*, had a knack for dialogue. Dubbed the "Dimestore Dostoevsky" his nihilistic novels really captured the vernacular of the street.

When Stanley Kubrick was in pre-production for his adaptation of the Lionel White novel *Clean Break*, he knew he needed someone with Thompson's unique ability to capture the rhythms of the underworld in words. Thompson had never written for the screen but jumped at the chance to make $1,000 and have Kubrick look at his novella *Lunatic at Large*, which he hoped to one day see on the big screen.

Checking into a seedy Manhattan hotel, Thompson pounded out a script that fleshed out Kubrick's ideas. His alcoholism made his work habits erratic, but there's no denying he delivered some classic hard-bitten dialogue. "It's not fair," says the wife of one of the characters, "I never had anybody but you, not a real husband, just a bad joke without a punchline." It's archetypal Thompson, an over-the-top toxic cocktail of cynicism and coarseness that oozes sarcasm.

Thompson, working in tandem with Kubrick and producer James B. Harris, fine-tuned the story of Johnny Clay (Sterling Hayden) a career criminal with one last job in mind.

Newly released from prison Clay has elaborate plans for a big score — $2 million in a race track heist — before he goes straight. His team is hand-picked, each possessing a special skill crucial to the plan's success. The inside guys — cashier George Peatty (Elisha Cook Jr.), bartender Mike O'Reilly (Joe Sawyer) and Randy Kennan (Ted de

Corsia), a policeman who will patrol the track area — are all clean and have no criminal records. Two shadier characters, wrestler Maurice Oboukhoff (Kola Kwariani) and sharpshooter Nikki Arcane (Timothy Carey), complete the team.

On the day of the theft the plan goes smoothly. During the seventh race of the day Maurice causes a diversion by starting a brawl in the bar while Nikki adds to the chaos by shooting the winning horse. During the ensuing melee George lets Johnny into the staff area where he picks up a gun left for him by Mike. He then disguises himself with a mask, steals the bet money from the till, completing the transaction by dropping the money down to Randy who, still dressed as a cop, takes the loot to a secret drop-off point, freeing up Johnny to leave the track unnoticed.

All accomplices resurface unscathed except Nikki, the sociopath who gleefully shot the horse. He is killed while trying to escape. At the rendezvous point, however, the situation turns ugly. While Johnny is en route with the money, the lover of Nikki's wife shows up and demands cash. Tempers flare, and a bloody shootout wipes out the whole gang.

Johnny, sensing that something is amiss bypasses the rendezvous and heads for the airport with his girlfriend Fay (Coleen Gray). He's committed the perfect crime. There are no witnesses or accomplices left, so he's scot-free. Or is he?

The movie more or less follows the script Thompson wrote between swigs of bourbon in his hotel in New York. Kubrick supplied instructions and notes, but the dialogue and the movie's characters — weak and vengeful flawed men and women — are pure Thompson, so you can imagine the writer's surprise when the finished film credits read: "Screenplay by Stanley Kubrick, Dialogue by Jim Thompson."

He threatened legal action, but was talked out of it by Harris and placated by the chance to work with Kubrick on his next film *Paths of Glory*. (Once again though, he would be sidelined in the credits.) In the end his contributions to *The Killing* went unnoticed by the public and press.

Unlike Thompson, Kubrick walked away from *The Killing* very much in demand. His other feature films, *Fear and Desire* and *Killer's Kiss* had been competent, but *The Killing*, his first professional outing, was a cut above. His deft mixing and matching of noir elements — the fatalism, the stylized camera work — with classic caper film conceits, was given an experimental twist by the addition of a (then fresh and new) non-linear narrative. It's a jigsaw puzzle of a movie that uses discordant staging to build suspense until the story falls into place in the final reel.

Quentin Tarantino has acknowledged *The Killing*'s fractured narrative as a major influence on his work, particularly *Reservoir Dogs* (another ex-con caper film) and once said that he would have cast Sterling Hayden in the Harvey Keitel role if he had still been alive. Hayden died in 1986, six years before *Reservoir Dogs* was released.

United Artists, who ponied up $200,000 of *The Killing*'s $320,000 budget (the rest came from Harris's friends and family), didn't understand the non-linear structure and insisted Kubrick recut the picture in a more coherent fashion. He complied, but when the reordered movie made even less sense than the original cut, the studio lost faith in the film and dumped it as the bottom half of double bill, paired with Richard Fleischer's *Bandido*.

Critics, however, recognized its worth, praising the film and its director. "*The Killing* announces the arrival of a new boy wonder in a business that soon separates the men from the boys," said *Time* on June 4, 1956. "Stanley Kubrick, in his third full-length picture, has shown more audacity with dialogue and camera than Hollywood has seen since the obstreperous Orson Welles went riding out of town on an exhibitors' poll."

A flurry of like-minded flowery reviews earned Kubrick a substantially larger budget for his next film, the acclaimed anti-war story *Paths of Glory*, which established him as an A-list filmmaker.

Thompson's two disappointing experiences with Kubrick didn't completely put him off the film business. In his later years he wrote for television and even wrote the script for an adaptation of his best known novel, *The Getaway*. Unfortunately history repeated itself when *The Getaway* star Steve McQueen rejected the script, saying it was dialogue heavy and didn't have enough action. Walter Hill stepped in, and despite using Thompson's script as a guide, was given sole credit.

Thompson's big moment on film would have to wait until after his 1977 death when no less than three of his novels — *The Kill-Off*, *After Dark, My Sweet*, and *The Grifters* (the latter of which earned four Academy Award nominations) — were adapted for the screen in a one-year period from 1989 to 1990. More than a decade after his passing, Hollywood finally gave him the credit he deserved.

Availability: On DVD

"Here the story should really end, for, in real life, the forlorn old man would have little to look forward to but death. The author took pity on him and has provided a quite improbable epilogue."
– TITLE CARD FROM *THE LAST LAUGH*

THE LAST LAUGH (1924)
▪ ▪ ▪ ▪ ▪ ▪ ▪ ▪ ▪ ▪

"Show Me, Don't Tell Me" is the golden rule of filmmaking. In other words it's always better to put the action on view rather than talk about it. For that reason film hard-liners often consider silent movies to be the purest form of film art. With no sound and just the odd title card thrown in to keep the story moving along, silent filmmakers had no choice but to use the language of the camera to show the action and the expressive faces of their actors to portray emotion.

One of the classics of the silent era takes the golden rule to the nth degree, eliminating all printed inter-titles save for one sarcastic title card near the end. Known for its beautiful camerawork and masterful performances, F. W. Murnau's *The Last Laugh* is a direct influence on the Italian neo-realist school of film and the work of German maestro Rainer Werner Fassbinder.

The story is a simple one. An aging doorman (Emil Jannings) is the front line greeter at the five-star Hotel Atlantic. He flamboyantly performs his duties, dressed in a flashy uniform complete with gold braid and buttons, military lapels and padded Joan Collins shoulders. The showy getup represents his power and station in the world. When decked out he gets respect — people in his apartment building wave as he struts by, saluting the importance the suit embodies.

The uniform is his everything, so when hotel management demotes him to the less than glamorous job of bathroom attendant, he is crushed. Rather than let his neighbors see him without the suit he risks getting fired and steals the uniform, wearing it on his walks to and from work. Of course his embarrassing secret is discovered and in a stunning kaleidoscopic montage the twisted faces of his former admirers mock him and his new-found insignificance.

Then comes the twist and one of the great cynical happy endings in movie history. Murnau wanted the story to end on a downbeat note with the death of the doorman in the bathroom, destitute and alone. However, his studio, UFA (Germany's national film production enterprise), had different ideas and insisted on an upbeat close to the film. To appease the moneymen Murnau goes over-the-top, as film historian Lotte Eisner writes in her seminal book on German film, *The Haunted Screen,* "he scamps it with disgust, pulling the coarsest threads of comedy and becomes as crass as the audiences that slapped their sides at *Kohlhiesels Töchter,* one of his least refined farces," by tacking on a rags-to-riches ending that changes the whole tone of the movie.

"Here the story should really end, for, in real life, the forlorn old man would have little to look forward to but death," reads the film's only title card.

The Last Laugh is forgotten today, relegated to limited DVD releases or a line or two in film textbooks, but for those who seek it out it remains a powerful examination of the frailty of self-worth. The tragedy of the doorman isn't that he lost his job, but that his self-esteem was so linked to something as external of a piece of clothing.

When critic Roger Ebert noted that when the doorman takes off the uniform, "he ceases to exist, even in his own eyes," Eisner put forth that *The Last Laugh* "could only be a German story. . . . It could only happen in a country where the uniform was more than God."

For its era *The Last Laugh* features dazzling camerawork by cinematographer Karl Freund. At a time when most films were shot on stationary cameras Freund utilized movement and some of the first point-of-view shots seen onscreen — certainly the first drunken, staggering POV shot ever — as the doorman performs his daily duties. Stories vary, but legend has it Freund achieved the film's astounding hotel interior shot by strapping a camera to his chest, riding on a bicycle down an elevator, across the lobby and through a revolving door as he followed the actors.

Most of the key players on *The Last Laugh* immigrated to Hollywood shortly after the film's production. Murnau continued to make innovative films in the U.S. — including 1927's *Sunrise*, sometimes cited as one of the greatest films of the silent era — before his untimely death in 1931. Freund, who also shot the legendary *Metropolis*, became an Academy Award–winning cinematographer and worked on many Hollywood classics including *All Quiet on the Western Front* and *Key Largo*.

Ironically the film's star Emil Jannings was to suffer a fate similar to the doorman, only without the happy ending. After a string of extraordinary performances in Germany he found success in Hollywood, and holds the distinction of winning the first Best Actor Academy Award. In those days actors received one Oscar for multiple films, and he won for *The Way of All Flesh* and *The Last Command*.

His American triumph, however, was short-lived. His thick accent and propensity for malapropisms made him unemployable in Hollywood talkies and by 1930 he returned to Germany. Several notable roles followed, including the self-important college professor smitten with Marlene Dietrich in *The Blue Angel*, before Jannings fell under the spell of Hitler in 1933, accepting an offer from propaganda minister Joseph Goebbels to appear in pro-German, anti-Semitic movies. He appeared in a number of these films throughout the '30s and early '40s and was named "Artist of the State" by Goebbels in 1941. After the war, metaphorically stripped of the Nazi uniform, the actor was shunned by the international film community and died of cancer in 1950.

The Last Laugh is an important film, influential in terms of its fluid cinematography, direction and performances. More than that, it is an entertaining, thought-provoking piece of pure, visual cinema.

Availability: On DVD

Davy (Vincent Winter): "Is this our baby now, Harry?"
Harry (Jon Whiteley): "No, it's mine, but you can have a loan of it while I'm on other business."
– DIALOGUE FROM *THE LITTLE KIDNAPPERS*

THE LITTLE KIDNAPPERS (1953)

In the cinematic universe, Canada often stands in for other countries. Toronto doubled for Baltimore in the musical *Hairspray*. Though set in Wyoming, *Brokeback Mountain* was shot almost entirely in Southern Alberta. Vancouver has subbed for any number of generic world cities in movies as diverse as *The X-Men* and *Fantastic Four* to *Hot Rod* and

Slither, but it's rare that other countries double for Canada. One such movie is *The Little Kidnappers*, a kids' film set in turn-of-the-century Nova Scotia but shot entirely in the U.K.

The Maritime province provides a vivid backdrop for the dark story of eight-year-old Harry MacKenzie (Jon Whiteley) and younger chubby-cheeked brother Davy (Vincent Winter) who relocate from Scotland following the death of their parents to live with their grandparents. They soon learn their new guardians are a bit of an odd couple. Grandma MacKenzie (Jean Anderson) is a dear old soul, while Grandpa (Duncan Macrae) is a bitter man, a bad-tempered Calvinist farmer deeply affected by the loss of his son in the Boer War. Gruff to the point of being abusive, he doesn't appear to want the kids around. When the boys, homesick and missing their parents, ask him to buy them a dog to keep them company, he crustily replies, "You can't eat a dog."

Their companionship problems are solved when Harry finds a seemingly abandoned baby (Anthony Michael Heathcoat) in the woods. Since they were denied a pet dog the boys decide to "adopt" the baby instead.

"We'll call it Edward, after the king," says Harry.

"I still think Rover's a very nice name," replies his younger brother.

Neither boy has an inkling of the gravity of their actions as they conceal the toddler in a shed, feeding it milk and generally supplying it with the love and attention they themselves crave.

The child, of course, wasn't a cast off, and is actually the daughter of the neighboring Hoofts family. Here another, darker aspect of the story comes to the fore. Because of his deep-set hatred for the Dutch — he claims it was a Dutchman who killed his son in the war — Grandpa MacKenzie has been at odds with the Hoofts. Tensions rise between the two families when Harry is taken to civil court, charged with kidnapping.

By the closing credits, however, the movie neatly wraps up all the loose ends with everyone — including Grandpa — learning the error of their ways.

The Little Kidnappers is a rare kids' film that avoids the diabetic shock-inducing sweetness of most children's stories. Everything works out for the best in the end but along the way the boys inherit the prejudices of their grandfather and seem to have little regard for the consequences of their actions. It's not typical kids' stuff but rather, an austere realistic look at poverty, loneliness and racial tension as seen through the eyes of children.

The two lead juvenile performances are the connective tissue here. Director Philip Leacock remembers casting the roles: "We brought the children in to test for the parts; we did play situations, as we did with the film itself. Vincent couldn't read so he had to be firmly taught lines — he had a memory like a computer. He would do his own lines aloud and then silently mouth everyone else's words."

John Whiteley had limited experience as a movie actor while Vincent Winter had never been on a film set before. Both give perfectly modulated natural performances without the preciousness of most child actors. Winter is a scene stealer with expressive eyes and a knack for underplaying his part, but both are effective because they seem like unaffected real kids, not the Hollywood version of what children in their situation might be like. Their easy-on-the-ear Aberdeen accents combined with their youthful charm earned them both honorary Oscars for their performances.

The Little Kidnappers is one of the best children's films to emerge from British cinema, and while the look of the film is more Pinewood Studios than authentic rugged Nova Scotia, it does provide an interesting time capsule of life in turn-of-the-century rural Canada.

Availability: Hard to find

"Running has always been big in my family. Especially running from the police."

— COLIN SMITH (TOM COURTENAY) IN OPENING VOICEOVER

THE LONELINESS OF THE LONG DISTANCE RUNNER (1962)

From 1959 to 1963, "It's grim up North" became a catchphrase for a particular brand of English filmmaking. The British New Wave — Angry Young Men Films, Social Problem Films or Kitchen Sink Cinema as they were sometimes called — challenged the status quo, exposing the harsh reality of life of the working classes, especially those in the North of England.

The leading directors of the movement, Jack Clayton, John Schlesinger, Karel Reisz and Lindsay Anderson, valued social realism above all else, using working class themes, dialogue and situations coupled with angry, alienated heroes. Looking to the French New Wave for inspiration, these filmmakers often shot in a pseudo-documentary style on gritty black and white film with non-actors blended into their casts for extra authenticity.

The most famous of the Brit Pack of directors was Tony Richardson, a former theater director and producer who contributed *Look Back in Anger, A Taste of Honey,* and the overlooked Kitchen Sink masterpiece *The Loneliness of the Long Distance Runner* to the genre. Based on a novella of the same name by Alan Sillitoe, Richardson was drawn to the gritty yet poetic story of the eldest son of a working class family from northern England, who falls into a life of petty crime but finds a complicated redemption through long distance running.

Colin Smith (Tom Courtenay) is a bored teenager with an unhappy family life. Unemployed, and unwilling to work himself to death in the local factory like his dad did, he and his mate, Mike (James Bolam), pass the time joyriding in stolen cars and picking up girls. "It's not that I don't like work," Colin says. "It's just that I don't like the idea of slaving me guts out so the bosses can get all the profits. Seems all wrong to me."

His life of Riley comes to a screeching halt after a bakery robbery goes bad and Colin is shipped off to a Borstal — a juvenile prison resembling the Tower of London, meant to reform seriously delinquent young people — called Ruxton Towers Reformatory.

In jail Colin maintains his cocky attitude and bristles with streetwise swagger. When asked how he came to be sent to the prison he replies, "I got sent, didn't I?"

"I know you got sent, but why?" asks his housemaster.

"I got caught. Didn't run fast enough."

Colin's redeeming feature is his athletic skill. Strong and wiry, he catches the attention of the Borstal's governor (Michael Redgrave) who believes that through the virtues of hard work and athleticism the boys in the prison can be rehabilitated. An upcoming foot race with a prestigious prep school seems like the perfect chance for the governor to showcase Colin's talents as a model of the therapeutic power of sport.

His athletic ability earns Colin special treatment from the fawning governor. Even though he's allowed to train unsupervised outside the prison walls and is given perks unavailable to the general population, Colin doesn't like the preferential treatment and is aware the other inmates resent him.

"I'm going to let them think they've got me house-trained," he says, "but they never will, the bastards. To get me beat, they'll have to stick a rope around my neck."

During his long, solitary training sessions he reflects on his situation and, through flashbacks, the journey that led him to the Borstal. In a surprise ending, on the day of the big race he makes a decision that will help him forge his own identity and gain independence.

Thoughtful and poignant, *The Loneliness of the Long Distance Runner* is a log of Colin's trip to self-discovery. Much of the film concentrates on Colin's training, but when it dips into a complex series of flashbacks recounting the events and relationships that formed him, he emerges as a complicated and interesting character.

Courtenay, in his debut as a lead actor (he'd later go on to earn two Academy Award nominations for Best Supporting Actor for his work in *Doctor Zhivago* and Best Actor in *The Dresser*), is an unconventional movie star, but his gaunt appearance perfectly captured the physique of a poor working class stiff and a long distance runner. He hands in a careful performance, slowly revealing the layers of the character, complete with the compromises, confrontations and rebellions that make up Colin.

Richardson makes great use of the cold, gray glens where Colin does his practice runs, using the endless running and stark backdrop as a metaphor for the futility Colin feels. The director further stylizes the film by borrowing heavily from the French New Wave and incorporating jump-cuts, dialogue that overlaps from one scene to the next and sped up action. These techniques may seem derivative (particularly of François Truffaut's *Les Quatre cents coups*) but Richardson makes them work, using them not simply for show but as tools to propel the story from one place to the next.

The Loneliness of the Long Distance Runner is very specific in its time and place. Set in England in the early '60s, with a very British pastime at its core — in the '50s and '60s long distance running was a popular British sport — the film seems as if it shouldn't have aged as well as it has, but because of its careful examination of the timeless themes of rebellion versus conformity and consumerism (Colin objects to television ads for fashions and useless thingamajigs) it remains a powerful and impressive film.

Availability: On DVD

"I don't want to kill Mailer, but I must kill Kingsley in this picture."
— RAOUL REY O'HOULIHAN (RIP TORN) IN *MAIDSTONE*

MAIDSTONE (1970)

"At the time, I thought it was a remarkable film," said Norman Mailer of *Maidstone*, his 1970 experimental movie. "No one else agreed with me."

Mailer had made two films before the rambling, disjointed *Maidstone*. The first, called *Wild 90*, was little seen, as was the second, *Beyond the Law*, despite Mailer's bloated claim that it was "one of the best pictures ever made about cops and crooks." By the time *Maidstone* came around Mailer was convinced, despite the abject failure of his two previous films, that he could change the way movies were made by staging an "attack on the nature of reality." His idea was to melt away the line between fiction and truth: to push actors to their limits and then film the inevitable emotional explosion.

The result is often more interesting than entertaining, but for all its pretension and strangeness, *Maidstone* has a kind of sloppy magnificence.

Mailer plays Norman T. Kingsley, a famous movie director along the lines of "Buñuel, Antonioni and Dreyer," who aspires to be president. At an estate in the Hamptons (shortly after Bobby Kennedy's assassination) he assembles a diverse cabinet to map out his journey to the White House. While they plot for — and some against — him, Kingsley (Mailer's middle name) auditions young starlets for his next sexually charged film. These sequences reveal him to be a loathsome character. In a series of apparently improvised scenes he abuses the young starlets, crudely commenting on their bodies and in one case, even her race.

"Good acting comes out of tyranny," he says in a phony southern accent to a young African-American woman. "I would say slavery."

Mailer frames the action with a series of mock interview segments hosted by a perky English reporter named Jeanne Cardigan (Lady Jeanne Campbell, a.k.a. Mrs. Mailer Number Three). She pops up throughout the movie, interviewing Mailer and cronies until near the end when, on live television, smeared in blood, she bares her breasts, licks the microphone and pronounces, "I love Norman T. Kingsley." Not everyone, however, loves Kingsley, and soon an assassination plot is afoot.

So far *Maidstone* plays like a self-indulgent art film, which it is, until a remarkable scene at the end involving Mailer and co-star Rip Torn. Torn, a frequent collaborator on Mailer's films, plays bodyguard and Kingsley half-brother Raoul Rey O'Houlihan. What actually happened on the day of filming is up for conjecture, but whether it was planned or not, it is compelling and just a bit crazy.

"You can't say that this is real now, what we're doing," Mailer says, piercing the fourth wall and addressing the cast and crew after the movie's main story has concluded. "You can't say what we were doing last night is real; the only thing you can say is that the reality exists somewhere in the extraordinary tension between the extremes."

In the film's defining sequence, moments after these words tumble from Mailer's mouth, Torn attacks him with a hammer, bashing him three times, yelling, "You're supposed to die, Mr. Kingsley! *You* must die, not Mailer." The ensuing fistfight, which only ends when Mailer bites a chunk off Torn's ear, is scored by the screams of Mailer's children and his hysterical wife.

"I'm taking this scene out of the picture," Mailer says after the brawl.

"The picture doesn't make any sense without this," Torn replies. "You know that."

In this one scene of realistic looking mayhem Mailer finally achieved what the preceding 105 minutes (culled from an estimated 45 hours of shot footage) couldn't, a baffling blend of illusion and reality.

Maidstone, like Mailer's other films, didn't capture an audience, but it satisfied at least one viewer — himself. He claimed to have watched it at least 150 times. "I love it," he said. "For me it ranks along with the best of my writing."

Availability: Hard to find

Marie Antoinette (Kirsten Dunst): "This is ridiculous."
Comtesse de Noailles (Judy Davis): "This, Madame, is Versailles."
– DIALOGUE FROM *MARIE ANTIONETTE*

MARIE ANTOINETTE (2006)
– – – – – – – – – – – –

Like the misunderstood queen the movie is based on, *Marie Antoinette* the movie has gotten a bad rap. It was met with boos at the 2006 Cannes Film Festival, blasted by critics and historians for not being an exacting look at the life of the teenaged queen. It may not get the details 100 percent right, but if you want accuracy watch the History Channel. Sofia Coppola's follow-up to the wildly popular *Lost in Translation* is more of a tone poem, a dreamy biography more concerned with feelings than facts.

"It is not a lesson of history," Coppola told reporters at the Cannes Festival. "It is an interpretation documented, but carried by my desire for covering the subject differently."

As with her two previous films, *The Virgin Suicides* and *Lost in Translation*, Coppola once again shows her skill in capturing the youthful perspective of odd circumstances. Just as the Lisbon sisters of *Suicides* felt alienated by their suburban surroundings and family, and *Lost in Translation*'s Scarlett Johansson suffered the isolation of an unhappy marriage and strange country, the youthful queen of *Marie Antoinette* must deal with isolation and rejection, Versailles style.

Brought from her native Austria at age 14 as kind of a "womb for hire" Marie Antoinette (Kirsten Dunst, who worked previously with Coppola on *The Virgin Suicides*) was thrust into a loveless marriage with Louis xvi, the boy king who had no interest in her, and the court of Versailles, a gossipy place so vicious they make the London tabloid press look like Miss Manners. As Antoinette attempts to acclimate to life in the court she embraces the decadence, spending lavishly while her subjects starve. Even her hair reflects her excess. As the film goes on her hair grows from a subdued hairdo to an outrageous bouffant that would make even Kim Jong Il green with envy.

"I had heard the usual clichés about Marie Antoinette and her decadent lifestyle," said Coppola. "But I had never realized before how young she and Louis xvi really were. They were basically teenagers in charge of running France during a very volatile period and from within an incredibly extravagant setting, the royal court of Versailles. That's what first interested me: the idea that these young kids were placed in that position and trying to find out what they went through trying to grow up in such an extreme situation."

Coppola's film is luscious. Shot on the world's most expensive film set — she was the first director given permission to shoot at Versailles — the movie is uncommonly beautiful. More controversially she chose British pop music as the key songs on the soundtrack. Now this is no *Knight's Tale*, a medieval tale where the new wave music seemed out of place and strange. Coppola's use of New Order and the Cure fit the mood of the piece perfectly. In one stunning scene Marie Antoinette is doing some at home shopping — merchants would bring their most beautiful and expensive baubles to Versailles for her perusal — and as the camera glides over the pink and blue shoes, Bow Wow Wow's "I Want Candy" pulsates on the soundtrack. Music and scene mesh perfectly as the ornate shoes look more like bonbons than footwear and Dunst's youthful enthusiasm is apparent.

"Everything we did is based on research about the period, but it's all seen in a contemporary way," said Coppola. "My biggest fear was making a 'Masterpiece Theater' kind of movie. I didn't want to make a dry, historical period movie with the distant, cold tableau of shots. It was very important to me to tell the story in my own way. In the same way as I wanted *Lost in Translation* to feel like you had just spent a couple of hours in Tokyo, I wanted this film to let the audience feel what it might be like to be in Versailles during that time and to really get lost in that world."

Marie Antoinette isn't strictly a biopic, or history lesson on the French Revolution. Instead it is a beautiful portrait of spoiled youth and the toxic culture of decadence that did her in.

"I really wanted to bring a little of the New Romantic spirit into it because I felt it had such a similar mix of youthfulness, color and decadence," says Coppola. "This is a more playful version of history that reflects teenagers in a decadent time. At the same time, there is always a sense that while they're partying into oblivion the revolution is right around the corner."

Availability: On DVD

> "You may come and go, but you will not take people from the city. If I hear of it, a single time, I will destroy you without salvation."
> — TADA CUDA (LINCOLN MAAZEL) IN *MARTIN*

MARTIN (1977)

— — — — —

Imagine George A. Romero going to a psychic early on in his career.

"There's good news and bad news," she might say, gazing into her crystal ball. "Which would you like first?"

"The good news," the *Dawn of the Dead* director would reply.

"You will make many movies . . ."

"That's great! What's the bad news?"

"The only ones people will go see have the words 'of the Dead' in the title."

That didn't happen of course, but the fact remains that zombie king Romero has had a rough time attracting audiences for his non–*Living Dead* efforts. Dig deep into the Romero bargain bin though, and there are a number of films that deserve a second look. *The Crazies* is a spooky thriller about a manmade combat virus that causes death and permanent insanity in those infected while *Knightriders* is a wild romp that can best be described as *The Legend of King Arthur* meets *Mad Max*. Best of all is *Martin*, an arty 1977 movie about a young man who believes he is a vampire.

The eponymous creature of the night, Martin Madahas (played by *Dawn of the Dead* casting director John Amplas), is a shy suburban teenager with a blood lust, but none of the usual trappings of the Nosferatu. Instead of fangs he uses razorblades and needles to do the dirty work and he isn't averse to garlic, sunlight or crucifixes. Despite no actual proof of his undead status, he is steadfast in his conviction.

Surprisingly he's not alone in his belief. Cuda (Lincoln Maazel), an elderly old-world cousin believes that vampirism is a family "shame" and makes it his calling to save Martin's soul by trying to arrange an exorcism with the local priest. He also takes the boy in and gives him a job at his neighborhood grocery store, but Martin can only control his cravings for so long.

Martin actually has more in common with *Taxi Driver* than it does with *Dracula*. Romero's films have always brimmed with social commentary, but his '70s work is especially ripe with societal resonance. In *Martin* he filters the post-Vietnam ills of drug addiction and urban decay through the lens of a vampire film, focusing on the reasons why Martin behaves the way he does and not the behavior itself. Compared to other horror films this one barely qualifies as a shocker. There are just three violent scenes and while they are bloody, the gore is used more as a measure of Martin's ineptness — his sloppy killing skills — than to scare.

Often labeled as horror, it's more accurate to call *Martin* a psychological drama since Romero spends the entire film flirting with the question of whether Martin is really a vampire, or just a drug addict with a vivid imagination. Eerie black and white flashbacks portray him as an undead creature, but the reality is a much different story. With these black and white sequences Romero muddies the water, never settling on a definitive answer, preferring to let the viewers decide for themselves whether there are supernatural forces at work, or if this is all the product of a diseased mind.

In Romero's world the notion that Martin might not be a vampire is scarier than if he was a certified bloodsucker. Romero uses the troubled mid-'70s and its products — drug-addicted youths, decaying cities and stultifying suburban life — as a catalyst for the kind of fantasy world Martin creates just to cope with his life. This reality, Romero seems to imply, is far more terrifying than a fanged man in a cape could ever be.

"I didn't try to come down on one side or the other," Romero said. "I like the lady or the tiger kind of thing. I tried to keep it ambiguous, but in my mind, he was a disturbed kid."

Martin is dense with the kind of social subtext that Romero favors in his films. His zombie movies have been thinly veiled comments on consumerism and the media, and *Martin* is no less layered. On the surface it seems to be a simple story, but push past the garish lighting and Romero reveals a mixed bag of metaphors regarding drug addiction, mental illness and the evil that humans do to one another. It's purposefully ambiguous. The director is asking the viewers to look inside themselves to decide what answer to Martin's status they are comfortable with. Is he a vampire or disturbed young man? Drug addicted or mentally ill? The answer you come up with — what you choose to believe — Romero implies, says as much about you as it does about Martin.

Availability: On DVD

"Sonny and Cher were kind of like my mom and my dad . . ."
– RODNEY BINGENHEIMER IN *MAYOR OF SUNSET STRIP*

MAYOR OF SUNSET STRIP (2003)

Rodney Bingenheimer is famous for being . . . well, Rodney Bingenheimer.

Since the mid-1960s he has been the Zelig of the Los Angeles music scene, an omnipresent figure who stood in for Davy Jones of the Monkees, got beaten up by Rolling Stone Brian Jones (who later apologized) and made a habit of knowing all the hippest people. He was such a man about town that Sal Mineo dubbed him "the Mayor of the Sunset Strip," a name director George Hickenlooper, the man behind the great documentary on the making of *Apocalypse Now*, *Hearts of Darkness: A*

Filmmaker's Apocalypse, borrowed as the title for his touching look at Bingenheimer's life and influence.

"I made this documentary so people would know about Rodney," said Hickenlooper. "It's a great journey through the history of rock and roll through the eyes of this unique Forrest Gump who sustained himself by living through the lives of celebrities and then becomes a celebrity himself. He's a metaphor for our obsession with the cult of celebrity."

Rodney may be a walking metaphor, but he's also a real person and Hickenlooper takes pains to explain where Rodney's celebrity mania came from. We learn that as a youngster he and his mother shared a fascination with movie stars and gossip columns. Old photos reveal a *TV Guide* cover mural on Rodney's bedroom wall — his celebrity obsessed way of sleeping under "the stars."

Mother and son shared many celebrity moments, but one likely defined Rodney's entire adult life. At age 16 his mother drove him to the house of his idol, Connie Stevens, with instructions to knock on the door and get an autograph. She then drove away and Rodney didn't see her for another six or seven years. Abandoned, he made his way to the Sunset Strip, at the time the most happening patch of pavement in America.

Instead of becoming a Sunset Strip statistic, soon, by virtue of his outgoing social-climbing nature Rodney was hanging out with Davy Jones, mixing it up with the brightest music stars on the Strip and making a name for himself as a tastemaker. If Rodney liked your band you were hip, if not, you just weren't cool. Through stints on radio and in print he championed everyone from David Bowie to Blondie to the Bangles, giving each of them their first big push in the all important Southern Californian music market.

In the early '70s he opened Rodney Bingenheimer's English Disco, a hip night spot and just about the only place to hear glam rock in So Cal.

"I went to London and met up with David Bowie," Rodney told me in 1994, "and he gave me the idea to open the club. In Britain there were a lot of these clubs that were playing records by the Sweet and bands called Mud and T. Rex. They had all these great records that people were dancing to, so I brought all these records back with me and opened the club with a partner.

"Of course we had a lot of celebrities who used to come in the club. Mackenzie Phillips was a regular. Linda Blair used to play records there. Joan Jett, Bianca Jagger, Angela Bowie, Shaun Cassidy used to play there. Iggy Pop, David Bowie, T. Rex and Led Zeppelin all used to go there," he says, the names pouring from his lips like quarters tumbling out of a winning slot machine.

A household name in music industry circles and hip L.A. society, Rodney's fame didn't extend much beyond the borders of the Sunset Strip. He was best known as a professional friend of famous people; a figure usually pictured standing next to, or just behind the rock and roll flavor of the day — although Robert Plant says that Rodney was so popular on the scene he bedded more girls than any of the guys in Zeppelin.

While making this clear, Hickenlooper's film takes on a wistful tone that elevates it beyond the level of a *VH1 Behind the Music* episode. Hickenlooper gives the highlights of Rodney's life, but doesn't shy away from showing us the disappointments and troubling side of being almost famous in a celebrity-obsessed world.

A visit to his father Bing and stepmother Zelda is heart-rending, as it becomes clear that they don't share his passion for celebrity culture and don't appear impressed or even interested in Rodney's place in the celebrity social strata. Coming across a signed photo of Kato Kaelin given to him by Rodney, Bing seems genuinely baffled. "He just sent it to us," he says, dismissing an importance that Rodney may have given the gift, instead treating it as an oddity, just one step away from the garbage can.

Even more heartbreaking is Rodney's interaction with a young woman named Camille Chancery. He mentions her several times throughout the film, and is clearly taken with her. When we finally meet her, sitting on a bed next to Rodney as he talks about love and relationships, it appears that they are a couple, except for the strained look on her face. When Hickenlooper finally asks her if she has feelings for Rodney she says they are just friends, that she has a boyfriend and she needs to focus on her music career. As the camera lingers on the two he sits there stone-faced, an inscrutable Warholesque figure who, although likely disappointed and hurt by her remarks, doesn't react. It's hard to watch, but doesn't feel exploitive because of Rodney's willingness to open his life for the camera. The very act of filming him at his best and worst is the fulfillment of his lifelong dream — to be a part of star culture, the star of a film about his life.

That said, there is a wistful quality to much of *Mayor of Sunset Strip*. He has friends — although by his own account not many close friends. While the celebrities he admires appear in the film singing his praises — David Bowie, Cher, Rob Zombie, Debbie Harry (who digs out an old Bingenheimer T-shirt for her interview), Courtney Love, Nancy Sinatra, Elvis Costello, super-groupie Pamela Des Barres (who says that Rodney was the first guy of many in Hollywood she made out with) and Mick Jagger — his best friend is an outsider musical artist who would be homeless if not for Rodney's generosity.

Mayor of Sunset Strip is a fascinating look at someone who has watched life in the fast lane from curbside. The beauty here is that Hickenlooper gets under his subject's skin and finds the real person behind the Rodney's often impenetrable facade. Rather than simply presenting a list of Rodney's accomplishments, Hickenlooper digs deeper, exposing an unhappy man who sits by helplessly as he fades into irrelevancy. Thankfully Hickenlooper doesn't allow his camera to mock Rodney. Instead his depiction of him is loving, a portrait of a man who gave his life to celebrity culture and got little in return.

Availability: On DVD

"It's Jurassic Park in your own backyard."
– ADVERTISING TAGLINE FOR
MICROCOSMOS: LE PEUPLE DE L'HERBE

MICROCOSMOS: LE PEUPLE DE L'HERBE (1996)

Although the stars of *Microcosmos: Le peuple de l'herbe* (*Microcosmos: The Grass People*) are tiny creatures, the emotions and drama contained in the story are as big as any Hollywood epic. French biologists-turned-filmmakers Claude Nuridsany and Marie Pérennou spent 15 years researching the lives of the bugs and developing the technology to properly capture their minuscule world. The result is a film that could simply be seen as a science project but is so much more.

Using specially designed cameras with magnifying lenses the filmmakers are able to get up close and personal with their insect subjects, transporting the viewer into a world where a blade of grass looks to be as tall as a skyscraper. Never before has a film given us such a clear view of a day in the life of the creepy-crawly community that exists just beneath our feet. "[It's] beyond anything that we could imagine," narrator Kristin Scott Thomas says, "and yet almost beneath our notice."

Call it "fly-on-the-wall" filmmaking or vermin vérité. *Microcosmos* was shot over the course of three years in the French countryside and has no plot, limited narration and little music. As an alternative it uses the sounds of nature, amplified but not changed, to create the soundtrack where bees' wings make a noise like an old prop plane. The choice to use natural sounds is sometimes relaxing, sometimes fascinating, and even sometimes silly, but always intriguing.

Shot up close these bugs take on the look of extraterrestrials but their everyday activities are anything but out of this world. Like all living things they are concerned with survival, providing food for themselves and their mates and, when the sun starts to go down, a little hanky-panky. Birds do it, bees do it, but do you know (how) snails do it? Nuridsany and Pérennou catch two snails engaging in some erotic foreplay that would make Hugh Hefner proud, and underscore the steamy moment with some fitting choral music.

Mixed throughout are light moments that infuse comic personality into the little critters. The filmmakers wisely choose not to manipulate or Disney-fy the insects with voices or computer-generated facial expressions. Instead they let nature take its course and the results are often surprisingly funny. A clumsy ladybird taking flight and the exploits of a determined sacred beetle's Sisyphean battle with a pellet of dung reveal the quirks of these remarkable creatures and provide a welcome dose of slapstick.

It is, however, the filmmakers' depiction of the daily life-and-death struggle in the insect world gives the film much of its oomph. Lethal-looking spiders trapping their prey in intricate webs that, magnified, resemble steel cable, a colony of ants decimated by a hungry pheasant and pelted by raindrops that proportionally are the size of basketballs become epic in scale when seen in close-up. Strangely, the real life trials and tribulations of these insects often pack as much emotional punch as human stories.

So many movies use computer generated effects to create images that aren't half as beautiful or interesting as the real ones on Earth that we never see. *Microcosmos: Le peuple de l'herbe* gives us a chance to explore our insect neighbors' lives and is a fascinating journey into an intricate and intriguing world.

Availability: On DVD

Richard's Favorite Big Bug Movies

1. *The Black Scorpion* (1957): Giant scorpions destroy Mexico City! Released from underground caverns, these deadly giant critters are on the rampage and only one man can stop them, American geologist Hank Scott (Richard Denning). Cool stop-motion monsters by legendary animator Willis O'Brien.
2. *Tremors* (1990): A throwback to the big bug movies of the 1950s, *Tremors* sees a small Nevada town terrorized by man-eating worm creatures with big fangs.
3. *Them!* (1954): One of the first atomic age big bug movies and still one of the best. Mutated oversize ants run riot in New

Mexico before migrating to the sewers of Los Angeles. Sharp-eyed viewers will spot a pre-Spock Leonard Nimoy in the cast.

4. *Mimic* (1997): Directed by Mexico's Maestro of Mayhem, Guillermo del Toro, the movie presents giant cockroaches that can mimic human form.

5. *Beginning of the End* (1957): Scientist Dr. Ed Wainwright (Peter Graves) must find a way to stop enormous flesh-starved grasshoppers from swarming Chicago.

6. *Starship Troopers* (1997): Based on a Robert Heinlein story and adapted for the screen by Dutch schlockmiester Paul Verhoeven, who claims not to have finished the book because it made him "bored and depressed," *Starship Troopers* is a wild shoot 'em up between the military and huge extraterrestrial insects. "These bugs are just like us," says General Owen (Marshall Bell). "Just as smart as we are. They want to study us. They want to know what makes us tick. They want to know our likes and dislikes. In short: they want to know about us . . . so they can kill us!"

7. *Mothra* (1962): The first sighting of the giant moth able to blow over buildings with the force of her wings who would later go on to co-star with a variety of J-Horror's greatest characters in films like *Mothra Versus Godzilla* (1964), *Ghidorah: The Three-Headed Monster* (1964), *Godzilla Versus the Sea Monster* (1966) and *Godzilla Versus Mothra* (1992).

8. *Eight Legged Freaks* (2002): A toxic spill in a rural mining town causes spiders to metamorphose into, well, bloodthirsty eight-legged freaks the size of Buicks. Good special effects and some great goofy dialogue. After one arachnid attack the sheriff's assistant explains what attacked him, "A spider, man . . ."

9. *The Deadly Mantis* (1957): Frozen for a million years, a gargantuan praying mantis is awakened by a volcano blast. The bug has a go at destroying both Washington, D.C., and

New York City before doing battle with the military. "In all the kingdom of the living," says Dr. Ned Jackson (William Hopper, best known as Paul Drake on *Perry Mason*), "there is no more deadly or voracious creature than the praying mantis."

10. *Empire of the Ants* (1977): Loosely adapted from an H. G. Wells novel, and definitely in the "so bad it's good" category, this one has a pre-*Dynasty* Joan Collins as a sleazy real-estate agent trying to bilk unsuspecting tourists into buying worthless land in the Florida Everglades. What she doesn't know is that the land is infested with nasty, whopping big ants who view Joan and company as tasty snacks.

"Where the hell am I supposed to find silver bullets? Kmart?"
— **RUDY (RYAN LAMBERT) IN *THE MONSTER SQUAD***

THE MONSTER SQUAD (1987)

Like many baby boomers reared on the *Famous Monsters of Filmland* magazine, Fred Dekker is a huge fan of the classic Universal horror movies. *Frankenstein, Dracula, The Creature from the Black Lagoon, The Mummy* and *The Wolf Man* inspire nightmares in most, but for Dekker they simply fire his imagination.

"As a kid," said the San Francisco born filmmaker, "I loved the Universal monster films of the '30s and '40s so obviously, getting the chance to play in their fictional universe was a dream come true."

The result of Dekker's reverie was the creation of *The Monster Squad*, a 1987 teenage horror comedy that owes a big nod to *Abbott &*

Costello Meet Frankenstein with a side order of *The Goonies* thrown in for good measure.

When Count Dracula recruits a posse of monsters — Frankenstein's Monster, the Mummy, the Wolf Man and the Creature from the Black Lagoon — to retrieve and destroy an ancient amulet that holds the key to controlling the balance of good and evil in the world, he didn't count on a band of fifth-graders (and one chain-smoking eighth-grade greaser) driving a stake through his plans.

The Monster Squad, a geeky group who wear T-shirts that say "Stephen King Rules" and spend their days obsessing over monster magazines and debating important topics like, "Who is the coolest monster?" and "Does the Wolf Man have the biggest nards?" have come into possession of the diary of famed Dracula hunter Abraham Van Helsing, a document that holds the secret to stopping the Count's army of darkness and thwarting his evil plan.

With the help of the local Scary German Guy (Leonardo Cinimo), who translates the book into English, they get the skinny on the amulet. According to the book it is composed of concentrated good, but for one day every century it is vulnerable and can be destroyed. If they can find the amulet and use it in conjunction with an incantation from the diary, they can create a swirling vortex which will suck the monsters away from Earth, condemning them to a metaphysical jail and saving the world from their reign of wickedness. If the monsters get to the amulet first, evil will win.

The first thing you'll notice about *The Monster Squad* is that the monsters don't look exactly the way you remember them from the old Universal movies. That's because this homage to those landmark films wasn't made by Universal, who still own the copyrights to the likenesses of those famous fiends. To get around that hurdle, special effects wizard Stan Winston — whose creature creations have been seen in everything from *Edward Scissorhands* to *Jurassic Park* and *Aliens* — took the original copyrighted designs and tweaked them just enough to avoid lawsuits.

"Although we were doing a movie that was a takeoff on the Universal classics, we had to be careful none of our designs infringed on the original designs of the Universal characters," Winston told *Rue Morgue* in 2007. "There were subtle changes; we had to be sure that nothing specific about them could be considered a copyright infringement of a design."

You'll notice Dracula still has a cape, but no widow's peak; Frankenstein's head is shaped differently and the neck bolts are gone, while the Wolf Man looks like his hair was blown dry and teased by a hairdresser with one too many Red Bulls under his belt. The changes are minimal, but spookily effective. The success of the makeup designs is further enhanced by strong creature performances by the actors, particularly Tom Noonan as Frankenstein's Monster, who brings a vulnerability to this familiar character.

"I think Tom Noonan brought just the right amount of conviction and gentleness and sadness to Frankenstein's Monster," says Dekker, "and Duncan Regehr was a terrific Dracula. He had just the right combination of nobility and evil and animal rage and all the stuff that are the hallmarks of that character."

In contrast to the supernatural showings of the older actors, the kids of *The Monster Squad* turn in nice, natural performances.

"It was really important to me that we had real kids and not movie kids," Dekker says. "You know, the kind you see in commercials who are too pretty and mug and overact? We didn't want that. We wanted them to be believable, and to seem like they were really friends. Luckily, they turned out to become a very tight-knit group."

Despite the salty language (the boys swear, Dracula calls a little girl "a bitch" and a preteen uses the word "chickenshit," no doubt courtesy of Shane Black who also wrote more adult fare like *Lethal Weapon*), the refreshing lack of political correctness, the violence and the presence of nightmare-inducing monsters, *The Monster Squad* is, above all, a kids' film. The youngsters are the heroes and battle the monsters in ways that only kids can. A garlic pizza proves to be Dracula's undoing, and in one classic scene the Wolf Man is felled by a well-placed kick to "the nards."

"I like to think that *Monster Squad*, in its own small way, says something about what it is to be a kid and to be afraid in the world," says Dekker, "and discovering the need for heroism."

Dekker adds that he set out to make an exciting teen adventure movie, but may have been a bit ahead of his time. In the post–*Buffy the Vampire Slayer* world we live in the mix of kids, humor and horror seems normal, but in 1987 it didn't click with audiences.

"When *Monster Squad* was released, we found that kids didn't go see it because their parents wouldn't let them. Mostly because they thought it was going to be too scary, and parents didn't see it because they thought it was a kids' film," he says. "In fact it took another several years before the combination of young people in jeopardy in genre-horror situations like *Buffy* and *Goosebumps* and *Harry Potter* really became acceptable. The audience wasn't ready for it in the '80s. Sure there was *The Lost Boys* and *The Goonies*, but specifically the kind of monster-slayer approach wouldn't be popular for another 10 or 15 years. So I like to think that we were a little ahead of the curve."

The movie's box office take, or lack of it, condemned the film to obscurity, but it didn't disappear altogether. Substandard video releases of the movie helped build a small cult audience for the flick, but fans had to wait 20 years for a deluxe DVD treatment. In 2007 Lionsgate released a sparkling two-disc set with lots of extras and deleted scenes. "The remastered print is so incredible that there are many shots that I hadn't seen since I saw them through the lens of my Panaflex," says Dekker.

Availability: On DVD

NARC (2002)

— — — — —

Narc is the kind of movie that makes you forget the dark patches on actors Jason Patric and Ray Liotta's resumés. One look at this and you'll stop thinking about Patric in *Frankenstein Unbound,* and forget all about Liotta in *Operation Dumbo Drop.*

The story is simple enough, almost clichéd. When the trail on a murder investigation of a policeman goes cold, an undercover narcotics officer, Detective Sergeant Nick Tellis (Patric), is teamed with loose-cannon Detective Henry R. Oak (Liotta) to solve the case. It's old hat — the good cop teamed with a out-of-control cop. We've seen it in movies and on television for as long as there have been police dramas, but when it is treated with the kind of conviction and intensity that Liotta and Patric bring to their roles, it seems fresh and compelling. Both play cops who cross the line into unlawful behavior in order to do their jobs, and both have become tainted by their experiences. *Narc* explores what happens to a good cop when he is forced to break the law.

"He's not Dirty Harry," said the movie's producer and star Ray Liotta about Oak, "and he's not a vigilante. He does things on his own. He has a 93 percent conviction rating, but his methods are not the department's. There's a great line in the film: 'It's not about rules and regulations, it's about right and wrong.' He crosses the line, but his reasoning is not wrong.

"*Narc* reminded me of a '70s movie. My idols from that time are Robert Duvall, Gene Hackman, Al Pacino and Robert De Niro. They were anti-heroes in their films. There was a lot of gray in what they did and who they were."

Both leads are treading in familiar territory. Patric starred as an undercover narcotics cop in 1991's *Rush,* and Liotta has played both sides of the law in innumerable cop dramas, but both bring something fresh to *Narc.* There's none of the fake witty banter between them that mars so many cop buddy movies. The funny back and forth has been replaced with grim, real-life dialogue and is well played by the two. This isn't *Lethal Weapon* or *Bad Boys* but a hard-edged cop drama made more believable by two actors who are both perfectly cast.

Liotta, who gained 25 pounds for the role, has the world-weary look of a man who has seen it all, and Patric's Tellis is like a cat ready to pounce. He radiates a quiet intensity that meshes perfectly with the unsentimental, tense tone of the film.

"When we met Jason we found that his energy is very different than mine," said Liotta. "He's very cerebral, he thinks things out. He knew what his part was. When I'm yelling at him, he knows he can only go to a certain degree because he knows I'm a live wire. When he tells me to get my hand out of his face, a lesser actor would want to show off that he's tough too. That wouldn't have made sense, because my guy would never have been talked to that way. To me, I can't think of anyone else in this role."

Visually director Joe Carnahan captures the feel of the mean streets. Shot in Toronto in just 28 days, he used a grainy film stock and hand-held cameras to underline not only the dirt, but the energy of the street and the sleazy underbelly in which these two men operate.

Narc is a great cop movie — *French Connection* director William Friedkin says it's one of the best he's seen — but it has a generic title, and a grainy feel to it that audiences didn't connect with. Perhaps it was too mean-spirited for mainstream viewers who prefer to have their cops cracking jokes instead of busting heads, something that is going to make them feel a little better. Hopefully it's the kind of movie that will build a cult following on DVD.

Availability: On DVD

NIGHT MOVES (1975)

■ ■ ■ ■ ■ ■ ■ ■ ■

Night Moves, the 1975 neo-noir from director Arthur Penn, represents the point at which the experimentation of the French New Wave intersected with the sensibilities of young Hollywood. Embracing the energy of the Nouvelle Vague masters Jean-Luc Godard and François Truffaut — jump-cuts abound — Penn brings a youthful iconoclasm to the movie. Rejecting most of the tried and true mores of the private investigator genre, he instead infuses the story with a very American dose of paranoia and acidity. Audiences rejected its cryptic story, but hindsight reveals it to be a fascinating look at the bitter taste left in the collective mouths of Americans post Watergate.

"I was in shock when I made this film," Penn told *Uncut Magazine.* "The assassinations had come tumbling down. Both Kennedys, Martin Luther King, even George Wallace. I don't embrace the conspiracy theories. I think far more there's an atmosphere of psychosis at a certain point that seems to take over in society that permits assassination — invites it — and I think we were in that kind of period and I had an immediate association with it, in that I had worked with both the Kennedys.

"I just had to do a film about it. It really was about the sourness I felt about all of that, and Watergate. That's why Gene's [Hackman] character doesn't realize he's part of a conspiracy — as we all were, by permitting the nonsense of Watergate to go on as long as it did."

When we meet former pro footballer Harry Moseby (Gene Hackman) he's a middle-aged Los Angeles private eye. Saddled with a cheating wife (Susan Clark) and a determination to make a go of his failing business, his life is in a tailspin.

Things don't improve any when he takes on what should be a standard missing person case, searching for Delly (Melanie Griffith in her first major role), the 16-year-old daughter of Arlene Iverson (Janet Ward), a faded Hollywood beauty who was once married to a big-time studio mogul and claims to have carried on with every power player in town.

Acting on a tip from Delly's ex, Quentin (James Woods), that the daughter has shacked up with a stuntman in New Mexico, Harry hits the road. That turns out to be a wild goose chase as Delly has already left, running to the Florida Keys and her pilot stepfather Tom Iverson (John Crawford). Harry tracks the girl in Florida and it is here that the movie really gets a head of steam.

As soon as Harry lays eyes on Iverson's sexy girlfriend Paula (Jennifer Warren) he is smitten. She's a sultry beauty that makes him forget all about his unfaithful wife and perhaps even his professional ethics. The plot thickens when, while swimming, they discover a body in the cockpit of a downed light airplane. The sight of the body is enough to shock Delly into returning to her mother in Los Angeles, but for Harry the case is far from closed. When his contacts start turning up dead he realizes this wasn't just a simple missing person case, but a vast conspiracy that may well cost him his life.

Night Moves features career topping work for several of the cast and crew. The dark, fearful tone established by director Penn is arguably his strongest and most fully realized vision ever on film. Warren, so scorchingly sexy in the role of Paula, never again displayed the kind of heat she emits here. Screenwriter Alan Sharp's script is letter perfect in capturing the feeling of unrest in America following Vietnam, Watergate and the Kennedy assassinations, but make no mistake, this is Gene Hackman's movie. Unfortunately since so few people saw this movie on release, Harry Moseby qualifies as Hackman's great lost performance of the '70s.

"Gene's just an absolutely wonderful actor," says Penn. "There isn't a dishonest bone in his body in front of the camera."

Hackman plays the kind of lead character in *Night Moves* you don't see much anymore in Hollywood films — a loser whose life only gets progressively worse instead of better. He's a lost soul wracked with anxiety and apprehension but Hackman's inherent machismo keeps him from appearing weak. It's a tough balancing act and he pulls it off magnificently. Hackman was nominated twice for Academy Awards for his acting in the '70s — *I Never Sang for My Father* and *The French Connection* — but to my mind he was nominated for the wrong movies. Perhaps his portrayal of Harry was too downbeat, too dark to appeal to Academy voters who seem to be drawn to chirpier, more heroic characters. Despite its lack of awards attention *Night Moves* remains a riveting piece of work from one of the icons of '70s cinema.

Overall *Night Moves* works not simply because of Hackman's strong central performance, but also for the movie's ability to take unexpected, but believable turns. Its plot is a curvy road that keeps you off guard right up until its surprisingly poignant ending.

Availability: On DVD

"What kind of job is this, anyway?
Garbage, that's all we handle . . . garbage!"
— JIM WILSON (ROBERT RYAN) IN *ON DANGEROUS GROUND*

ON DANGEROUS GROUND (1952)

Martin Scorsese calls it one of his biggest influences. Its shy psychopathic killer character may have partially inspired the portrayal of Norman Bates in Alfred Hitchcock's *Psycho* and years later its themes of police alienation and displacement resurfaced in Christopher Nolan's

Insomnia. On Dangerous Ground is a great lost classic from a director about whom Jean-Luc Godard once said, "Nicholas Ray *is* cinema." A run-through of any of Ray's 28 films — *Rebel Without a Cause, The Savage Innocents* or *Bitter Victory* for example — shows Godard's comment to be more than sheer hyperbole.

Based on the novel *Mad With Much Heart* by Gerald Butler and made for Howard Hughes' RKO Pictures in 1950, but not released until 1952 after Hughes fiddled with the ending, the film is broken into two distinct parts. The first is a gritty urban noir that sees former local high school football hero Jim Wilson (the Oscar-nominated Robert Ryan), now an 11 year ticking-time-bomb veteran of the NYPD, grappling with the unsavory aspects of his job. Dealing with lowlifes and criminals has eroded his ability to trust anyone, including, it appears, women, as he is a committed bachelor.

Around the precinct he has a reputation for being a dedicated but unstable force to be reckoned with. Even his partners, Pete Santos (Anthony Ross) and Pop Daly (Charles Kemper) think he's on the verge of a nervous breakdown, and his increasing bent for police brutality isn't going over well with the higher-ups.

He's having an increasingly difficult time separating work from his personal life, and soon the demons that torment him on the job invade his home. Even the simple task of washing his hands takes a nasty turn as he squeezes his fingers together as if he was wringing the neck of an imaginary suspect.

When he brutally beats a stool pigeon to get info on two cop killers his methods are called into question, but because his tactics lead to the arrest of the murderers he's let off with a warning. When he slaps around another suspect, Captain Brawley (Ed Begley) transfers him out of New York City to work on a small town rape and homicide case in hopes that the rural surroundings will chill him out.

Wilson doesn't want the assignment — "Siberia," he calls it — but given no choice he packs his bags and heads upstate, and the second, and more interesting, part of the movie begins.

In an isolated snow covered small town — never identified by name, but it's noted that the village is seventy miles north of the city, although the scenes were actually shot in Colorado — Wilson meets his match in a man even more consumed with rage than he. Walter Brent (Ward Bond) is the father of the young victim, who vows to get revenge on the suspect — trial or no trial — and doesn't trust anyone from "the city."

The investigation leads Wilson to a remote cabin, nestled in the hills outside of town. There they find the blind Mary Malden (Ida Lupino) and her disturbed brother Danny (Sumner Williams), who committed the crime and is now in hiding. Mary's main concern is for her brother's welfare. She wants for him to turn himself in — peacefully — so he can get the help he needs in an institution. Mary fears Brent and his vengeance, but has seen the long hidden good side of Wilson and trusts that he will help her resolve the case in her brother's best interests.

Not only is *On Dangerous Ground* two movies in one — the bleak hard edge of its first couple of reels compared to the redemptive rural drama that makes up the end of the film — it also isn't easily pigeonholed. It's a psychologically dense drama, an action flick, a crime story, a romance (almost), and a mystery all rolled into one. Only a director as skilled as Ray could juggle all these elements successfully without turning the film into an incomprehensible stew of styles.

Some credit probably belongs to Howard Hughes who tinkered with the story, particularly the final moments of the film, which, by all reports, solidified the action and cleaned up a few ambiguous elements. But make no mistake, this is a Nicholas Ray film. He specialized in stories about loneliness, pain and alienation, all of which play prominent roles here.

The redemption of *On Dangerous Ground*'s main character is an obvious plot point, so while you may innately know he will be saved from himself in the end, the question that remains is how. In many ways the journey to recovery from his torment is the film's unexpected gotcha. Frequently redemption in the movies is found through the love of a good woman, but here Ray sets it up so that Wilson's relief comes from an unlikely source. Wilson is a law-and-order kind of guy who falls for the sister of a known criminal, and to boot, a sister who is trying to get him to go easy on a guy who raped and killed a young girl. Their relationship is chaste, but burns up the screen nonetheless. The heat in this coupling is generated by the two actors — Ryan and Lupino — who manage to take stock characters and humanize them, he making his spiritual awakening seem tangible and real, she gorgeous and heartfelt. Lupino's sultry presence is underscored by a rich minor-chord musical motif, courtesy of Bernard Herrmann's score, which plays when she is onscreen.

On Dangerous Ground is a taut, economical 80 minutes that, when seen, should push you in the direction of other works by its two under-appreciated collaborators, Nicholas Ray and Robert Ryan.

Availability: On DVD as part of the Film Noir Classics Volume 3 set

"If I could sing, I'd sing. I can't sing, Frannie!"
— HANK (FREDERIC FORREST) IN *ONE FROM THE HEART*

ONE FROM THE HEART (1982)

In 1981, we saw video kill the radio star. Using dry ice and artifice, loud colors and quick cuts, MTV revolutionized the way we experience music. Twenty years later the high concept musicals *Moulin Rouge!* and *Chicago* translated that aesthetic to the big screen, earning big bucks and Oscar nods in the process.

While those films may have won raves from the critics and scored at the box office, two decades earlier a similar movie had financially and creatively sent one of America's best known filmmakers into a tailspin. The story of Francis Ford Coppola's *One from the Heart* is a saga of the right idea at the wrong time.

After completing the grueling *Apocalypse Now* shoot the maverick director was burned out. "I was frightened and personally kind of depressed," he told me in 2003. "It had taken a big toll on everything in my life — certainly on my finances, my family life, everything."

In an effort to bring some stability to his chaotic life he decided to make a small film that he could shoot in at his own facility, American Zoetrope Studios in Hollywood.

"I could remember being a teenager when I first started to do the college musicals and that had been a very happy period for me. My father had been a conductor of Broadway shows and I wanted very much to make a musical. The musical I was writing or trying to write, which was *Tucker*, was far from being ready and I had to make another film to support my family. I thought that *One from the Heart*, which was a very simple fable love story, could be a kind of experimental musical, in that it would use song and dance and scenic elements of a kabuki play, you know, rather than a conventional musical, which was not permitted in Hollywood at that time."

The "simple fable love story" Coppola chose to bring to the screen was a standard issue romance where the visual and emotional elements mattered more than the plot. Filmed completely on a sound stage, *One from the Heart* contains no exteriors or location shots. Coppola had clearly been stung by his arduous experience on *Apocalypse Now* in the Philippines during which costs had spiraled out of control and his star Martin Sheen almost died after suffering a stress related heart attack. This time out Coppola was determined to control every aspect of the shoot from the relative calm of a high-tech control room built specially for the production.

Ensconced in a trailer jammed with experimental video equipment, Coppola was able to see on a monitor what the director of photography was seeing through his lens. It's standard procedure today, but at the time it was a revolutionary process. The set-up allowed the director to view each shot in real time without having to wait for dailies and gave him the opportunity to consider various editing combinations on the spot. From that vantage point Coppola said he was able to "compose" the film during production.

"My mindset was to make *One from the Heart* as kind of an experimental film," said Coppola, "since we had the wonderful opportunity of buying a Hollywood studio and equipping it as a modern digital studio.

"I viewed electronic cinema, or what you might call today digital cinema, not so much as a cheap solution to edit more quickly, or to do special effects more inexpensively. I thought it would change the form, the language of cinema. It would evolve it because the electronic cinema is much more genie-like, much more elastic and you would be able to compose movies rather than assemble them as we went from a mechanical cinema, which is photochemical, to electronics."

Not everyone was onside with Coppola's brave new method. When the simple movie the director had in mind started to balloon into a well publicized debacle, word leaked to the press and the knives came out.

"He took an $8 million project and used the latest advances in video to bring it in for $23 million," went one dismissive wisecrack. It was also suggested that the movie wasn't coming from the heart, but from the lab.

The resulting two years of bad publicity before the film hit screens sunk any chance of it finding an audience. Coppola tried to position the film as a special event, premiering it at a reserved seat run at New York City's legendary 6,000-seat Radio City Music Hall. When it failed to attract an audience — it grossed only $900,000, a fraction of what it cost to produce — Coppola pulled it from theaters.

Critical response was less than welcoming. *New Yorker* doyenne Pauline Kael compared the film's look to that of a Dr Pepper commercial, and wrote, "A man who can say, with the seriousness of a hypnotist, that the new movie technology is 'going to make the Industrial Revolution look like a small, out-of-town tryout' seems to have lost the sense of proportion that's needed for shaping a movie." Other, less vitriolic critics said it had "all the warmth of neon," and was "an ambitious misfire."

But did *One from the Heart* deserve the critical ass-whooping it took at the hands of writers and commentators?

Yes and no.

The story of Frannie and Hank (Teri Garr and Frederic Forrest), a couple who split up after celebrating their fifth anniversary on the eve of the Fourth of July, only to discover that their new, beautiful partners (Raul Julia and Nastassja Kinski) don't fulfill them emotionally is, at best, a dreamy trifle. It was a complete departure for the director from the heavy themes that informed his work for most of the '70s and critics and audiences expected more depth from a filmmaking Goliath like Coppola.

The clunky performances (we're looking at you, Ms. Kinski) may be attributed to Coppola's new work method. Traditionally directors directed from the floor, spending time with the actors, helping them mold their performances, but in this instance Coppola rarely left his trailer, preferring to tinker with the technology rather than guide his cast.

On the upside Coppola and cinematographer Vittorio Storaro (one of Bernardo Bertolucci's favored collaborators) imbue every frame of the picture with a wonderfully artificial look and feel that echoes the large-scale abstract sequences Gene Kelly made famous in movies like *Singin' in the Rain* and *An American in Paris*. (Kelly actually worked as an unaccredited technical advisor on the film's musical numbers.)

It's an entirely cinematic experience, one that challenges the preconceived ideas of what makes a musical. There are songs, but the characters don't sing them. The Oscar-nominated soundtrack by Tom Waits (who met his wife Kathleen Brennan when she worked as a script analyst at Zoetrope) and Crystal Gayle was described by Coppola as a "cocktail landscape," and provided an emotional musical dialogue that underscored the lovers' downward spiral.

"I wasn't used to concentrating on one thing for so long, to the point where you start eating your own flesh," said Waits, who wrote some of his most heartfelt songs to date for the film.

The simple little film that was meant to rescue Coppola from the brink of financial and emotional ruin did just the opposite. The enormous cost of *One from the Heart* — reported to be somewhere between $23 and $26 million at a time when the average movie cost half that amount — bankrupted his little dream factory, American Zoetrope, robbing him of his independence and his chance to challenge the movie establishment.

The price may have been high, but time has been kind to *One from the Heart.* The radical video technology Coppola used is now the standard; the then experimental style of the film has been adopted by other filmmakers; there are hints of it in everything from *Chicago* to Lars Von Trier's *Dogville.* Tom Ohanian, one of the creators of the Avid nonlinear editing system, credits Coppola and *One from the Heart* with inspiring him.

Twenty-five years after the release of the film Coppola was philosophical about risking it all on *One from the Heart.*

"I imagine at the moment of my death as I'm smiling and thinking back on the wonderful life I've had and the great things I did; the wonderful people I've known and loved and the only bad thing would be to say, 'Well, I didn't do this, and I didn't do that.' I have maybe two things I didn't do. Most people have a hundred things, or a thousand things they didn't do, and I think you should live your life to the fullest because it is terminated eventually and a happy death is the end of a happy life."

Availability: On DVD

Richard's Favorite
Actors Turned Singers

1. Burt Reynolds cracked the *Billboard* Hot 100 single chart at number 88 in 1980 with the song "Let's Do Something Cheap and Superficial" from the film *Smokey and the Bandit II*. The song, written by Richard Levinson, clocked in at number 150 on a list of the Worst Country Titles Ever next to "Mama Get the Hammer (There's a Fly on Papa's Head)."

2. Hot off the success of *Beverly Hills Cop* Eddie Murphy teamed up with Rick "Superfreak" James on the good-time anthem "Party All the Time," which entered the *Billboard* charts in November 1985 and spent 14 weeks in the Top 40, reaching the number two spot. In *Beverly Hills Cop II* Murphy pays tribute to his musical collaborator by using the undercover name "Richard James" in the gun club scene.

3. "I don't sing very well – I have a horrible voice – but I get a big kick out of it," says Bruce Willis. "Early in my career," he continues, "I was given the opportunity by Motown to do a couple of albums that really sucked. Most of the songs were somebody else's idea of what songs I should be singing. I wrote a couple myself and those are the ones that I liked . . ." The albums were *Bruce Willis: The Return of Bruno*, which went platinum on the strength of the single "Respect Yourself," and the considerably less successful *If It Don't Kill You, It Just Makes You Stronger*.

4. "The bar is set pretty low – I'm fully aware of that," Minnie Driver says. "There aren't too many actors who've made good records." Driver, who sang as a teen in London's jazz clubs, took a break from Hollywood in 2004 and released her debut album, *Everything I've Got in My Pocket*. Featuring a cover of Bruce Springsteen's "Hungry Heart," the album earned Driver some new fans – including Springsteen himself. "He was trying on jeans [in a store in Boston] when he heard [my version of] 'Hungry Heart' and he told his wife to buy a couple of copies. It's so cool."

5. Everyone knows that Sissy Spacek was nominated for a Grammy for her rendition of the title song of the movie *Coal Miner's Daughter*. What is less known is that she also once made a record under the pseudonym Rainbo. "I met these guys [in 1968] who ran Roulette Records and recorded two songs for them. They had a gimmick and a song and they needed a girl. They even had a name: Rainbo. The song was 'John, You Went Too Far This Time,' a commentary on John Lennon's nude album cover. I can't tell you how long it took to live that one down."

6. Movie tough guy Robert Mitchum developed a love of calypso music while filming in Trinidad. In 1957 Capitol Records, was enthusiastic enough about Mitchum's "authentic flavor, beat and vitality" to sign him to record an album called *Calypso Is Like So*. Despite a fair amount of hype the album failed to burn up the charts. The next year, however, Mitchum hit musical gold co-writing and performing the theme song for the film *Thunder Road*.

7. "I put [singing] aside to learn how to act," Gina Gershon says. "So I put it aside until I auditioned for *Cabaret*. When I sang, the musical director and [director] Sam [Mendes], said, 'Why aren't you singing?'" That, she continues, "is when I realized how much I loved it." Gershon belonged to a band when she was 15, but didn't go on the road as a musician until she was 41 years old. To promote the movie *Prey for Rock and Roll* she hit the road with New York indie outfit Girls Against Boys. "Acting is not as freeing. At the end of the day, I'm a song-and-dance girl."

8. Robert Downey Jr. had written and performed songs for soundtracks but didn't consider making a record until later in

life. "I'm pushing 40," he said, "it's time to do something more courageous than just make faces for cash and chicken." The result was 2005's *The Futurist*, an album consisting of eight of the actor's own pop ballads as well as two cover songs, including "Smile," a Charlie Chaplin composition. "Music is great therapy," Downey Jr. says.

9. In the early '90s, Keanu Reeves, drummer Rob Mailhouse and guitarist Gregg Miller (later replaced by Bret Domrose) formed a jam band called Small Fecal Matter, a charming name later changed to Big Fucking Shit and then, finally to Dogstar. Their best known recording, 2000's *Happy Ending* features the group's cover of the Carpenters' ballad "Superstar." "I admit that my acting career has given us some opportunities to be heard," says Reeves, "but in the end it comes down to the music, and I feel good about what we are doing."

10. In 1994, after years of jamming together, Michael and Kevin Bacon were invited to play a charity gig in their hometown of Philadelphia. "And then we got another gig and we started doing a lot of writing," says Michael. "Three and a half years later, we put out the first CD, and now we can play all the time if we want to. When we first started, the people who attended our shows came strictly to see Kevin Bacon, the movie star. Now people come to see and hear the Bacon Brothers."

Dr. Neil Connery (Neil Connery): "It's going to blow up soon, maybe even tomorrow, with you on-board."

Maya Rafis (Daniela Bianchi): "You read too many novels by Fleming."

— DIALOGUE FROM *OPERATION KID BROTHER*

OPERATION KID BROTHER (1967)

▬ ▬ ▬ ▬ ▬ ▬ ▬ ▬ ▬ ▬ ▬ ▬ ▬ ▬

Sean Connery was not too happy with his kid brother, Neil, when he starred in the 1967 James Bond parody variously known as *Operation Kid Brother, OK Connery, Operation Double 007* and *Secret Agent 00.* Advertised with the awkward tagline, "Operation Kid Brother is too much for one mother!" the movie saw Neil Connery playing a plastic surgeon inventively named . . . Neil Connery. The younger Connery, who looks like his famous brother with a beard, is informed that because his brother is out on a routine mission, her Majesty's Secret Service has to assign him to an important mission — the investigation of the actions of the crime syndicate Thanatos and their attempts to take over the world by using a magnetic wave generator!

Oddly, several other Bond veterans pop up in the cast. Bernard Lee, who played M, Bond's superior in the legit Bond films, shows his campy, comic side playing Connery's boss. Canadian-born actress Lois Maxwell, known for playing Miss Moneypenny in the first 14 Bond films, is the secretary, although she is a little more proactive here than in the Bond films. Here she mows down bad guys with a machine gun, and she actually kidnaps another character. Adolfo Celi, the villain with the eye patch in *Thunderball*, plays the number two villain of Thanatos who wants to be number one. Daniela Bianchi, the Bond girl in *From Russia With Love*, is the bad girl turned good in this feature while Anthony Dawson, who was Dent in *Dr. No* and also provided the body for bad guy Ernst Stavro Blofeld in *From Russia With Love* and *Thunderball* plays a Blofeld clone named Alpha.

Operation Kid Brother is one of the more blatant attempts to cash in on the 007 craze, and while it doesn't really make a great deal of sense, it is entertaining and fascinating for its sheer chutzpah. This Italian production seems cobbled together with little regard for story or deference for the James Bond legend. Take for instance Dr. Connery's unique skill sets. Unlike his more famous brother, Neil doesn't have a license to kill, just a degree in plastic surgery and a habit of reading lips. His main strength is his ability to use hypnosis to incapacitate his enemies. It's not quite as exciting as James Bond tearing apart a hotel room while doing hand-to-hand combat with Goldfinger's henchmen, but it has a certain B-movie charm.

Operation Kid Brother appears to exist solely for the purpose of exploiting the Connery name. Neil can't act, but he is a Connery and I would guess the filmmakers figured that had enough cachet to put bums in seats. (Brother Neil was not the only member of Sean Connery's family to have a Bond movie connection; in 1990 Sean Connery's son, Jason Connery, played 007's creator in a TV movie called *The Secret Life of Ian Fleming*.) It's classic exploitation filmmaking, and a study in how to cash in a fad. *Operation Kid Brother* is the kind of movie that would make Roger Corman proud.

The soundtrack, unlike the rest of the film, is on par with a real James Bond film. Ennio Morricone, years before he became well known for his spaghetti western soundtracks, co-wrote the score with Bruno Nicolai. Big and brassy, for sheer sonic pleasure it rivals the music of '60s-era Bond films. One writer called it "among the best non-Barry spy scores ever." (John Barry did 11 of the first 14 legit Bond films.)

Apparently one Connery was enough for moviegoers, and the film flopped so badly it could have been the reason the bargain bin was invented. After a few more movies the wheels came off the fun bus and Neil Connery retired from film to become a full-time plasterer.

Availability: Hard to find

Walter Fane (Edward Norton): I knew when I married you that you were selfish and spoiled, but I loved you.

Kitty Fane (Naomi Watts): I married you even though I didn't love you, but you knew that. Aren't you as much to blame for what has happened as I?

— DIALOGUE FROM *THE PAINTED VEIL*

THE PAINTED VEIL (2006)

Pre-release publicity for *The Painted Veil* hinted that Edward Norton's performance was so strong he may earn an Academy Award nomination for Best Actor. His two previous Oscar outings — *Primal Fear* and his searing portrayal of a former neo-Nazi skinhead in *American History X* — hadn't netted him a trophy, so perhaps the third time would be a charm. Yet, when the nominations were announced there was no sign of Norton . . . or the movie for that matter.

There could be a number of reasons for that. It was a strong year for male performances, and Norton simply could have been bested by Forest Whitaker, Leo DiCaprio, Peter O'Toole, Ryan Gosling and Will Smith. Strong performances all, but Hollywood insiders hinted that maybe a conspiracy more devious, more worthy of tabloid headlines, was afoot. Gossip floated around the web that Norton may have been snubbed by Oscar because of his hard-line stance on the practice of giving celebrities elaborate gift baskets at award shows.

"Gift baskets, worth amounts of money that a low income family could live on for a year [are given to] people who have so much already," he said. "It gets depressing. You sit there, going, 'This is an embarrassment.'"

He reportedly spoke to the Academy about the practice and was instrumental in getting the baskets eliminated, which may have alienated some of the more swag-hungry Academy voters. It's too bad because he hands in a powerful performance in this little seen but deserving film.

The Painted Veil, W. Somerset Maugham's novel about a dysfunctional British couple who travel to rural China in the early part of the twentieth century, has been brought to the screen twice before. Greta Garbo's 1934 version used the title but little else from the book, while a 1957 take on the story, titled *The Seventh Sin*, skirted around some of the more unsavory aspects of the story. The 2006 version, starring Norton and Naomi Watts, has the epic old-fashioned feel of its predecessors, but is far more frank than either of the first two films could ever be.

"You know you don't run into stuff that's complicated and rich like that every day," Norton told me in 2006. "I mean it's not like you're choosing between phenomenal parts. When you get a good one, or you see one that you think you understand on some levels you hold on to it. In part too, to be totally honest, everybody can imagine when you're watching a move like *Out of Africa* or *Lawrence of Arabia* you think, 'Wow, that's gotta be so fun to make a movie like that' and again you don't see these great epic films all the time.

"For me I just thought I wanted to make one of those kinds of movies, and have that kind of experience and work with an international crew and go somewhere. It felt a couple of times like we were cooked on it. It just wasn't going to come together and I definitely had a few moments where I thought, I'm banging my head against the wall on this, it's just not happening and maybe we should just move on. But, eventually we got Naomi and she was so responsive to it, so that sort of reinvigorated me. It did reaffirm for me that sometimes you just have to persevere with something."

Norton and Watts play Walter and Kitty Fane, an unhappily married couple who stay together out of habit rather than love. He is an unaffectionate biologist who is married to his work, she a shallow party girl who craves attention. When she has an affair with one of her husband's colleagues, Walter explodes, showing real passion for the first time in their marriage. He cruelly offers her an ultimatum: she can either follow him to a cholera ravaged village in rural China where he will study the disease or suffer the indignity and ensuing scandal of being sued for divorce on the grounds of adultery. She chooses the former and while in the dangerous rural village, away from everything and everyone they know, the couple discovers forgiveness and is able to reconnect. Both Norton and Watts hand in solid performances that really get under the skin of a relationship that is in serious trouble.

"I feel like the characters almost get exfoliated by China," he said. "They get beaten down and humbled by what they go through until all of their illusions about self and each other have been stripped away and they're forced to actually take a look at each other, which is really interesting to confront as an actor."

Shot on location in mainland China, *The Painted Veil* looks spectacular.

"John [director John Curran] and I were in China about five months and the filming was four months of that. It was a great adventure but it was fraught with many things. There was no way to predict certain things that happened. You're dealing with the inherent inefficiency of working through translators. We had a camera crew that were Kiwis, the sound guys were Australian, the wardrobe designer was British, and we had mutts like me and John and then all of our Chinese cast and crew.

"The Beijing crews all speak Mandarin, and people that came on from the south speak Cantonese, and then out in the river towns they spoke a dialect that I wasn't exactly clear what it was called. John being John was shown many places that had roads and were accessible but he didn't feel they captured the compositions that he wanted in the river valleys, and so he kept pushing further and further out and ultimately we were working in places where there was no word for pavement. It was worth it because it looks unlike almost any place I had been. Making a movie in a place like that it's like an Army operation, half of it is the logistics of just getting all the people and things where you need them to be and that was challenging."

Another of the challenges faced by Norton was easily solved in the usual Hollywood way — with money. When the production ran into rice harvest season, Norton, as one of the film's producers, persuaded farmers to cooperate with them so the crew could get a shot they needed for the film.

"We had to avoid the rainy season, but we still wanted to have the big, beautiful green rice," he told World Entertainment News Network. "Earlier we went into the valley and spoke to the provincial head and he said, 'You can't cut the rice.' I said, 'We've got to have rice for these shots. What do we have to do?' We ended up buying the rice crop of the entire county in advance to get them to plant it a month late. We gave it back to them to sell it — so they got a two-for-one deal. They thought we were insane!"

Set in post-Victorian times, *The Painted Veil* adheres to the etiquette of the day, but also shows the passion that boils just beneath the mannered facades of Norton and Watts. It achieves something remarkable — making an 80-year-old story set nearly a century ago feel up-to-date and modern.

Availability: On DVD

"If there's a plague here, you're the most important guy in this town."
— NANCY REED (BARBARA BEL GEDDES) IN *PANIC IN THE STREETS*

PANIC IN THE STREETS (1950)
▬ ▬ ▬ ▬ ▬ ▬ ▬ ▬ ▬ ▬ ▬ ▬ ▬

When the Academy of Motion Picture Arts and Sciences paid tribute to director Elia Kazan at the 71st Annual Academy Awards with a montage of his greatest moments on film, one movie was surprisingly over-

looked. *Panic in the Streets*, a low-budget film noir from 1950 is significant not because it broke box office records (it didn't) but because it
was the film that saw Kazan break free of the studio system and forge
the naturalistic style that made his later films distinctive. "Making *Panic
in the Streets* was a fantastic liberation for me," he said, "because I was
such a dutiful boy before that."

After immigrating to the United States from Istanbul, Elia Kazan
(born: Elias Kazanjoglou) was drawn to the theater, first as a stage manager for New York's famed avant-garde Group Theater in the 1930s and
later as the co-founder of the Actors Studio and Broadway director. He
spent the 1940s split between the Great White Way, where he ushered in
a new era of theater, mounting the first stage productions of *A Streetcar
Named Desire*, *Death of a Salesman* and *The Skin of Our Teeth*, and
working in Hollywood.

His first directorial assignment for 20th Century Fox was *A Tree
Grows in Brooklyn*, a lyrical film that won best acting awards for James
Dunn and Peggy Ann Garner. Over the next five years Kazan became
one of the most sought-after directors in Hollywood, helming a series
of stagy but politically charged films that touched on the hot-button
topics of the day like political corruption (*Boomerang!*), anti-Semitism
(*Gentleman's Agreement*) and race relations (*Pinky*). By 1950 he was
ready for a change and *Panic in the Streets* was his turning point.

"I was from the theater and I was deep — loaded up with the first
film that said 'Nigger,' the first film that said 'Jew,'" he told writer Jeff
Young. "I finally rebelled. In this picture I broke out of it, and it saved
me . . . really. Otherwise, I could have been a bore all my life. I can't
imagine anything more than *The Sea of Grass* or *Pinky*. That amount of
righteousness is tedious. It hasn't got the breath of life in it."

Panic in the Streets takes place in 1950s New Orleans. It's dirty, dangerous and claustrophobic — the perfect setting for a film noir. When
we open, a recent illegal immigrant is playing poker with some local
toughs. Just as the newcomer hits a lucky streak he becomes ill. Dizzy
and nauseous he decides to leave the game, leaving Blackie (Jack

Palance) and his two thugs (Zero Mostel and Tommy Cook) a little lighter in the pocketbook. Blackie demands his money back, and when the immigrant refuses, the gangster has him shot down in the street, robbed and dumped in the water, his lucky streak at a permanent end.

At first light the body is discovered floating by the New Orleans docks. Dr. Clinton Reed (Richard Widmark) of the Public Health Service is called away from a day he promised to spend with his wife to perform the autopsy on the John Doe. The doctor has done hundreds of these procedures, but never one like this. It turns out the poor unfortunate floater was destined to die the night before, one way or another. He is infected with a highly contagious form of bubonic plague — yes, *that* plague — and would have been dead a few hours after the card game, bullet or no bullet.

Dr. Reed calls an emergency meeting of health officials and the police to convince them of the severity of the situation. He explains that this disease has an incubation period of 48 hours and they must track down everyone who came into contact with the dead man so they can be quarantined and inoculated before they become contagious. Trouble is they don't know who the man is or how he ended up in the water with two holes blown in his chest. The only thing they do know is that if they go to the papers, the killers will likely go on the run to avoid being caught and spread the disease wherever they go.

Dr. Reed and Police Captain Tom Warren (Paul Douglas) have just 48 hours to put the pieces of this man's life and death together, or they might have another Black Plague on their hands.

I have a hunch that the scare tactic of a biological threat plays better now, post-9/11, than it did when this film was released in 1950. In an age of big diseases with little names — AIDS, SARS — and deadly airborne viruses like Ebola, the menace of becoming ill by tiny microbes or spores seems altogether too real. Back in the days of the Cold War *Panic in the Streets* was seen as a thinly veiled Red Scare allegory. The police interrogation scene could be a vision out of Joe McCarthy's commie witch hunts, while the rapid spread of the disease plays like a paranoid metaphor for the proliferation of communist ideology.

In light of the political undertones of the film, it is interesting to note that just two years later Kazan would sit before McCarthy's House Committee on Un-American Activities and name eight of his old friends from the Group Theater who, along with him, had been members of the American Communist Party. Kazan saved himself from being blacklisted by Hollywood, but destroyed the careers of the people he named. Ironically one of those blacklisted was *Panic* co-star Zero Mostel, who despite denying any political connections was unemployable in Hollywood for most of the 1950s.

Political nuances aside, *Panic in the Streets* is a first-rate procedural thriller. Shot on location in New Orleans, the film feels freer than any of Kazan's movies to that point. Unencumbered by a studio set, *Panic* feels less like a filmed play than *Splendor in the Grass* or *Gentleman's Agreement*. It's as though the freewheeling attitude of the city loosened him up a bit. It was, by his own admission, the first film he enjoyed making.

"I went wild," he said to writer David Lee Simmons. "There were all kinds of girls on our set, visitors and extras. It was a carny atmosphere or like that around a second-class rock band on tour today. All this was a fantastic liberation for me . . . I got everything I wanted. In one sequence, for extras we emptied a whorehouse of its girls; that was a jolly day . . . Living irregularly, I was in heaven."

The laissez-faire attitude and risk-taking learned on this set directly influenced his best work. Gone were the days of staid studio work. *Panic in the Streets* heralded a new natural method of directing for him. There could not have been the Kazan classic *On the Waterfront* if he hadn't used this film as a test run.

Kazan is known as an "actor's director," and true to form he pulls good showings from his cast and doesn't let the atmosphere of New Orleans overshadow the performances.

Widmark, in a rare sympathetic role, brings a steely resoluteness to Dr. Reed while at the same time displays real warmth with his wife Nancy and young son Tommy (Tommy "Lassie" Rettig). The interplay between Widmark and his movie family feels particularly genuine in the scene where he comes home after being awake for 24 hours straight and Nancy puts her exhausted husband to bed.

As is often the case in film noir, the thugs are more colorful than the straights. "I never had much affection for good guys," said Kazan. "I don't like puritans. I don't like guys who are rigid and have one point of view, who squeeze the complexities out of life. I like hoodlums and gangsters. Not only that, I like women who leave home, men who leave their wives and people who express the impossibility of living in a constricted eighteenth- or nineteenth-century religious bind."

Jack Palance, in his screen debut as the cold-blooded sociopath Blackie, plays the bad guy with extreme relish, both brooding and unpredictable with a side order of paranoia thrown in for good measure. Palance first came to Kazan's attention in 1947 when the young actor was hired to be Marlon Brando's understudy in the stage version of *A Streetcar Named Desire*. One night before the show Brando and Palance were working out backstage, taking turns hitting a punching bag. Palance swung hard, missed the bag and punched Brando square in the nose. While Brando was hospitalized Palance took his place onstage and earned rave reviews. Those reviews landed him a contract with 20th Century Fox and the role in *Panic in the Streets*.

In one of his last films before being blacklisted Mostel plays Blackie's sidekick, the snivelling Raymond Fitch. Mostel has a manic energy here that bounces nicely off Palance's studied calm. It's an excellent pairing, one tall and slim, the other short and stout — kind of the Laurel and Hardy of crime, except you won't die *laughing* with these two. Kazan does occasionally play off Mostel's natural comic ability, particularly in a chase scene where Palance makes Mostel run faster by slapping him on the butt as though he were a thoroughbred racehorse.

"I tried to balance a sense of levity so that the violence would not be taken too seriously. So all of it, villains included, was treated with affection because, after all, you can't take the plot too seriously. You know the plague isn't going to spread. It's a springboard for a sort of caper. . . ."

Fifty years after making *Panic in the Streets* Kazan praised his cast, all save for one. "I hand-picked everybody because I liked them," he said, "The only one I didn't like much was Paul Douglas [who played Captain Tom Warren]. He wasn't really an actor, you know. He'd been a football announcer. He was a front man. He should have been the host of a steak joint."

Panic in the Streets wasn't as financially successful as its predecessors in the Kazan canon, but it did win an Academy Award for Best Writing, Motion Picture Story. While it may not have been as socially profound as his other work, it is the film on which he says he truly became a film director. "This isn't very deep," he admitted. "It has other virtues. It has lightness of foot, it has surprise, it has suspense, it's engaging."

Availability: On DVD

"The press is good or evil according to the character of those who direct it."
— **PHINEAS MITCHELL (GENE EVANS) IN *PARK ROW***

PARK ROW (1952)

Maverick director Sam Fuller was so passionate about the script for *Park Row* he was willing to do almost anything to get it made. Anything, that is, except take 20th Century Fox head honcho Darryl F. Zanuck's advice and turn it into a musical. Fuller balked at the suggestion, instead deciding to finance the $200,000 film himself. It flopped and he lost every penny, but he got to make the movie he wanted. The action-packed ode to the birth of yellow journalism in New York is sometimes thought of as a poor man's *Citizen Kane*, but is actually an exciting ride into the very heart of the Fourth Estate.

At age 17 Fuller began his career as one of the youngest crime reporters in the United States working for the *New York Daily Graphic*, making his mark covering "strikes, executions and that kind of thing." He used this experience and his love of the newspaper game to craft a story set on New York's late nineteenth-century Park Row, "the most famous newspaper street in the world where giants of journalism mix blood and ink."

In the first reel of *Park Row* Phineas Mitchell (Gene Evans) gets the boot from big time newspaper the *Star* after questioning the integrity of owner Charity Hackett (Mary Welch). Unemployed, he gets drunk and launches into an idealistic rant about the newspaper business. Impressed by Mitchell's tirade, his honesty and gumption, Charles A. Leach (Forrest Taylor) fronts Phineas the money and equipment to start his own broadsheet.

He quickly prints the first edition of the *Globe* on butcher's paper and soon Mitchell has made a name for himself as an ethical and innovative newspaperman. He helps with the invention of the linotype, pioneers the use of newspaper stands and launches a campaign to raise funds to bring the Statue of Liberty to New York. Along the way Fuller delves into the finer points of the publishing process with the kind of details that can only come from someone who understands both newspapers and filmmaking. "Every newsman is a potential filmmaker," he once said.

As sales of the *Globe* pick up the ironically named Charity does her best to destroy the rival paper. Making things more complicated is a cat-and-mouse romance between Mitchell and Hackett, proving there is only a thin line between love and hate.

Fuller never shied away from using a jackhammer when a rubber mallet would have done the job. That is to say he's heavy-handed, but it is that conviction that gives *Park Row* its kick. For instance, visually he uses the camera to accentuate the importance of publishing giants

Benjamin Franklin and Horace Greely by including low-angle shots of their statues that quite literally make them look like towering figures.

Also not so subtle is the film's most famous sequence, once again involving the statues. When one of Hackett's thugs attacks Mitchell he bashes the guy's brains out against Franklin's statue, using the image of Franklin as a paragon of integrity to violently protect freedom of the press. These scenes are beautifully filmed by cameraman Jack Russell, who would later go on to shoot Hitchcock's *Psycho*, using amazing tracking shots and inventive framing, giving *Park Row* a distinctive visual flair that contradicts its low-budget.

Fuller, who would go on to explore mental illness with the same kind of gusto in the infamous *Shock Corridor*, crams *Park Row* with comments on hot button ethical issues such as censorship of the press, check book journalism and corporate corruption. These were timely messages in 1886 when the movie is set, 1952 when the movie was released and even today. By taking a high moral stance he celebrates the folks who fought for freedom of the press, and sends a valentine to the business he loves, while simultaneously pointing out the industry's biggest flaws.

Whether seen as an ode to a lost idealistic era of journalism or a cautionary tale for today's news people, Fuller's *Park Row* remains a powerful film filled with passion.

Availability: Hard to find

PASSPORT TO PIMLICO (1949)

A fanciful English comedy about a London district that becomes its own sovereign state was actually inspired by a little-known event that occurred in Canada. During World War II and the German occupation of the Netherlands, Princess Juliana and her two daughters left her home for Ottawa to represent the State of the Netherlands in exile.

When the Princess's third child Margriet was born, the Governor General of Canada ceded her hospital rooms at the Ottawa Civic Hospital to the Dutch, so that the child could be declared to have been born on Dutch soil and therefore be the heir to the throne. To celebrate, the Dutch tricolor flag was raised on the Canadian Parliament's Peace Tower while its carillon played Dutch music at the news of the birth.

The idea that a small patch of land could be declared independent of its country sparked the imagination of longtime Ealing Studio writer T. E. B. (Tibby) Clarke, who wrote 15 films for the studio between 1943 and 1957.

The story he came up with is fairly simple. When an unexploded wartime bomb is detonated in the cockney parish of Pimlico, fish shop proprietor Arthur Pemberton (Stanley Holloway) finds an ancient land charter and buried treasure in a hidden vault at the bottom of the crater.

Professor Hatton-Jones (Margaret Rutherford) authenticates the document as a royal charter that relinquished Pimlico to the last Duke of Burgundy 500 years ago. The charter, never having been revoked, is still valid, making Pimlico a part of Burgundy. "Blimey! I'm a foreigner!" says amazed policeman P. C. Spiller (Philip Stainton).

The locals — just 19 families — quickly set up shop, creating a committee of elected officials — for instance bank manager Mr. W. P. J. Wix (Raymond Huntley) becomes the Chancellor of the Exchequer — but soon a newfound feeling of freedom takes precedence to building their state. Not bound by the austere English laws that applied after the war, the new Pimlico cuts loose. Pubs stay open late, cafés and patios pop up and even the weather clears up. The formerly strict inner London area becomes a continental oasis in an otherwise glum, post-war city, but under siege their resolve to remain free Burgundians is put to the test.

At the time of *Passport to Pimlico's* release England was still rebuilding after the devastation of World War II, so the idea of a colorful Burgundian republic in the middle of London where it doesn't rain and, at least for a time, food and drink wasn't limited, must have seemed almost like science fiction to the British people. It is a whimsical idea, brimming with sweet humor, but under the jokes and Swiftian critiques of bureaucracy and isolationism are ideas that were perfectly suited to the mood of post-war England.

At its core *Passport to Pimlico* is about human spirit and what it means to be English. The people of Pimlico may have called themselves Burgundians for a time, but at their core they show the determination, spirit and stiff-upper-lip that characterized post-war Britain. At the end, when the Burgundians rejoin the U.K., the film subversively suggests that the only way Britain will be rebuilt to its former glory is by creating a sense of community in which everyone works together and makes the same sacrifices.

Ealing Studio head honcho Michael Balcon categorized their post-war output as "our mild revolution," but *Pimlico* is anything but mild. The humor may be gentle, but the subtext is as steely as the British spirit.

Availability: On DVD as part of the Ealing Comedy Collection

"The only performance that makes it, that really makes it, that makes it all the way, is the one that achieves madness."
— TURNER (MICK JAGGER) IN *PERFORMANCE*

PERFORMANCE (1970)

Performance is a head-scratcher of a movie that blends a straight-ahead British gangster story with a hallucinogenic head trip.

James Fox is Chaz, a sadistic mid-level East London thug who revels in "putting the frighteners on flash little twerps." Good-looking, charming and lethal, he's an enforcer for Harry Flowers (Johnny Shannon), a hardman who uses intimidation and his fists to get the job done. When a bit of ultra-violence goes too far and the wrong man ends up dead Chaz must hide out not only from the law, but from his own gang. He finds refuge in a rented room in the Notting Hill home of Turner (Mick

Jagger), a reclusive, sexually ambiguous, washed-up rock star. The other occupants, Turner's junkie girlfriend, Pherber (Anita Pallenberg), and her French lover, Lucy (Michèle Breton) help initiate the gangster into Turner's anti-establishment lifestyle where drug libertarianism and psychosexual gender-bending are the norm. At this point the film's linear structure dissolves as the house's psychedelic and dangerous world becomes Chaz's undoing, when he loses his grip on reality and swaps personalities with the singer.

For years arguments over what the movie actually means have been thrown around like toast at a midnight showing of *The Rocky Horror Picture Show*. *Performance* is deliberately obtuse, a hallucinogenic stew of sex, drugs and rock and roll that disturbs, exhilarates and confounds in almost equal measures. The film's tagline, "See them all in a film about fantasy. And reality. Vice. And versa," should be an indicator that this isn't going to be an easy ride, but really, it only hints at the twisted psychological wreckage that lies within.

"I always thought *Performance* was a comedy," says writer and co-director (with Nicolas Roeg) Donald Cammell. Perhaps a comedy of modern manners, psychedelic '60s style, but certainly not the kind of comedy that inspires knee-slapping.

Marianne Faithfull may have more put it more accurately when she said it "preserves a whole era under glass." It's the Swinging London that lit up the tabloid headlines in the late '60s. It's about the decadent lifestyles of rich rock stars who wore expensive clothes, trotted the globe and took mountains of drugs. It's about the violence of the notorious twin Kray Brothers, who ruled East London with an iron fist. It's about sexual experimentation and the relationship between sex and death. In short it's about the hedonistic stuff that made the '60s swing. It's the end of that era, a startling portrait of the Age of Aquarius in decay.

"Donald Cammell was always aware of posterity as a director," said Jagger. "He always thought of film as this thing that freezes time. He was very aware of historical authenticity."

Mick Jagger, in his film debut, is perfectly cast as Turner. It may not have been much of a stretch for him to play a depraved rock star, but his take on Turner is fascinating. The story's bohemian character brought to life the media's perception of Jagger as a rock and roll Lucifer, an androgynous pleasure-seeker of the highest order who exuded pure, raw sexual energy. Although his dialogue occasionally falls into a druggy slur, he commands every scene he's in, bringing nuance to a character that could easily have been a caricature. Jagger allows the insolent aggression that made him famous to guide the character and the result is his best onscreen performance. "Because I'm not in the whole movie," said Jagger in 2007, "there are whole chunks I can watch without cringing."

Jagger was at the height of his power as sex symbol in *Performance*, but in a great bit of foreshadowing Chaz says to Turner, "You're a comical little geezer. You'll look funny when you're 50." Bang on, brother. Bang on.

Legend has it that James Fox was so affected by the degenerate atmosphere on the *Performance* set, he quit acting and became a Christian missionary after the film wrapped. It's true that he left acting for 10 years and became an evangelical Christian, but he says the movie was simply a trigger for him to re-examine his life.

"*Performance* gave me doubts about my way of life," he said. "Before that I had been completely involved in the more bawdy side of the film business. But after that everything changed."

Whatever happened on the set didn't prevent him from handing in a marvelous performance that shimmers with narcissism — he even looks into a mirror admiringly during sex — power and eventually sexual self-doubt. It's a haunting meditation on human identity and a challenging, difficult role, but he devours it, playing it with dark menace.

Performance sat on the shelf for two years while Warner Bros. fretted about what to do with it. Brimming with explicit sex, brutal violence and drug use, the film was deemed too wild for release in its original form, so a re-edit was ordered. Cammell spent a year locked in a

Hollywood studio fiddling with the film, reordering an already non-traditional story into a one-of-a-kind cinematic experience. Employing jump-cuts, elliptical storytelling and surreal imagery he instills a kinetic energy to the story propelling the viewer to abandon traditional ideas of movie watching and accepting the disjointed narrative as reality skewed by the haze of fading memory or drug use.

It's baffling and bizarre, a movie that refuses to be pigeonholed. It isn't exactly a youth exploitation movie, or a crime drama or a drug movie, but in a way it is all of those and more. *Performance* is a challenging experience and one that hasn't lost one iota of its power in the decades since its initial release.

"I've seen a lot of films from that period again and they all seem to live in a time warp," said Pallenberg. "*Performance* is completely timeless, it's extraordinary — you always discover something new and that's what makes a great film."

Availability: On DVD

> "In the period of which we speak, there reigned in the cities a stench barely conceivable to us modern men and women. Naturally, the stench was foulest in Paris, for Paris was the largest city in Europe. And nowhere in Paris was that stench more profoundly repugnant than in the city's fish market."
> — NARRATOR (JOHN HURT) IN THE OPENING MINUTES OF
> *PERFUME: THE STORY OF A MURDERER*

PERFUME: THE STORY OF A MURDERER (2006)

This is one strange movie. Directed by *Run, Lola, Run* helmer Tom Tykwer and based on the 1985 bestselling novel by Patrick Süskind, *Perfume* is the story of an eighteenth-century serial killer obsessed by smell. With international sales in excess of 15 million, the book is the most successful German language novel since Erich Maria Remarque's *All Quiet on the Western Front.* Cited by Nirvana's Kurt Cobain as his favorite book, *Das Perfume* was the inspiration for the tune "Scentless Apprentice" from the band's *In Utero* album.

Popular as the book is, it took a long and circuitous route to the screen. So extraordinary, in fact, was the trip from the page to the stage that Süskind wrote a thinly veiled account of producer Bernd Eichinger's efforts to turn *Das Perfume* into a film. Süskind's account resulted in the movie *Rossini*, about a shy author who pens a number one bestseller and came out a decade before *Perfume* finally made it to theaters.

Many A-list directors were connected to the *Perfume* project over the years, including Ridley Scott, Tim Burton, Martin Scorsese, Milos Forman and Stanley Kubrick, who pronounced the book unfilmable.

Finally producer Eichinger settled on Tykwer as co-writer and director. "Tom has a distinctly artistic and innovative vein, but he also has a very popular understanding of film," said the producer. "Because of those two components — the experimental and the popular — he's the ideal director for this film."

Tykwer, with co-writers Andrew Birkin and Bernd Eichinger, spent two years honing the script before rolling camera in July 2005 on the $80 million film, said to be the most expensive German movie ever.

The picture tells the curious story of Jean-Baptiste Grenouille (Ben Whishaw), a bastard child born in the foul fish market of Paris with two disquieting traits — he has an astonishingly developed sense of smell but no personal smell of any kind. Rejected as "devil-spawn" by the wet nurses hired to care for him, he is placed in an orphanage and put to work in a tannery. After years of toil there he ends up in a job that suits him to a tee, as an apprentice to master perfume maker Giuseppe Baldini (Dustin Hoffman).

He becomes an expert perfumer but his overdeveloped olfactory sense pushes him to a darker place. He kills women to harvest their scent in the demented hopes of making the ultimate perfume.

In due course Grenouille is captured and put on trial for his crimes, but in a sequence that must be seen to be believed he unveils his secret weapon, a perfume so transcendent it casts a spellbinding power over all who breathe in its aroma.

This is an ambitious, big budget film — 67 principal actors, 520 technicians, more than 100 sets and a total of 5,200 extras — that manages to capture the novel's world of scent.

Luckily the film isn't in Smell-O-Vision because Tykwer nails the odorific lifestyle of eighteenth-century France. The movie employed 60 set dressers known as the Dirt Unit whose sole job was to convincingly and accurately recreate the filthy conditions of the time.

"This was France before there was a system for how to keep the streets clean or how to wash clothes every week," said Tykwer, who was dubbed Lord of the Dirt by co-workers. "In fact, most people washed their clothes once a year. They didn't undress for sex, they didn't undress for sleeping, they just kept their clothes on because that's the way they lived."

"While Süskind used the clear and exact power of words, we use the power of image, noise and music," Eichinger said cryptically. "When filming a lawn in sunlight, or even a single tree, all that is needed is absolute optical precision and then smells are created."

It's this eye for detail that *Perfume* co-star Alan Rickman noted when working with Tykwer. "It's like you're not just in control of every frame of every film," he said to the director, "you're in control of the milliseconds within a frame." Whishaw concurs. "Tom is kind of fanatical in a Grenouille-ish kind of way," he said.

Perfume: The Story of a Murderer is a strange movie, chock full of abrupt changes in tone, magic realism and characters who appear and disappear just as quickly, but Tykwer has taken the unfilmable novel and captured the wonky spirit of the book with a vision that is vivid and disturbing. This film isn't for everyone, but should thrill adventurous viewers.

Availability: On DVD

Astronaut number one: "What's going on?"
Astronaut number two: "I wish I knew."
— DIALOGUE FROM *PLANET OF THE VAMPIRES*

PLANET OF THE VAMPIRES (1965)
■ ■ ■ ■ ■ ■ ■ ■ ■ ■ ■ ■ ■ ■

"People, and critics too, should know about the circumstances under which I had to shoot my films," said Mario Bava. "On *Terrore nello spazio* (*Planet of the Vampires*) I had nothing, literally. There was only an empty sound stage, really squalid, because we had no money. And this had to look like an alien planet! What did I do then? I took a couple of papier mâché rocks from the nearby studio, probably leftovers from some sword and sandal flick, then I put them in the middle of the set and covered the ground with smoke and dry ice, and darkened the background. Then I shifted those two rocks here and there and this way I shot the whole film."

Planet of the Vampires is a low-budget film, but the visual style of Italian maestro Mario Bava elevates what could have been a forgettable B-movie into a memorable movie experience.

American International Pictures, the house that entertainment lawyer turned Hollywood showman Samuel Z. Arkoff built by churning out cheaply produced exploitation films with grabby titles like *I Was a Teenage Werewolf* and *Invasion of the Saucer Men*, had distributed two of Bava's best known films, 1960's terrifying fairy tale *Black Sunday* and '63's *Black Sabbath* (Ozzy Osbourne and friends lifted their band's name from this movie). Those films had filled AIP's coffers, so Arkoff and collaborator James H. Nicholson felt it was time to co-produce a movie with Bava, rather than simply distribute the finished product. They'd make more money and be able to shape the story according to the ARKOFF Formula, which was the former lawyer's recipe for B-movie success.

Action (exciting, entertaining drama)
Revolution (novel or controversial themes and ideas)
Killing (a modicum of violence)
Oratory (notable dialogue and speeches)
Fantasy (acted-out fantasies common to the audience)
Fornication (sex appeal, for young adults)

AIP provided the services of *Robinson Crusoe on Mars* screenwriter Ib Melchior to help form the "haunted house in space" tale based on the short story "One Night of 21 Hours" by Renato Pestiniero into a screenplay.

An international cast was assembled, headed by American Barry Sullivan, Brazilian actress Norma Bengell, Italian starlet Evi Marandi and Spanish actor Ángel Aranda. Co-writer R. J. Dalvia remembers it was a confusing shoot, with each cast member using "their own native tongue on the set, in many cases not understanding what the other actors were saying."

Sullivan plays ever-so-serious Captain Mark Markary of the exploratory space ship *Argos*. In orbit over a newly discovered planet, the fogbound Aura, the *Argos* begins receiving odd electronic signals. Forced to crash land on the desolate planet by a radiation overload, the troop turns on one another. Once restrained, the aggression disappears and the crew members have no memory of their violent behavior.

Markary, puzzled by the feral behavior of his crew, doesn't have time to get to the bottom of the mystery before he receives a distress signal from their sister ship, the *Galliot*. Leading a small search and rescue party Markary braves a hallucinatory landscape of psychedelic swirling colors and molten lava flows only to find that most of the *Galliot*'s crew has already massacred one another, and those who survived are badly injured, or worse, experiencing scars that are psychological. In other words, they've gone crazy from fear.

It's a grim discovery, made all the worse when it is revealed that the deceased *Galliot* crew members are having a hard time staying dead. In one of the film's most eye-popping sequences the undead rise from their makeshift graves with a taste for living flesh.

Bava, working with no money but lots of ingenuity, isn't so much a cinematographer as he is a cinemagician. For once, Arkoff's penny-pinching ways actually served the movie. Optical special effects are expensive so Bava created the world of Aura using nothing but minia-tures and old-school forced perspective shots. The two papier mâché rocks — "Yes, two," he said years later, "one and one!" — were maxi-mized with the use of mirrors and multiple exposures to give the illusion of a rocky landscape. It's hard to know for sure, but it's possi-ble that if Bava had access to a larger bankroll he might not have been so imaginative in his execution of the look of the film.

As much as possible the special effects were done "in camera," that is utilizing the camera's operations such as stop-motion, slow shutter tricks and multiple exposures in lieu of special effects, which are typically added to the film once the shooting is complete.

Bava further masked the cheapness of the set with a rainbow of colored lights filtered through fog. "To assist the illusion I flooded set with smoke," he said.

It's this sense of style that makes *Planet of the Vampires* so enjoyable. Bava injects great atmosphere into every frame, turning a sow's ear into a silk purse. The film's simple B-movie premise doesn't promise much in the way of originality, but Bava's unerring eye elevates the material, giving us an alien world unlike any seen on film to date.

Fangoria's Tim Lucas wrote, "*Planet of the Vampires* is commonly regarded as the best SF ever made in Italy, and among the most convincing depictions of an alien environment ever put on film."

The images are striking, none more so than the scene where the *Argos* astronauts discover a derelict ship in a huge ruin on the strange new planet's surface. Climbing through the skeleton of the ship they uncover the gargantuan remains of mysterious creatures. If this sequence looks familiar, it's perhaps because it appears that Ridley Scott borrowed from it while shooting *Alien*. Although Scott and screenwriter Dan O'Bannon deny having ever seen *Planet of the Vampires* at the time they made their film, the similarity between Bava's vision and a long sequence in the 1979 movie cannot be disputed.

Bava died in 1980, and even though he made all kinds of films during his career, his name has become synonymous with horror. It's ironic that the maker of such classic horror films as *Kill, Baby . . . Kill* and *Twitch of the Death Nerve* was a bit of a 'fraidy cat in real life.

"I make horror movies," he said, "my aim is to scare people, yet I'm a faint-hearted coward; maybe that's why my movies turn out to be so good at scaring people, since I identify myself with my characters . . . their fears are mine too. You see when I hear a noise at night in my house, I just can't sleep . . . not to mention dark passages. Sure, I don't believe in vampires, witches and all these things, but when night falls and streets are empty and silent, well, sure I don't believe . . . but I am, frightened all the same. Better to stay home and watch TV!"

Availability: On DVD

"Passion at ten. Envy at eleven. Murder at noon."
— ADVERTISING TAGLINE FOR *PLEIN SOLEIL*

PLEIN SOLEIL (1960)

In the 1960s few international stars were more successful — or better looking — than French-born Alain Delon. As an unknown his chiseled boyish features — which later earned comparisons to James Dean and the nickname "the male Brigitte Bardot" — got him noticed by a talent scout for legendary producer David O. Selznick. Selznick offered Delon a contract, provided he could learn to speak English.

The young man, who had never acted before, signed up for ESL classes in Paris, but before he could finish the course was plucked from obscurity by French director Yves Allégret, who convinced him to stay at home and build a career in France. Small roles in a handful of films built a buzz for the actor, but it wasn't until 1960's *Plein soleil* that he arrived as a star and became typecast in a certain kind of role.

Plein soleil (released in Australia as *Full Sun*, in the U.K. as *Blazing Sun* and in the U.S. as *Purple Noon*) was the first big screen adaptation of the Patricia Highsmith novel *The Talented Mr. Ripley*. Delon plays Tom Ripley, a character described by Highsmith as a "suave, agreeable and utterly amoral" con artist, and more bluntly explained by critic Roger Ebert as "charming, literate and a monster." He has been offered a sizable reward from a wealthy businessman to bring his son, Philippe Greenleaf (Maurice Ronet), home to San Francisco after several years spent gallivanting in Europe.

Once in Italy, instead of persuading his charge to return home, Tom quickly adapts to the decadent lifestyle, carousing, spending his rich friend's money and generally living *la dolce vita* with Philippe and his girlfriend Marge (Marie Laforêt). The arrogant Philippe quickly bores of Tom, makes him the butt of cruel jokes and once even stranding him on a rescue boat, leaving Tom to bake in the sun, alone, for several hours.

Despite the cruel treatment — or perhaps because of it — it soon becomes clear that Ripley not only wants the *kind* of life Philippe has, he literally wants Philippe's life. When the two have a falling out Tom comes up with a plan. He manages to separate Philippe and Marge and then stabs Philippe in cold blood before throwing his body overboard to become fish food. He concocts a cover story to throw Marge off the scent and then embarks on a wild journey to Italy's hotspots, using Philippe's name and forged signature to acquire money. Soon he's even talking, dressing and behaving like Philippe. The poor Tom Ripley, once a plaything for the spoiled millionaire, has almost completely disappeared, replaced by a reasonable facsimile of Philippe.

The charade goes according to plan until Tom bumps into one of Philippe's friends, Freddy Miles (Billy Kearns). Suspicious, Miles unravels Ripley's game and soon Tom has to dispose of him. The second murder doesn't put a crimp in Tom's plans. He continues the sham, and even puts the moves on Marge.

The murder of Miles, however, gets the police involved and when Philippe's body turns up, tangled in his yacht's anchor it seems like the whole scheme will come tumbling down. Or will it?

Plein soleil established Delon's onscreen persona as the angelically handsome but dangerous sociopath — one writer called him "a saint made of ice" — a role that he would return to time and time again. His steely, emotionless facade recalled the great film noir characters of the

1940s, and no less an authority than Highsmith herself said that Delon's cold-hearted characterization was the performance that closest portrayed her idea of Tom Ripley.

Directed with tense, brisk precision by René Clément *Plein soleil* is faithful to the source material. Intact is the sexual tension from the book and the ambiguity of Tom's motive — it's implied, though never stated, that Ripley has sexual feelings for Philippe. We're never sure whether Ripley is simply interested in Philippe's money, or actually *becoming* him. It's the fine line that makes Ripley such a compelling character — is he simply a thief and murderer or is there something psychologically darker at work here?

There have been plenty of *Ripley* adaptations that have come to the screen — *Ripley Under Ground* (Barry Pepper as Ripley), *Ripley's Game* with John Malkovich as the killer, *The Talented Mr. Ripley* starring Matt Damon and *Der Amerikanische Freund* with Dennis Hopper. *Plein soleil* is the best of them, because of Delon and his undeniably dangerous charisma in the main role.

Availability: On DVD

"Write it. Live it. But try not to be it."
– ADVERTISING TAGLINE FOR *PULP*

PULP (1972)
■ ■ ■ ■ ■

Pulp was one of the most anticipated films of 1972. Following hot on the heels of the iconic British gangster film *Get Carter*, it reunited that film's creative core, director Mike Hodges and star Michael Caine, in

My Favorite Movie You've Never Seen

"There is one movie that I think is absolutely amazing and it is the only true piece of 'cinema' cinema that I have ever seen and I have my own 35 mm copy of it. . . . I don't have a 35 mm projector so I can never look at it but I certainly got it. It is Alain Resnais' *Last Year in Marienbad* (1961). *L'Année dernière à Marienbad*. It is an extraordinary piece. An amazing film. It's a film about memory. It's going to really upset all the purists. It's a story but it is told in a peculiar order. It tries to replicate how selective our memories are. Did it happen? Or didn't it happen? Did it happen like this? Or did it happen like that? It is a sort of dissertation about memory. To explain again how unorthodox it is all the characters are simply known as A, B, C and D, which is going to turn thousands of people off. It has a magnificent organ soundtrack — again, church organs aren't everyone's cup of tea. The dialogue is incredibly stilted, the action and the drama is very self reflexive, but all these artificialities, as you can imagine if you've seen any of my movies, are just up my street. Film is a deeply artificial medium. How can we pretend that anything is real? Go for the artifice. If you go for the artifice to the nth degree you're going to end up with a brilliant film."

— Peter Greenaway, Golden Palm nominee and
director of *The Cook, the Thief, His Wife & Her Lover*

a story that promised the same kind of hard-hitting underworld punch. Expectations were high, but Hodges and Caine didn't want to repeat the gritty violence of *Get Carter*. Taking their lead from *The Maltese Falcon* team of John Huston and Humphrey Bogart who added a dash of humor to their 1953 collaboration, *Beat the Devil*, Hodges and Caine took the crime genre and turned it on its head. "I wanted to make a film about why people see violent films," said Hodges, "and I wanted it funny."

Audiences in 1972, still clearly hungry for more *Get Carter*–style violence and mayhem, stayed away from *Pulp* in droves, but years later the film gained cult status on video and DVD.

Shedding the steely tough guy of *Get Carter*, this time around Caine plays Mickey King, a wannabe tough guy who has run away from his ho-hum life in England. He's left behind a wife, kids and job as a funeral director for the more glam-dandy life of a pulp fiction writer based in the Mediterranean. "I am famous for such books as *My Gun Is Long*," he says in a noirish voiceover. "I have many aliases. I am authors Susan Eager and Paul S. Coming. I am those and others. I am Paul Strong, Gary Rough and Les B. Han."

The story kicks in when Mickey is offered big money to ghost write the memoirs of washed-up movie star Preston Gilbert (Mickey Rooney). Gilbert made his name playing criminals onscreen and is rumored to have Mob connections in real life. Think George Raft, only really short.

Gilbert is an obnoxious chatterbox who berates his staff and talks endlessly about himself. After giving Mickey the bizarre opening line of the book, "We all passed a lot of water since then," Gilbert weaves a tale about a hit man who has been following him. Mickey doesn't buy it, but he goes along with Gilbert's self-important rant in the hopes of cashing in when he writes the book. The actor invites Mickey to a party later that night, and while at the party mysterious gunshots cut short Gilbert's days. Mickey's life begins to imitate his art when he puts in some hours of amateur detective work to solve the murder, but ends up putting his own life in peril.

Pulp tanked because audiences and critics expected the same hard edge of *Get Carter*, but instead were confronted with a film that dulls that movie's blunt edge with humor, substituting slapstick for violence and the bright sunshine of the Mediterranean (it was actually shot in Malta) for the dreariness of *Get Carter*'s industrial England. Hindsight, however, allows us to compare the two films — one a classic, the other an obscure gem — and find points of intersection.

The tone of the films are complete opposites, but if you look past the veneer at the subtext you'll discover that Mickey, much like Jack Carter, is a character mired in a world of dubious morality and duplicity. In both stories nothing is quite what it seems and the only real difference is how the characters react. Carter responds violently while Mickey passes out at the sight of blood. They're different people but they breathe the same rotten air. In addition both characters believe they can control the events that finally overshadow them.

In his portrayal of Mickey, however, Caine seems, on some levels, to be trying to distance himself from Jack Carter. He played Carter as an English hard man allowing the action and not his emotions to move the story along. *Pulp*, on the other hand, is all Mickey. Caine hands in a flamboyant performance, heavy on the physical comedy that keeps the movie zipping along at a breakneck pace.

A layer of humor is added to Mickey's character with the use of a heavy-handed film noir voiceover that wouldn't be out of place in one of his hard-boiled pulp novels. Trouble is the action onscreen rarely lives up to the gritty promise of the narration. It's a funny way of exposing the clichés of noir films, while still maintaining the aesthetic of the form. Hodges affectionately turns the genre inside out, deftly using the trappings of noir to parody itself.

The plot is complex, besieged with red herrings and dead ends, but Hodge keeps the witch's cauldron of sardonic humor and noir truisms together, lovingly stirring the pot to create something unique and fresh. His inspirations are clear — throwaway pulp novels and 1940s noirs — but he uses those simply as starting points for a wide-ranging exploration of the boundaries of the crime drama and the limits of human corruption.

Pulp can't be categorized easily, and perhaps that was its downfall. It is, however, much better than the detective novels that inspired it. "I really want to take the audience by the hand and take them somewhere they haven't been before," Hodges once said, and with *Pulp* he succeeds.

Availability: On DVD

Anthony Hancock (Tony Hancock): "I'm an impressionist!"
Mrs. Crevatte (Irene Handl): "Well, it don't impress me!"
– DIALOGUE FROM *THE REBEL*

THE REBEL (1961)

Unknown in North America, comedian Tony Hancock is a legend in Britain and was voted Favorite British Comedian in a 2002 BBC poll. Not bad for a guy who died in 1968. It's generally agreed that his best work was on radio and television, but his first film — he only appeared in five throughout his career — is a classic that still raises a laugh.

The Rebel (renamed *Call Me Genius* in the U.S. to avoid confusion with the Nick "Johnny Yuma" Adams television series of the same name) sees Hancock play a browbeaten London bookkeeper with artistic aspirations. Trouble is, he has more gusto than actual artistic talent. Never one to let a thing like that stand in his way, Hancock quits his job and moves to Paris where he hopes his work will be appreciated.

He begins wearing a beret, falls in with an arty crowd of surrealists and existentialists — including an artist played by a young Oliver Reed — and even shares a Montmartre garret with Paul (Paul Massie), a talented, but undiscovered painter. Hancock, believing his work to be superior, condescends to Paul as he looks at his paintings, "It's just quite not there yet, is it?"

Hancock's world is upended when noted art snob and impresario Sir Charles Broward (*All About Eve* Academy Award–winner George Sanders) mistakes Paul's good paintings for Hancock's work. Suddenly he is the toast of the town and worse, begins to believe his own hype as the founder of the Infantile School of Art, hence the film's U.S. title *Call Me Genius*. When he is commissioned to create a statue of a Greek tycoon's vampy wife the results are disastrous.

Back in London he is pushed into quickly creating a series of paintings for a show arranged by Sir Charles. In over his head, and hoping to avoid a replay of the statue debacle, he calls in his old friend Paul to help with the work. Paul, now painting in Hancock's folk art style, causes a sensation with the new childlike paintings. In the end Hancock realizes he can no longer take credit where credit isn't due and takes steps to set things right.

There's loads of funny business in *The Rebel*. For those not familiar with Tony Hancock, the first thing that stands out is an unerring sense of comic timing that would give Jack Benny a run for his money. The character was a riff on Hancock's well-known television persona, Anthony Aloysius St John Hancock, a haughty bore with aspirations to greatness who was always and inevitably thwarted in the end, so the characterization is letter-perfect. Mix that with a script tailored for him by long-time writers Alan Simpson and Ray Galton and his ability to twist a line or get a laugh from a sigh or even just a sideways look and you get a lesson in comic precision.

Much of the humor is derived from Hancock's unique personal style and wordplay, but there is no lack of inventive sight gags that also amuse. Not to be missed is Hancock's creation of a modern art piece by splattering paint on a canvas and then bicycling over it.

The Rebel premiered at the Beirut Film Festival, where it was greeted with kind reviews, which translated into good box office in the U.K., but a resounding thud everywhere else. The failure of the film to launch his international career prompted Hancock to fire his long-time collaborators Simpson and Galton. Without those two at his side his career faltered and he only made one more film as a lead character, the disappointing *Punch and Judy Man* in 1962.

His career limped along, damaged by poor choices and alcoholism until his death by overdose in Sydney, Australia, on June 25, 1968.

In the years since his death his popularity has increased. His legendary radio shows have remained bestsellers on vinyl and CD while DVD releases of his television shows and two films have kept him in the public eye. Despite being dead for over four decades he still has a fan club, The Tony Hancock Appreciation Society; has a bronze and glass sculpture on display in Old Square, Corporation Street, Birmingham; was the subject of a 1991 biopic starring Alfred Molina; has no less than five books; and counts among his fans young whippersnappers like Pete Doherty and rock groups Manic Street Preachers and Pop Will Eat Itself, all of whom have referenced Hancock in their songs.

Dan Peat of the Tony Hancock Appreciation Society said that if Hancock was still alive he would react to the attention with "some kind of dry crack, but in truth he would have been chuffed."

Availability: Out of Print VHS

"As unique as the paradise she lived in . . ."
— ADVERTISING TAGLINE FOR *RESPIRO*

RESPIRO (2002)
▬ ▬ ▬ ▬ ▬ ▬

In Lampedusa, a tiny island off the coast of Sicily, they tell a story about a woman who is brought back from the dead by the prayers of the villagers who condemned her while she was alive. *Respiro* (Italian for "to breathe") updates that legend, setting it in modern day.

Valeria Golino — the beautiful Italian star of everything from Lina Wertmüller's *A Joke of Destiny* to Barry Levinson's *Rain Man* — plays Grazia, a free spirit whose conduct crosses the line of acceptability in the small fishing community in which she and her family live. She bathes naked in front of the fishermen, lets stray dogs loose from the pound and radiates a reckless energy. Her unruly behavior confounds her husband, who tries to control her mood swings with drugs. After one particularly nasty incident it is decided that she will be sent to a hospital in Milan for treatment.

With the help of her son she escapes being sent to the big city head-shrinker, and hides in a cave by the ocean. After an exhaustive search she is presumed dead. Just as Joni Mitchell said, you don't know what you've got till it's gone, and once Grazia is out of their lives her husband and the citizens of the small village realize what a force of nature she was.

Director Emanuele Crialese clearly finds Grazia fascinating. His camera adores her, lovingly and carefully detailing her every move. "We have this weird tendency as human beings to look for the black sheep," he says, "they're the ones who get the blame, but it's through their sacrifice that we understand more about ourselves." When Grazia is ostracized by her traditionally minded neighbors, the viewer actually learns more about their fears and prejudices than Grazia's perceived shortcomings.

Crialese takes his time with the story, allowing us to get a good sense of the village and the people. The slow pace of the film reflects the pace of life in Lampedusa, but like a Mediterranean *Blue Velvet*, the ugly side of the beautiful village is exposed. *Respiro* is one of those films with a slight story that succeeds because of its sense of place. It is a cliché to say that the location is a character in the film, but in this case it is true.

"I knew that the director was going to set the tone of the movie — like a cadence in a poem — and that what I needed to do was get in sympathy with that pulse and not interfere with it," Golino told *Film Freak Central*'s Walter Chaw. "My character is so elemental, and she's in her element among the rocks and the water. There's something hypnotic about the movie. It's such a simple storyline, but it has so many rich opportunities to attach meaning and metaphors. Those scenes feel so natural that a lot of people think that the picture wasn't scripted, but almost everything was — the script was so good, but I think that during the shooting Emanuele didn't know what he was making, where he was going. He was working on his gut and he found the heart of the movie while he was editing."

In a film like this the viewer must understand where the story is taking place in order to understand *why* the story is taking place. In this, and the wonderful performance of Golino and the cast of non-actors, *Respiro* succeeds wonderfully well.

Availability: On DVD

"Rififi . . . means Trouble!"
— ADVERTISING TAGLINE FOR *RIFIFI*

RIFIFI (1955)
■ ■ ■ ■ ■

The epic 30-minute safe cracking sequence in *Rififi* is so detailed in its construction that Paris police had the movie banned in the fear it would serve as an instructional guide for would-be robbers. Directed by the Hollywood blacklisted Jules Dassin for just $200,000, *Rififi* is the father of the modern heist film.

Based on a book called *Du Rififi chez les hommes* by Auguste Le

Breton, which François Truffaut called the worst crime novel he'd ever read, *Rififi* (that's underworld slang for a violent confrontation) begins, as so many heist films do, with a freshly released con. Aging thief Tony le Stéphanois (Jean Servais) gets out of jail after a five-year stint to discover his girlfriend Mado (Marie Sabouret) living with Louis Grutter (Pierre Grasset), the gangster owner of the nightclub L'Âge d'Or. Despondent, he turns back to a life of crime.

When his friends Jo le Suedois (Carl Möhner) and Mario Ferrati (Robert Manuel) propose a simple snatch and grab jewelry robbery, Tony suggests they think bigger. Why take a few trinkets when there is a safe full of priceless gems for the taking at the Paris branch of Mappin & Webb? With the help of Cesar le Milanais (the director Jules Dassin as Perlo Vita), Italian safe cracker extraordinaire, they execute a flawlessly planned robbery that yields 240 million francs worth of jewelry. It's thumbs-up all round until Cesar gives a valuable ring to his mistress and everything goes south.

At the heart of *Rififi* is a bravura half-hour safe cracking sequence played without dialogue or music. The only sounds are the noises created by the robbers themselves — heavy breathing, coughs, the whirr of a drill and the gentle rustle of a light shower of plaster as it falls into an umbrella set up to catch the dust. It is a knuckle whitening scene that grows in tension as the silence becomes almost deafening.

Dassin, an American B-movie director forced to find work abroad after being named as a communist by director Edward Dmytryk for the House Un-American Activities Committee in 1952, underlines the soft underbelly of his movie by using a semi-documentary style similar to the one he developed with photographer Weegee on *The Naked City*. Shooting on location, his bleak view of Paris's streets, bars and clubs predates the New Wave's break with studio shooting. It gives the film a realistic feel uncommon to crime dramas of the day.

Also interesting is Dassin's break from Hollywood moral mores. Working outside the studio system for the first time in five years, the director was no longer bound by the strict Hays Code and felt free to push the envelope, including scenes of misogyny and sadism. One disturbing sequence sees Tony punish his ex-girlfriend for cheating on him. He humiliates and beats her (off camera) in a cruel and disturbing way that simply would not have made it past the Hollywood censors of the day.

Rififi set the mold for many heist flicks that came after, but because of Dassin's inventive direction and no-nonsense approach to the crime in the story, it still seems fresh and exciting more than half a century after its release.

Availability: On DVD

"There's one thing to pass a law and another thing to enforce it. There'll always be fellows wanting a drink."
— GEORGE HALLY (HUMPHREY BOGART)

THE ROARING TWENTIES (1939)

Director Raoul Walsh was one of a kind.

When a car accident cost him his eye his doctor asked if he wanted a glass prosthesis. "Hell, no!" he said. "Every time I get in a fight, I'd have to put it in my pocket." He opted for an eye patch instead.

In May 1942, Walsh and heavy-lidded actor Peter Lorre played a macabre trick on aging swashbuckler Errol Flynn. According to legend the juiced jokers "rented" the dead body of John "The Great Profile" Barrymore — grandfather of Drew — for $200 from the Pierce Brothers Mortuary in Los Angeles and secretly took the cadaver to Flynn's home in the Hollywood Hills. They propped the not-yet-embalmed body up in an easy chair with a drink clenched in his hand and waited for Flynn to return home. The idea that Barrymore had come back from the grave freaked the actor out so much he ran screaming from the house, only to be told by his giggling "friends" waiting outside that it was a prank. "You missed the old boy and I brought him up here," Walsh said. "At least come in and say hello to him." When Walsh and Flynn's butler Alex returned the body and told the owner of the mortuary what they had been up to, the mortician said, "Why the hell didn't you tell me? I would have put a better suit on him."

Walsh was a flamboyant man who, in a 52-year career, brought his innate sense of showiness to every one of his projects. A case in point is *The Roaring Twenties*, his first gangster film (a 1915 outing, *Regeneration*, is often mistakenly identified as such, but is a crime drama, not a gangster movie), and a visually spectacular look at Prohibition. Filling the screen with interesting characters — probably the kind of men the rough and tumble Walsh would have liked to hang out with in real life — the director brings a sense of humor to a genre not known for laughs. Decades later Amy Heckerling would complete an unofficial remake of *The Roaring Twenties* called *Johnny Dangerously*, which played up the original's lighthearted flourishes.

The story is typical mobster stuff enhanced by Walsh's deft touch. Based on Mark Hellinger's experiences as a New York City reporter during the Jazz Age, it echoes the true-to-life rise and fall of bootlegger Larry Fay, a colorful character arrested 41 times during Prohibition.

The screen's quintessential tough guy James Cagney plays Eddie Bartlett, a World War I vet who builds a fleet of cabs during Prohibition by using the cars to deliver illegal liquor.

"And so the Eddie of this story joins the thousands and thousands of other Eddies throughout America," bleats the narrator. "He becomes a part of a criminal army — an army that was born of a marriage between an unpopular law and an unwilling public. Liquor is the password in this army. And it's a magic password that spells the dollar sign as it spreads from city to city, from state to state. The public is beginning to look upon the bootlegger as something of an adventuresome hero, a modern crusader who deals in bottles instead of battles. And so, because of a grotesque situation, this new kind of army grows and grows, always gaining new recruits who care nothing about tomorrow just so long as money is easy today."

Eddie's rolling in it, and cuts two army buddies, lawyer Lloyd Hart (Jeffrey Lynn) and George Hally (Humphrey Bogart), in on the action.

With money in his pocket Eddie tries to romance Jean Sherman (Priscilla Lane), a "cute blonde" woman with whom he had corresponded while he was stationed overseas. Jean, however, is more interested in the handsome Lloyd. Meanwhile Eddie ignores the advances of the woman who gave him his start as a bootlegger, the tart with a heart of gold, Panama Smith (Gladys George playing a character based on "Queen of the Nightclubs" Texas Guinan, a hardnosed woman who also inspired Whoopi Goldberg's bartender Guinan on *Star Trek: The Next Generation* and the *All That Jazz* number in the musical *Chicago*).

When Jean and Lloyd marry, romantic rivalry starts to erode the effectiveness of Eddie's racket. The business suffers another blow in 1929 with the crash of the stock market and is destroyed by the repeal of Prohibition in 1933. The vicious and ambitious George picks up the pieces, edging Eddie out of the scam. Soon the former Mob boss is destitute, alcoholic and reduced to driving a cab to make ends meet. On Christmas Eve the fickle finger of fate pokes him in the face when he picks up Jean in his cab, leading to the tragic end of the story.

Walsh kicks off the whole thing with an interesting historical montage, working backwards through recent history to establish a context for the film's action. This documentary style timeline not only sets the date and place, but also gives the viewer insight into the trio of leading players. Following the timeline back to World War 1, we meet Eddie, George and Lloyd in a foxhole on the Western Front in France.

The quick scene with Eddie stumbling into the hole sets up the dynamic between the three. George is short-tempered and edgy ("Do you always come into a rathole like that?") while Eddie's reply, "What do you want me to do, knock?" is tough, but with a sense of humor. When Lloyd says, "Ten thousand shellholes around here and everybody's got to come diving into this one," it sets him apart from Eddie and George, using dialogue, not action to show us that unlike the other two, Lloyd's no tough guy.

Throughout the film Walsh employs visual metaphors in ways not usually seen in gangster movies. His Wall Street crash montage is memorable, not only for the scene where a giant tickertape appears to crush people, but for the animated dollar signs that spin downwards, literally showing us money going down the drain.

There are a number of these tightly edited minute-long tableaus in the film, mixing stock footage with new material and adding considerable visual excitement to the film. Backed by a barking informational voiceover they also keep the story moving along at breakneck speed.

Cagney's energetic performance keeps pace with the action. As Eddie he's a fast talking hood, but he's not all bad — he has a conscience. This pliable morality makes Eddie one of Cagney's more interesting onscreen gangland creations and one of the most complex crime characters of the 1930s. In one great scene three ex-cons approach him looking for some under the table work. Eddie is a gangster and lives on the wrong side of the law, but he only hires the two men who admit their guilt and kicks the third to the curb when he insists that he was framed. Apparently he'll hire criminals, but only honest ones.

Bogie, in his third and final outing with Cagney — they appeared in Michael Curtiz's *Angels With Dirty Faces* and *Oklahoma Kid* — is in fine form. His George is a cold-blooded killer who easily murders an ex-army sergeant who gave him a hard time in the service. In his final scene in the film Bogart plays a wide range of emotions, from swaggering top dog to sniveling coward and everything in between. It's melodramatic, but his facial expressions are interesting and entertaining.

Walsh breaks the movie's occasionally grim, violent tone with snappy, humorous dialogue. When a club owner wonders if Jean can "out talk" Eddie, Panama replies, "I hope she can outrun him." Walsh peppers the movie with these moments; the kind of lines designed to get a laugh and sharply contrast with the fatalistic atmosphere of the rest of the film.

The Roaring Twenties, Warner Bros.' final gangster film of the 1930s, was slammed by the critics on release. *Variety* thought it was "overlong," while the *New York Times* called it "egregiously sentimental" and said it brimmed with "annoying pretentiousness." The movie's reputation has improved over the years, but despite great, inventive direction from Walsh, interesting performances and a solid story it remains seriously underappreciated.

Availability: On DVD

My Favorite Movie You've Never Seen

"There's one called *The Night They Raided Minsky's* (1968). It's a wonderful film about burlesque. Very, very funny. Directed by William Friedkin, it stars Jason Robards and was Bert Lahr's last movie (he died during filming). It is a hilarious film. It is a musical, and has some great numbers in it. This is one of Friedkin's best pieces and it just sort of got lost and I can't understand why. It's as funny as *The Producers* in my opinion."

– *Re-Animator* writer/director Stuart Gordon

"I had everything worked out but nothing's gone the way I planned."
— **MAJOR CHARLES RANE (WILLIAM DEVANE) IN** *ROLLING THUNDER*

ROLLING THUNDER (1977)

In an age of stadium seating, digital projection and multiple screens it requires a bit of doing to remember a time when not all movie theaters had uniformed staff and five kinds of topping for your popcorn. In the days before multiplexes dotted the landscape, most big cities had at least one movie palace that showed first-run films, while its dirty doppelganger — a seedy theater playing B-movies, usually as double bills — often resided down the street on the wrong side of town. They were called grindhouses, so named because usually they were housed in former burlesque theaters that at one time had featured "bump and grind" dancing.

What exactly is a grindhouse you ask? You may have been in a grindhouse theater and not even known it.

If the ushers in the theater carried a flashlight in one hand and a two-by-four (known as the "peacekeeper") in the other, chances are, you were in a grindhouse.

If they played *Santa Claus Conquers the Martians* in July, you were in a grindhouse.

If there were sections missing from the film, or if the reels were out of order, you were in a grindhouse.

"One of the bigger deals is the fact that the grindhouse cinemas were the ones in the big cities . . . a Cleveland, a Chicago, a Detroit," grindhouse connoisseur Quentin Tarantino told me in 2007. "They had the grindhouses and the films that would be coming in were the one-week-only exploitation movies. Whatever kung fu movie or whatever they knew would do well from the rental exchange, they'd just send them. Or whatever big movie on its way out of town, on the way to oblivion before it stopped playing at any theaters, the last stop was the grindhouse."

Most of those grubby theaters are gone now, but their legacy lives on. Classic exploitation titles like the sexually charged *Coffy*, starring grindhouse legend Pam Grier and the psychodrama *Fight for Your Life*, once called "the least politically correct movie ever to play in American theaters" can help you relive those down-and-dirty days on DVD . . . the only thing missing is the usher with the two-by-four.

One film that isn't available on DVD, although it is a staple of late night television, is *Rolling Thunder*. Named by both Robert Rodriguez and Quentin Tarantino as their favorite grindhouse movie, this hyper-violent 1977 flick about a Vietnam veteran (William Devane) hell-bent on revenge for the murder of his family was scripted by *Taxi Driver*'s Paul Schrader.

Devane (six years before finding fame as the nasty Greg Sumner on the night-time soap opera *Knots Landing*) plays Air Force flier Major Charles Rane, a recently released Vietnam POW, who, after spending years in a prison camp, returns home to San Antonio to a hero's welcome. The good folks of Texas reward him for his service with a Cadillac and 2,555 silver dollars, one for every day he was confined, plus one for luck.

His happiness at being on familiar turf soon dissipates as feelings of despair overtake him. Emotionally devastated from his experience in Vietnam, it is impossible for him to fit in. He feels that no one understands him, and slowly becomes detached, distant.

His problems with readjusting to civilian life are compounded when he realizes that his young son doesn't remember him and his wife has developed a wandering eye. Things go from grim to grimmer when a group of psychos (among them, James Best, *The Dukes of Hazzard*'s Sheriff Rosco; and Luke Askew, best known as the "Stranger on Highway" in *Easy Rider*) invade his home, determined to steal his silver dollars.

Despite taking a horrific beating — in flashbacks we see he survived worse torture in Hanoi — he won't tell the bad guys where he hid the loot. As the bandits are putting his hand in the garbage disposal, his wife and son return home. While he lies bleeding on the kitchen floor, his son gets the coins, handing them over to the thieves. The gang then shoots the wife and son, and leaves Rane for dead.

After recuperating in the hospital and getting used to the hook that replaced his hand, Rane and fellow heavily armed former POW Johnny Vohden (a young looking Tommy Lee Jones) hunt down and dispatch the thugs with brutal efficiency.

Co-written by Paul Schrader, *Rolling Thunder* breathes the same merciless air as *Death Wish*, another, better known film from the 1970s heyday of payback movies. Revenge, or badass cinema, was a staple of the grindhouse, and it's easy to see why. They're straightforward. Someone gets killed and someone else seeks vengeance and will stop at nothing until the bad guys have paid the ultimate price. They're gratuitously bloody (losing a hand to an InSinkErator!) and in the end the "good guys" generally came out on top, perhaps with their morality a little muddied, but otherwise intact.

In most cases revenge dramas are pretty cut and dried — search and destroy — and while *Rolling Thunder* more than delivers the badass thrills essential for the genre, Schrader and director John Flynn do something rare — they inject substance into an exploitation flick by exploring the rough repatriation of Vietnam vets who felt alienated by a society that didn't understand what they had been through.

The returning vet angle is clarified by the strong performances of Devane and co-star Jones who embody men who served their country, only to lose themselves and their souls in the process. Each actor delivers a sensitive portrayal of a man wrestling with demons, their emotions covered with a thick layer of scar tissue. Scenes of Jones trying to relate to his family, even though they won't discuss the war with him, are harrowing.

Later the Vietnam vet as vigilante would become its own sub-genre, with movies like *Good Guys Wear Black* and *The Exterminator* riffing off the ideas first (and best) presented in *Rolling Thunder*.

The big payoff in *Rolling Thunder* happens in the last 10 minutes. The showdown between Rane and the men who killed his family crackles with energy. Director Flynn, working with a shoestring budget, paces the movie carefully, slowly edging up to the final and vicious face-off. When Rane says, "It's your time, boy," before blowing one of the baddies away (in a Mexican whorehouse no less) it's a cathartic, crowd-pleasing moment that only could have come from the macho typewriter of Paul Schrader.

Once seen *Rolling Thunder* leaves an impression. "I saw it on a double feature with *Enter the Dragon*," said Tarantino, who named his DVD distribution company Rolling Thunder Pictures after the movie, "and [Rolling Thunder] was better."

Availability: Out of Print VHS

"It's a Lloyd film — that's enough!"
— ADVERTISING TAGLINE FOR *SAFETY LAST!*

SAFETY LAST! (1923)
■ ■ ■ ■ ■ ■ ■ ■

Safety Last! is on *Premiere Magazine*'s 50 Greatest Comedies of All Time list and contains one of the most famous images of the silent era, but remains a little seen classic from a man who was, at the time, more popular than Charlie Chaplin and Buster Keaton. Harold Lloyd's masterpiece *Safety Last!* is a classic, but more people have seen the famous poster image of Lloyd hanging 12 stories above a city street, clinging to the minute hand of a clock than have ever seen the film.

Lloyd resurrects his most famous character in *Safety Last!*, the bookish eager-to-please everyman with round horn-rimmed glasses and boater hat. Known only as The Boy, he's a young, naive guy from rural Great Bend, California, who sets out to make his name in the big city. He travels west to Los Angeles with dreams of wealth rattling around his head, hoping to make good so he can marry his sweetheart (Mildred Davis, Lloyd's real-life wife).

Like so many before him, he finds success in the City of Angels elusive, and he finds himself living hand to mouth, struggling to pay the rent. While working at the ladies material counter in the De Vore Department Store — several pay grades below his desired management position — he writes glowing letters to his girl, amplifying his degree of success. Impressed, she dashes off to the city to be with her supposed bigwig, while in reality he and his roommate are broke and dodging their landlady, who wants to get paid.

Desperate to appear successful he impersonates the store's manager. She buys the charade, but he still has to come up with some cash to back up his outrageous claims of prosperity. When his boss asks him to come up with a publicity gimmick to draw people to the store our hero cooks up a thrilling stunt that will draw loads of attention. He convinces his roommate to play a human fly and crawl up the side of the department store — all 12 stories. Unfortunately when the day comes the roommate is nowhere to be found, so The Boy must take his place.

Inch by inch he climbs the 12-storey building while a mounting crowd watches his progress. His advancement is almost thwarted at every step by a variety of obstacles including flapping pigeons, a mouse that crawls up his pant leg, a revolving weather vane, a flagpole and finally a giant clock.

The business with the clock is the thing that makes *Safety Last!* a classic. As he hangs precariously from the minute hand — in reality he was dangling above a ledge covered in mattresses, but clever camera angles made it look much more dangerous — The Boy has almost completed his climatic climb, and if he can make it to the top he just might get everything he ever wanted: the girl, the money and respect.

At the time the movie was made Lloyd's Boy character was extremely popular because he embodied real people's dreams and aspirations; he appealed to audiences then, and I imagine still will today. The trip to the top of the building is tense, funny and outrageous, but in its own way it's also heartwarming, and one of the great sight gags of early cinema.

Availability: On DVD as part of Harold Lloyd Comedy Collection

"All these adventures begin simply. The listener thinks it'll soon be over, but one story creates another, and then another . . ."
– DONNA REBECCA UZEDA (BEATA TYSZKIEWICZ)

THE SARAGOSSA MANUSCRIPT (REKOPIS ZNALEZIONY W SARAGOSSIE) (1965)

A brutal editing job performed by distributors for *The Saragossa Manuscript*'s release in the U.K. and U.S. cut nearly a third of the action away from this three-hour Polish masterpiece, rendered it unwatchable and doomed it to failure. If not for the efforts of Grateful Dead guitarist Jerry Garcia (who called it a major influence on his music) and directors Francis Ford Coppola and Martin Scorsese, the unexpurgated film might have been lost to time.

Set in Spain during the Napoleonic Wars, *The Saragossa Manuscript* is one of the most elliptical stories ever put on film. Scheherazadian in nature, the story makes the *Arabian Nights* seem positively terse or *The Canterbury Tales* merely wordy. The adventure begins when a Napoleonic officer, separated from his troop, finds refuge in an abandoned inn. There he passes the time reading a strange old book, filled with even stranger tales. He is joined by an enemy soldier who is supposed to capture him, but instead tells his adversary about a personal connection to the volume. It seems the tome is based on the exploits of his grandfather, Alfonse Van Worden, a captain in the Walloon Guard (Zbigniew Cybulski, a popular actor known as "Polish James Dean").

From this point on the movie becomes a flight of fancy, literally going off in all directions at the same time as filmmaker Wojciech J. Has weaves together the many tangential story shards of Van Worden's escapades skipping through the Sierra Morena mountains of eighteenth-century Spain while trying to avoid the Inquisition.

Along the way we meet a demonically possessed hermit, seductive Islamic princesses, gypsies, priests who are really disguised sheiks and many others, all of whom tell their own tales in what becomes a nesting narrative that keeps turning in on itself, at one point going seven levels deep. To label it convoluted is to call the Grand Canyon wide or the first bite of a Snickers bar delicious — it's obvious — and while it stretches the elasticity of most people's attention spans, for those willing to give their heads a workout, it is rewarding and great fun.

Based on a loopy 1813 novel of the same name by Polish Army captain of engineers, ethnologist, Egyptologist, linguist and nobleman Jan Nepomucen Potocki, the movie is a condensed version of the book, which was long thought to be unfilmable. In cutting down the rambling doorstopper of a novel into a merely epic script, director Has managed to maintain the novel's stream-of-consciousness storytelling and its sardonic humor.

It's a tricky balance to juggle the insanely complicated story with a hodgepodge mix of reality and fantasy and one of the longest cast lists this side of *Ben Hur*, but Has keeps all the balls in the air with the help of beautiful cinematography and a rollicking score by Krzysztof Penderecki, who also contributed compositions to the soundtracks of later films *The Shining*, *The Exorcist* and *Inland Empire*.

Despite the butcher job performed by the U.K. and U.S. distributors, *The Saragossa Manuscript* did manage to find some fans upon its release. Surrealist filmmaker Luis Buñuel, who rarely watched movies, liked this film so much he screened it over and over again. Jerry Garcia was such a fan he financed part of the restoration of the director's cut. Unfortunately the guitarist died before the refurbishment was complete, but the cause was picked up by Martin Scorsese, who helped preserve and restore the film, and Francis Ford Coppola who teamed with Scorsese to present the film in its complete form in 1997 before ushering it to a long-awaited release on DVD in 1999.

Availability: On DVD

"This is the captain. We have a little problem with our entry sequence, so we may experience some slight turbulence and then . . . explode."
— CAPTAIN MALCOLM REYNOLDS (NATHAN FILLION)

SERENITY (2005)

When the movie version of *Buffy the Vampire Slayer* tanked at the box office, its writer, Joss Whedon, was convinced it still had some life left in it. He took the concept and shrunk it down for the small screen, turning it into a massive cult hit that ran for seven seasons. Then when another show, *Firefly*, failed to click with audiences and was canceled after only 11 episodes aired, Whedon (who is often called the Geek Guru) utilized the *Buffy* theory in reverse. The result is *Serenity*, a big screen blow-up of the failed television series.

The film, which was shot on the sets of the canceled show, tells the story of Captain Malcolm Reynolds (Nathan Fillion) who was on the wrong side of a galactic war, escaping with only his broken-down ship, *Serenity*, and his devoted crew. When he picks up two new passengers, a young doctor, Simon Tam (Sean Maher) and his occasionally violent and telepathic sister River (Summer Glau), he gets much more than he bargained for. The two are on the lam from the Alliance, the evil conglomerate that controls the galaxy. The moon-eyed River has learned something no one was ever supposed to know and the Alliance will stop at nothing to make sure the secret dies with her.

Like *Buffy* and the other shows Whedon has been involved in, *Serenity* takes the conventions of its genre and turns them on their head. This is science fiction filtered through John Wayne westerns with a touch of *Spaceballs* thrown in for good measure — it's action-packed, funny and just when you think the movie is about to dip into a cliché it rounds another unexpected corner.

The thing that sets *Serenity* a galaxy apart from so many of the other recent sci-fi films is its emphasis on character over effects. Sure, there are the obligatory big intergalactic action sequences involving space-ships and lasers, but they are secondary to the relationships of the people aboard the ships. Whedon understands that action and adventure are more exciting if you actually care about the characters, and gives us characters that are by turns hilarious, heartbreaking and occasionally creepy.

The difficulty of adapting a television series to film lies in finding the right balance of exposition to open the story up to newbies without alienating viewers who are familiar with every nuance of the original show. Here again Whedon nails it. Aficionados of the original series will be pleased with this adaptation — in fact a group of überfans called the Browncoats actually helped the studio with the film's marketing by hosting surprise screenings and spreading the word on the Internet — but *Firefly* virgins like myself can also enjoy it.

Availability: On DVD

"You know what you remind me of? In Tangiers there was a bartender. His name was Mumbo Charlie and he used to make a cocktail, and this cocktail was as sleek as satin, but there was just one thing wrong with it. About two hours later it snuck up on you and you wished you were dead."
— PAUL MASON (ROD STEIGER) TO MELANIE DE LA CRUZ (JOAN COLLINS) IN *SEVEN THIEVES*

SEVEN THIEVES (1960)

Joan Collins became a television icon in the 1980s on the basis of one role. As Alexis Morrell Carrington Colby Dexter Rowan on the night time soap opera *Dynasty* she redefined bitchy for a whole new genera- tion. In 193 episodes Alexis was a glamorous, larger-than-life villainess who jumped from bed to bed, smoked cartons of her signature black Nat Sherman cigarillos and, most famously, provoked a catfight that ended up in a mud pool. But before the outrageous shoulder pads, the big hair shellacked with gallons of ozone layer–destroying Aqua Net and the sour attitude, Collins was a sultry starlet who appeared in dozens of movies.

Usually cast in window-dressing roles requiring little more than an alluring pout and a low-cut dress, Collins was better known for her stormy personal life than her onscreen acting chops. A mid-career caper film called *Seven Thieves* did little to change the public's perception of her — she plays a burlesque dancer — but hindsight (and a reissued DVD) reveals a strong performance without any of the camp that marred most of her work.

Predating the other great Swingin' '60s caper films — the original *Ocean's 11*, *The Italian Job* and *Topkapi* — *Seven Thieves* stars Edward G. Robinson as Theo Wilkins, a disgraced scientist who masterminds the robbery of $4 million in French francs from the underground casino vault in Monte-Carlo, Monaco. He's put together a crew of co-conspirators and planned the heist "as I would a chemical experiment." That is to say down to the last molecule. This will be his nest egg and he's taking no chances. To lead the team of troublemakers he recruits Paul Mason (Rod Steiger), a sophisticated thief who is savvy enough to pull off the elaborate raid and tough enough to keep everyone in line while doing so.

It's an intricate plan involving classic film noir standards: assumed identities (Eli Wallach is the colorfully named Baron von Roelitzl; Robinson is Dr. Vital), glamorous parties, cyanide and a long walk on a narrow window ledge. Mason ensures that the burglary goes as planned, but as in any good caper flick, it's not the robbery he should have been worried about, but the behavior of his accomplices once the money is in hand.

Robinson leads the fine ensemble cast. The veteran actor is particularly comfortable in the charming old codger role he perfected in his later years. His Wilkins is a thief, but he is a sympathetic one and the audience gets on side with him as he prepares to make his last big score.

Steiger isn't his usual bombastic self, instead choosing to underplay Mason, giving him an interesting aura of quiet menace.

Collins wins the audience over in a restrained performance (no cat fights or Nat Shermans in sight) that reveals a layered character — simultaneously hardened and forlorn, but with a compassionate soul. Her performance is highlighted by two memorable dances that showcase her best assets. A third, more risqué striptease (choreographed by famed stripper Candy Barr) was shot but consigned to the cutting room floor when it was declared too steamy for 1960s audiences.

Seven Thieves is a handsome-looking film, with production standards in line with the movies of the day. The obvious rear-projections look a little stagy seen through modern eyes, but if I have one real complaint it's that director Henry "*True Grit*" Hathaway chose to shoot the movie in black and white to play up the noir aspects of the story, rather than film in Technicolor and take advantage of the beautiful Monte

Carlo scenery and elaborate interiors of the casinos. Otherwise he handles the set-up of the plan well, keeping the story taut, while the heist itself is a real nail-biter with a good twist at the end.

Seven Thieves didn't make Joan Collins a household name — she'd have to wait until *Dynasty* would make her the Queen of Mean — but is a fine addition to her body of work.

Availability: On DVD

"It seems I'm filming my life in order to have a life to film, like some primitive organism that somehow nourishes itself by devouring itself, growing as it diminishes."
– DIRECTOR ROSS MCELWEE IN *SHERMAN'S MARCH*

SHERMAN'S MARCH (1986)

The original plan was for documentarian Ross McElwee to make a film that examined the enduring effects on the southern psyche of William Tecumseh Sherman's devastating "scorched earth" Civil War march. On the eve of this adventure McElwee's girlfriend dumped him, leaving him despondent and feeling hopeless. Rather than abandon the project in the wake of his breakup, he retooled his idea, and set off in Sherman's footsteps, this time to film his search for the perfect southern woman.

The resulting 157-minute travelogue is an epic journey not only into the lives of the women he meets along the way, but also into his psyche. He's an interesting dude. Imagine a southern Woody Allen type, with a halting drawl that rarely rises above the volume of a whisper and a passing facial resemblance to Burt Reynolds. He's obsessed with nuclear war and unlucky with women, but luckily for us, somewhat fearless and a good listener.

Using his camera as a tool to pick up women he allows the subjects to talk . . . and talk and talk. His cinema-vérité style — a rough-hewn technique that in his hands almost resembles home movies — suits his homegrown approach to filmmaking. It's sloppy, but his lack of polish gives the proceedings an intimate feel that draws the viewer into the action. When he speaks to self-described female prophet Pat or to dim-bulb Winnie who believes "that the only important things in life are linguistics and sex," his informal filmmaking shows real affection for his subjects. He pushes buttons, for sure, (one good old boy asks, "You sure you never had anybody hit you?") but his genuine charm wins the day and *Sherman's March* never feels manipulative or forced.

Like Michael Moore or Nick Broomfield, McElwee places himself at the center of the film. The characters he meets along the way are interesting, but it is the way he deals with and contextualizes them that makes the documentary fascinating. The strong, tough women he showcases have their roots in the Civil War, when mothers, wives and daughters ruled the roost while the men were busy getting blown to bits. McElwee, in his desperation to meet women, may have inadvertently stumbled on a little recognized aspect of Sherman's southern legacy.

On a more personal note we're told that Sherman, much like McElwee, began his march from a place of failure, leaving behind a series of belly-up businesses in Ohio. McElwee brings Sherman alive by drawing comparisons between their lives and journeys, and in doing so blows the dust off the traditional portrait of the general.

Ed Gonzalez, writing on Slant.com, called McElwee "the Mark Twain of documentary filmmaking, a purveyor of American dreams whose wit is surpassed only by his uncanny knack for observation." In *Sherman's March* he uses that keen sense of observation, coupled with gentle humor and his search for meaning to miraculously connect past and present.

Availability: On DVD

STALKER: A FILM BY ANDREI TARKOVSKY (1979)

Patience, we were all told as children, is a virtue. It's a virtue that will stand you in good stead while watching the sprawling 163 minutes of *Stalker* (Russian title: *Cта??ep*), a punishing but fascinating Russian art sci-fi film.

Phrases like "mind-bending" and "head trip" are often used to describe the plot of *Stalker*, Andrei Tarkovsky's last film in his native Soviet Union before he defected to the West. Basing his movie on the short story "Roadside Picnic" and clearly drawing inspiration from *The Wizard of Oz* and the 1957 catastrophe in the Mayak nuclear plant, which resulted in several thousand square kilometers of deserted "zone" surrounding the reactor, Tarkovsky weaves an intriguing tale set in a post-apocalyptic totalitarian society. The title character, the bald Stalker (Aleksandr Kajdanovsky), illegally leads two men known simply as The Writer (Anatoli Solonitsyn) and The Scientist (Nikolai Grinko) into a shadowy wasteland called The Zone. Created by a meteorite and thought to be under alien control, The Zone is a lush landscape littered with the waste of modern society — burned-out shells of automobiles and military vehicles sit alongside flaccid telephone poles. They pass pools of water contaminated with waste — syringes and even a painting of John the Baptist. At the end of their journey, in the middle of The Zone is a room where all one's wishes can be fulfilled.

Stalker isn't a science fiction film in the traditional sense, it doesn't have the usual bells and whistles — there are no special effects or E.T.s — just smartly wrought ideas about fundamental questions of existence and the human condition. Not much happens. It's extremely slow paced, uncompromisingly uneventful and pensive, and therein lies its beauty. It's about beliefs and ideas, not action.

As the trio venture toward the starkly beautiful Zone it becomes clear they are on a religious pilgrimage and the film ripens into an allegorical depiction of nuclear fallout, government secrecy, the need for faith and the existence of God. By extension it becomes a harsh comment on Tarkovsky's native Communist Russia of the 1970s.

One of the film's fans, *Eastern Promises* director David Cronenberg, called *Stalker* "a difficult but rewarding pseudo-sci-fi movie which manages to be more revealing of Russia in 1979 than any documentary." The viewer doesn't have to work too hard to see The Zone, a government controlled oasis of hope in a bleak world, as a metaphor for life under the oppressive Communist regime.

Tarkovsky was an extremely cerebral filmmaker, but the feel of *Stalker* may have had as much to do with a film stock problem as with the director's brainy point of view. Tarkovsky shot all the movie's outdoor scenes before it was discovered that the film stock was defective. Rather than abandon the project the director convinced the Soviet film board to give him more money and he re-shot the material that had been lost. During the second kick at the can he rewrote much of the script toning down the expensive science fiction elements and giving it a more philosophical slant.

Although *Stalker* was an award winner at the Cannes Film Festival, and is revered by fans of intellectual speculative fiction, its legacy for those involved in the production is rather dark. Several of the cast and crew died of related illnesses after shooting the film on location near power plants.

"We were shooting near Tallinn in the area around the small River Pirita with a half-functioning hydroelectric station," said soundman Vladimir Sharun. "Up the river was a chemical plant and it poured out poisonous liquids downstream. There is even this shot in *Stalker*: snow falling in the summer and white foam floating down the river. In fact it was some horrible poison. Many women in our crew got allergic reactions on their faces. Tarkovsky died from cancer of the right bronchial tube. And Tolya Solonitsyn too. That it was all connected to the location shooting for *Stalker* became clear to me when [assistant director] Larissa Tarkovskaya died from the same illness in Paris."

On the nuclear front, life imitated art seven years after *Stalker* first hit the big screen following another nuclear meltdown, the Chernobyl disaster. The workers hired to take care of the radioactive nuclear power plant took to calling themselves "stalkers," and the area around the wrecked reactor was known as The Zone.

The film's history only deepens one's appreciation of it, and while *Stalker* isn't for everyone, adventurous viewers will find beauty in the film's thought-provoking depiction of man's effect on the planet.

Availability: Out of Print vhs

My (Three) Favorite Movies You've Never Seen

"I suggest *Solyaris* (1972), the Andrei Tarkovsky original. I saw this film in Spain. I was in Spain with *Shallow Grave*, the first film I made. It was in the film festival there, San Sebastián. I woke up on a Sunday morning and I wanted to see a film. Everyone else was asleep and I wandered up the street and there was this screening of this Russian film with Spanish subtitles. Neither language I speak, but I went in and it was the most extraordinary experience I've ever had. I completely followed it despite the language being incomprehensible.

"We have such a limited appreciation of what has consciousness and what doesn't. That film defines the idea that a planet has a consciousness and can read you and find what you want and what is most precious to you. It is just wonderful. I love that and I think it is a great movie because of that. He did it also with none of the resources that Kubrick had on *2001*. He had to find ways to present the film without those kind of resources and it's a brilliant film.

"The second one I would recommend is a film by the Russian filmmaker Elem Klimov. It's a film called *Come and See* (a.k.a. *Idi i smotri*, 1985) which is the most extraordinary film I've ever seen for sound. It's set in the wartime in Russia and it's about a Nazi atrocity in a village as seen through the eyes of a little boy. It's the most extraordinary use of sound I've ever experienced. The Russians will come back as filmmakers. They disappeared for a while because of the turmoil in their country, but it's in their blood in the way that it is in the American blood and the French blood to make movies.

"The third one I'd recommend is by a British filmmaker called Nic Roeg. . . . It's called *Eureka* (1984) and it's got Gene Hackman as the lead in it. The first hour of that film is as good as it gets. It is the story of a man who has everything. He's the richest man in the world. He's like Murdoch or Bill Gates. He has everything and yet he has nothing. The first hour is pure Nic Roeg. It's assembled through all sorts of abstractions and the weirdest kind of stuff and yet it is a comprehensible and emotional story. The second half is a trial, which doesn't work quite as well because it is much more rigid but it is an extraordinary film . . . Universal withdrew it because it bombed and it cost a lot of money to make, but it is a brilliant film."

– Danny Boyle, *Trainspotting* director and BAFTA Award winner

STRAIGHT TO HELL (1987)

The press release for *Straight to Hell* was prefaced by a quote from the movie's star, punk rock legend Joe Strummer. "Yuppies are gonna hate it" was his take on this twisted spaghetti western. He might have been on to something. At the time of its release the movie was met with howlingly bad reviews and audience apathy. No less a critic than Roger Ebert suggested that it wouldn't just be yuppies that hated the movie. "In fact," Ebert wrote in the *Chicago Sun-Times*, "if he finds a demographic group that does not hate it, he should phone in a new quote for the ads." And at least one of the film's stars was in agreement with the critics. "*Straight to Shit*'s what I call it," says Kathy Burke, who played Sabrina.

When asked why people had such strong reactions to the film, director Alex Cox said, "I don't know. Perhaps it was a little ahead of its time; there was not then a vogue for jokey films about black-suited professional hit-men *à la* Jean-Pierre Melville. Certainly some people didn't 'get it.'"

Among those who didn't get it was the film's distributor, who dumped the movie on the public with so little promotion and flourish it was as if they were trying to keep the release a secret. Time, however, has been kind to *Straight to Hell*. Now seen as a forerunner to the smirky, violent movies of Guy Ritchie and Quentin Tarantino — Sy Richardson's Norwood is a dead ringer for the Samuel L. Jackson character in *Pulp Fiction* — it is hailed in some quarters as a postmodern cult masterpiece.

Starring a who's who of English musicians, *Straight to Hell* (named after a song on the Clash's *Combat Rock* album) came into being after a proposed punk rock package tour fell apart.

"While we were editing *Sid & Nancy*, Commies From Mars Inc. organized a concert at the Fridge, in Brixton, in support of the FSLN [Sandinista National Liberation Front] in Nicaragua," Cox told AlexCox.com. "The Pogues, Elvis Costello and Joe Strummer played to a full house and we made a couple of thousand quid for the Nicaragua Solidarity Campaign.

"Eric Fellner, the producer of *Sid & Nancy*, came up with a grander scheme: since the public clearly loved the musicians and was sympathetic to the Nicaraguan cause, why not organize a rock and roll tour of Nicaragua, involving the same guys? Eric figured that a video deal would pay for it, and we persuaded the musicians in question to sign up for a month-long acoustic Nicaragua Solidarity Tour in August 1986. The bands agreed; but, as time went by, we couldn't find a video company that would fund the tour.

"Eric's solution? Make a film instead: as he predicted, it was easier to raise $1 million for a low-budget feature starring various musicians than to find $75,000 to film them playing in a revolutionary nation in the middle of a war."

Written in three days and filmed over the course of three weeks in Tabernas, a ghost town in southern Spain's desert badlands originally built as sets for the Charles Bronson film *Chino*, *Straight to Hell*'s shoot was chaotic and, while not exactly in a war zone, it took on a combative tone as the conditions on set grew almost unbearable. A temperature of 110 degrees Fahrenheit and Cox's insistence on realism — he covered several actors with sugar water to attract flies — combined with almost constant drunkenness from several of the cast give the film a punk rock sheen that is the visual equivalent of listening to hard and fast guitar rock.

The plot — if you can call it that — revolves around three inept hit men, the hotheaded Simms (Strummer), newbie Willy (Dick Rude) and the cold blooded Norwood (Richardson), who decide to rob a bank and go on the lam after bungling a job for their boss, Amos Dade (Jim Jarmusch). Cash in hand they head for the Mexican desert to hide out from the Dade and the police. After burying their booty they come across a strange town populated by cowboys and run by coffee swilling killers.

Not immediately accepted by the townsfolk, once the trio off a few people, the locals warm to the newcomers. Just as things seem to be going well Dade shows up, looking to settle a score with the hit men turned robbers leading to a bloody free-for-all gun battle.

If you listen carefully to the dialogue, the first thing you'll notice about *Straight to Hell* is that there is no bad language in the film. The "hell" in the title is about as raunchy as it gets, and in fact much humor is derived from these rough-and-ready characters not swearing. Where else would you find banditos telling someone to "go boil your head" or asking "Wot the *heck* is going on here"? The lack of language didn't impress the censors, however, who still gave the film an R rating.

Looking past the quaint language the film is admittedly muddy, with a silly spaghetti western–inspired plot, some dodgy performances — although Strummer's charisma shines through and Elvis Costello is a guilty pleasure as Hives the coffee-serving butler — but it's also really fun. Loose-limbed and sloppy, it's been called a "great terrible movie" and if nothing else is worth checking out as a kind of time capsule to a moment in history before Courtney Love (in her first film lead performance) discovered plastic surgery, and the punk ethos — whether in music or on film — was still on the fringes of society and not yet gobbled up and spit out by corporations looking to cash in on the punk subculture.

"*Straight to Hell,* for better or worse is my film," says Cox, who turned down the chance to direct ¡*Three Amigos!* to make this one, "and I like it very much."

Availability: On DVD

John L. Lloyd "Sully" Sullivan (Joel McCrea): I want this picture to be a . . . document. I want to hold a mirror up to life. I want this to be a picture of dignity. A true canvas of the suffering of humanity.
Mr. Lebrand (Robert Warwick): But with a little sex in it.
Sullivan: But with a little sex in it.
– DIALOGUE FROM *SULLIVAN'S TRAVELS*

SULLIVAN'S TRAVELS (1941)
■ ■ ■ ■ ■ ■ ■ ■ ■ ■ ■ ■

Since the first time anyone threaded film through a camera Hollywood has played a tug-of-war between art and commerce. Film is an art form, but it's also a business and sometimes the line between the two becomes blurred. I'll never forget being on a sound stage in Culver City while a stagehand showed me around. "Here's where they shot the bridge scene in *It's a Wonderful Life*," he said, gesturing to a corner of the massive stage. "Over here they shot some of the scenes for the original *King Kong*."

My eyes widened as he continued, taking me through a laundry list of great movies that were birthed on that stage. *Gone With the Wind. A Few Good Men.* The list went on and on. Then, just as I thought the tour was over, he added, "Oh, and you'll want to check out the next stage," he said. "They shoot *Deal or No Deal* over there."

I laughed, but then realized he wasn't kidding. At the time *Deal or No Deal* was the most successful game show on television, and while it may not have the historic cachet of *Gone With the Wind*, it was lining the studio's pockets. Art versus commerce. They are the dual forces of which Hollywood dreams are made.

Director Preston Sturges understood that dichotomy and put it to terrific use in one of the great films about Hollywood, *Sullivan's Travels.* In a way it's the film he was predestined to make, having been raised by an arts-loving mother who took him to the great museums and opera houses of the world, and a successful father who was all business.

Sturges drew from his split upbringing when creating John L. Sullivan (Joel McCrea), a successful director of light comedies. The character is the Judd Apatow of his day, only without the fart jokes. His previous film, *Ants in Your Pants of 1939* — the follow-up to *Hey, Hey in the Hayloft* — breaks box office records, so naturally the studio wants a follow-up. Fast. Sullivan is keen to get back to work, but aspires to do something different, something important. His next project, he tells his bosses, will be *O Brother, Where Art Thou?*, a pretentious breadline story brimming with social comment.

The studio honchos are dismayed and, in an effort to dissuade him, suggest that he can't possibly make the movie because he doesn't understand what it's like to be poor. To research the movie he vows to embark on a journey of self-discovery, starting life again, only this time at the bottom of the economic food chain.

The studio throws a monkey wrench into his plan when they try to capitalize on his trek. They turn his heartfelt search for enlightenment into a publicity stunt, providing him with a luxury motor home, complete with an entourage including a butler (Robert Grieg) and valet (Eric Blore).

On the advice of his servants who school him in the ways of the needy, he ditches the fancy studio transportation and sets out incognito. He learns first hand of real hardship when he meets The Girl (Veronica Lake), a failed actress who must now scrounge for food.

After experiencing the downside of life he returns to Hollywood wearing his heart on his sleeve. In short order he arranges for a screen test for The Girl, then heads to the rail yard to hand out $10,000 in small bills to those less fortunate than him.

His act of charity goes awry when he is mugged by a hobo who steals his clothes and identification. Later when the tramp is killed by a speeding train there's a case of mistaken identity and it's assumed that the mangled body on the tracks is John Sullivan.

In the movie's grim closing moments the real Sullivan, his memory wiped clean by the blow, and wearing the tramp's raggedy clothes, is arrested and thrown in jail where he finally realizes that the fluffy comedies he used to make as a famous director had some value after all.

In *Sullivan's Travels* Sturges takes a standard movie device in which a person of power and privilege disguises himself to see how the other half lives and tweaks it by adding delicious dollops of satire and thought provoking comedy to create a film rich with social context, but without a heavy-handed feel. *Sullivan's Travels*, he says, was "the result of an urge, an urge to tell some of my fellow filmwrights that they were getting a little too deep-dish and to leave the preaching to the preachers."

Like Charlie Chaplin, much of whose work was focused on the poor, Sturges doesn't judge his subjects. He portrays the underprivileged with dignity and grace, particularly in a stunning seven minute, entirely silent tour of a shantytown. It's a powerful sequence that contrasts the hedonism of Hollywood to the reality of living with little or no money. *Sullivan's Travels*'s hard-edged satire aims to pierce the bubble of rich directors (we're looking at you Frank Capra!) who try to assuage their class guilt by making films as "commentary on modern conditions." Sullivan is portrayed as a director who wants to outright reject the commerce that made him a rich man, and try to make art in the form of a film that will benefit mankind. The clash of art and commerce seen here is a humbling one for Sullivan.

The beating heart of the film is McCrea in the title role. Best known as the star of westerns, McCrea was often written off as a one-note actor, but Sturges pulls a great performance out of him. As Sullivan he is required to wrap his tongue around sophisticated, witty dialogue as well as perform slapstick and lead the audience down the path to despair as his plan to help the poor backfires. He displays a nimble touch as he plays Sullivan not as a boy wonder — he's no Orson Welles — but as a modestly talented man who lucked into his lucrative career. It is the single best performance of his career and one that shows what a gifted comedian he was.

Playing opposite him in her first major role was Veronica Lake, who, at 4′11″, was 16 inches shorter than McCrea and had to stand on a box for most of their scenes so her head would appear in the frame alongside his. Acting-wise she's not particularly memorable — she isn't given that much to do — but she does lend a certain charm to the proceedings. Most notable is her peekaboo hairstyle, a cleverly combed lock of her long blonde hair which covered one eye. The fancy do became a craze and her signature look for the rest of her career.

In *Sullivan's Travels* Sturges mixes Shakespearean tragedy with pratfalls and wordplay that would make Noel Coward proud to craft a movie that is at once very funny and deeply moving.

Availability: On DVD as part of the
Preston Sturges: The Filmmaker Collection

> "You know, sooner or later every woman's bound to find out — the only thing a man's got below his belt is clay feet."
> — MUFF (MARLENE CLARK) IN *SWITCHBLADE SISTERS*

SWITCHBLADE SISTERS (1975)

"It originated the way a lot of pictures I did originated," said director and B-movie legend Jack Hill. "The distributor had an idea to do a street gang movie with girls so he had a poster made up with the title *The Jezebels*. When I saw the poster I said, 'Yeah, I can do that.'

"We worked with the writer [F. X. Maier] and developed a script and we shot it. It did not do well, so the producer and everybody went into a panic. They came up with the title *Switchblade Sisters* and gave it a new campaign."

Still, not even the snappier title could improve the movie's fate. After a lackluster run — and subsequent banning in several key overseas markets — it disappeared from screens, only to be hailed as a lost classic in the new millennium by fans of trash cinema.

Joanne Nail plays Maggie, the new girl in town. A recently transferred high school student, she's a tough cookie who doesn't take shit from anyone. When she butts heads with the female auxiliary of the school's toughest gang she holds her ground, impressing the gang's leader, the squeaky voiced Lace (Robbie Lee). The newcomer is invited to join the Dagger Debs and soon rises through the ranks, becoming Lace's new BFF.

Things really get revved up, however, when gang member Patch (Monica Gayle), so named because of a pirate patch she wears over one eye, drives a wedge between the new best friends. Iago-like she poisons their relationship with lies and sexual innuendo, morphing their friendship into a bitter rivalry. When a Dagger Deb plan to eliminate rival gang the Crabs goes awry and Lace ends up in the hospital, Maggie assumes control of the Debs, changing the name to the Jezebels and severing their ties to the male gang.

With the help of an African-American mob led by a Chairman Mao–spouting revolutionary, Maggie plans bloody revenge against the Crabs for their treatment of Lace, but instead ends up fighting the very person she had tried to avenge.

Shot in just 12 days for $320,000, *Switchblade Sisters'* rough and ready reworking of *Othello* — "I've always tried to emulate Shakespeare in my own way," said Hill — is action-packed fun. Check out the final battle between the two gangs and the skating rink scene; they're breathless romps through the kind of juvenile delinquent culture that only ever existed in exploitation films. It is the logical extension of the biker movies that had proved popular at drive-ins in the early '70s, with an added sprinkle of women's lib in the form of the Deb's rejection of traditional male chauvinist authority. The script crackles with ideas of the importance of female solidarity, which in 1975, when Helen Reddy's feminist anthem "Ain't No Way to Treat A Lady" was topping the charts, was a hot button topic.

Switchblade Sisters' girl power angle is a perfect exploitation hybrid — combine good-looking women with hard-hitting urban violence and you could at once appeal to the female viewers who would gravitate toward the girl power portrayed onscreen, while the guys in the audience would respond to the women and the action. It should have been a surefire recipe for success, but never got traction at the box office.

"Either you buy into the style of that kind of movie or you don't," said Hill. "Some people don't."

Availability: On DVD

TAMPOPO (1985)

▬ ▬ ▬ ▬ ▬ ▬ ▬

Tampopo's plot splinters off into several tangents, but the main thrust of the story begins when truck driver Goro (Tsutomu Yamazaki), a mysterious Shane-like character with a weathered face and a cowboy hat, pulls into a decrepit roadside noodle restaurant run by Tampopo (Nobuko Miyamoto), a widowed fast food cook. When the trucker badmouths the restauranteuse's cooking to a group of rowdy regulars he is pummeled, five against one. Tampopo, stung by his words, but moved by his honesty, plays nursemaid. While he recovers they mutually decide to seek out the perfect ramen recipe and turn Tampopo's place into a shrine to the "art of noodle soup making."

Interspersed in the main narrative are a series of lateral subplots which stress the importance and value of food in Japanese society. In one a yakuza gangster (Kôji Yakusho) and his moll (Fukumi Kuroda) find inventive ways to use food to spice up their love life. Much whipped cream is dispensed and eggs become sex toys as the randy duo pass an egg yolk seductively back and forth between them in a drawn-out kiss.

Another digression sees a young executive upstage his bosses at a fancy restaurant by ordering in perfect French as they struggle with the menu, while other plotlines involve a housewife who leaves her deathbed to prepare one last meal for her clan and an enigmatic Noodle Master who lives with a group of street vagabonds.

Tampopo becomes an anarchic concoction of the crude and the transcendent. Over the movie's 114-minute run time director Juzo Itami skillfully folds together the various vignettes, blending such diverse tributes to food as the outrageous sex play of the yakuza and his gun moll with a Zenlike examination of the noodle as a philosophical way of life. "The new noodles have more substance," says one customer after slurping a bowl, "but they still lack the necessary depth." The free association of these stories and ideas creates a pace and rhythm to the film that feels more like beat poetry than traditional storytelling.

As a topper Itami pays tribute to the great westerns, spaghetti and otherwise. Goro is the mysterious stranger who rides into town, rights a wrong and moves on. He's the Japanese equivalent of the Clint Eastwood *Man With No Name* character popularized in the Sergio Leone movies while the final noodle test feels like a good old-fashioned shootout via *The Seven Samurai.*

It's a rambunctious stew that examines the importance of food from the cradle to the grave, from a mother breast-feeding her newborn to the housewife who makes one last meal for her family before passing to the great beyond. Many movies — *Babette's Feast, Like Water for Chocolate* and *Eat Drink Man Woman* — feature food as a metaphoric central theme, but none are as loving, as loopy or libidinous as Itami's singular vision for *Tampopo.*

Availability: On DVD

"The music he created was strange. His life was even stranger."
— ADVERTISING TAGLINE FOR *THEREMIN: AN ELECTRONIC ODYSSEY*

THEREMIN: AN ELECTRONIC ODYSSEY (1994)

We've all heard the sound. It's the ethereal howl that heralds the entrance of the extraterrestrials in the sci-fi classic *The Day the Earth Stood Still* and personifies the Summer of Love in the Beach Boys tune

"Good Vibrations." It's the theremin, the only musical instrument you play without touching. Using rare archival footage, home movies, still photographs and diagrams, Steven M. Martin's *Theremin: An Electronic Odyssey* recreates the stranger-than-fiction life of Leon Theremin, a Russian mad scientist who created an electronic machine that looks like a wooden box with antennae and produced otherworldly sounds when he waved his hands near its metal appendages.

A musical Zelig, Theremin showed his experimental instrument to Lenin in the 1920s before immigrating to the United States. While in New York he fine-tuned the Theremin for public consumption. Perfected, it was featured in concerts at Carnegie Hall and for the next 10 years or so Theremin toured with his creation, earning rave reviews — even on the front page of the *New York Times* — mentoring a young protege named Clara Rockmore, who was known as "The Virtuoso of the Theremin" and marrying a ballerina named Lavina Williams. His fame grew until he was labeled "the prophet of the future of music" and "the Soviet Edison."

Then, one day, he disappeared. Gone without a trace, none of his American friends, including his wife, ever heard from him again.

The amazing revelation of *Theremin: An Electronic Odyssey* is the discovery of Dr. Theremin alive in Russia. Turns out he had been abducted in 1938 by Soviet secret agents and smuggled back to the Soviet Union where he was imprisoned under the Stalinist regime. Out of prison he was forced by the KGB to develop electronic eavesdropping devices and eventually was "rehabilitated" and given a job at the Moscow Conservatory where he continued to work on electronic music even though Stalin disapproved, saying that electricity was better suited to executions.

Martin brought the inventor back to the United States. On his first trip to New York since his mysterious disappearance Theremin, now a frail 95, is reunited with his protege (who plays for him), but not his wife, who died without ever discovering what happened to him.

Martin weaves Theremin's story together with a parallel history of electronic music, featuring talking heads like synthesizer inventor Robert Moog — who calls the Russian innovator's work the cornerstone of modern electronic music — and musicians Todd Rundgren and Brian Wilson.

Director Martin's obvious affection and enthusiasm for the topic gives the film much of its appeal and energy. The discovery of Theremin, old and infirm, however, deepens the movie, bringing with it a wistful tone as the story shifts from straightforward doc about a obscure, eccentric man to a contemplation on the ups and downs of life and how the fickle finger of fate sometimes pokes you in the eye.

Availability: On DVD

"Why's your room so filthy, Jim? What's that you said, Jim?"
— A GUARD OF STATE HOSPITAL FOR THE CRIMINALLY INSANE AT BRIDGEWATER, MASSACHUSETTS TO A PATIENT IN *TITICUT FOLLIES*

TITICUT FOLLIES (1967)

One of the most notorious documentaries of all time is also one of the least seen movies of the 1960s. *Titicut Follies*, which depicts the cruel treatment of patients at a Massachusetts asylum, was pulled from distribution shortly after its debut at the 1967 New York Film Festival. Critics raved about director Frederick Wiseman's unflinching exposé of human rights abuses of the mentally ill, but the Attorney General for Massachusetts, Elliot Richardson, wasn't as impressed. Claiming the film violated the prisoners' right to privacy, he sought a court-ordered banning of the film.

Amazingly the Massachusetts Supreme Court agreed with Richardson, despite the fact that Wiseman had consent waivers from all involved and their guardians. They ruled it could only be shown in small non-theatrical screenings for selected legal, educational and medical professionals, thus making it the first film in American history to be banned for reasons other than obscenity or national security. When the embargo was lifted in 1992 Wiseman chose to keep it under wraps, allowing only one airing on PBS and slapping a whooping $500 "educational license" price tag on DVD copies.

So what's all the fuss about?

Simply put, *Titicut Follies* — the name comes from a strange musical revue staged by the inmates and guards that bookends the film — is one of the most harrowing cinematic experiences you're ever likely to have. Wiseman uses a bare-bones direct-cinema technique to take us inside the Bridgewater State Hospital, a branch of the Massachusetts Department of Corrections where criminally insane prisoners were housed. He employs hand-held cameras, available light and sound, grainy black and white film stock and no musical soundtrack — this guy was doing Dogme 95 while Lars Von Trier was still in short pants.

Wiseman's camera unflinchingly shows the inhuman treatment of the inmates — called "charges" in the film — and the often patronizing and bullying attitudes of the doctors and guards. We see a starving man force-fed through a tube in his nostril by a less than compassionate doctor who casually smokes a cigarette while performing the operation. We're shown naked inmates forced to live in empty cells with a bucket in lieu of a toilet and a mattress on the floor. Wiseman gives us long takes of prisoners babbling incoherently about religion or Communism, occasionally bursting into song and roaming aimlessly.

It's not hard to see why the Commonwealth of Massachusetts wanted to keep *Titicut Follies* out of the public eye. It's often said that the measure of a society is in the way it treats its prisoners and, frankly, the most shocking thing about the film is the astonishing lack of humanity on display. State guards and doctors treat their charges as things rather than people, overmedicating patients simply to keep them alive rather than actually trying to help them get better. It's unnerving and explicit, but more than that, it's a powerful condemnation of human callousness.

Availability: Hard to find

> "It's typical of my career that in the great crises of life, I should stand flanked by two incompetent alcoholics."
> — OSCAR JAFFE (JOHN BARRYMORE) IN *TWENTIETH CENTURY*

TWENTIETH CENTURY (1934)

These days John Barrymore is primarily thought of as the grandfather of Drew Barrymore, but during Hollywood's Golden Age he was regarded as one of the finest actors on stage or screen. His matinee idol good looks earned him the title The Great Profile, and while he was never nominated for an Academy Award (both his siblings Ethel and Lionel are Oscar winners), he left behind a vast back catalogue of memorable performances. His personal favorite — he called it "a role that comes once in a lifetime" — and one of his best received outings was as Oscar Jaffe, the pompous Broadway director in the Howard Hawks production of *Twentieth Century*.

The role seems tailor-made for Barrymore, who was himself a larger than life character. As legend has it when the actor asked director Howard Hawks why he should play the role, Hawks replied, "It's the story of the biggest ham on earth and you're the biggest ham I know."

Twentieth Century is based on *Napoleon of Broadway*, an unproduced play about Charles Bruce Millholland's time spent working for eccentric impresario David Belasco. The film begins with Oscar (Barrymore playing a thinly veiled Belasco) plucking Mildred Plotka (Carole Lombard) out of his chorus with the plan to remold her into a star. Even though his partners Oliver (Walter Connolly) and Max (Charles Lane) don't believe she has a lick of talent, Oscar gives her the more marquee-friendly name of Lily Garland and ushers her to stardom.

Soon she heeds the call of Tinseltown, where she becomes an even bigger star. Unfortunately for Oscar her departure marks a downturn in his career and after a road production of *Joan of Arc* closes early he skips town, jumping aboard the Twentieth Century Ltd. to New York. Coincidentally — this is a screwball comedy after all — Lily is on the same train. Oscar sees her as another shot at the big time as he tries to convince her to sign an exclusive contract with him. Standing between him and reconciliation is George (Ralph Forbes), Lily's jealous boyfriend, and the fact that she hates Oscar's guts.

Released the same year as *It Happened One Night, Twentieth Century* was overshadowed by the flashier Clark Gable movie. While some of the references have not aged well — I'm still not sure what "He can't do this to me; I'm no Trilby!" means — the screwball comedy and sight gags hold up as well as its more famous rival. Barrymore's masterful handling of the train sequence equals anything in the screwball vein by the acknowledged masters of the genre like Cary Grant or William Powell and the natural comic gifts of Lombard are evident.

She was a rare Hollywood star — beautiful but silly. She never shied away from the joke, even if it meant looking ridiculous onscreen. I can't imagine Lombard's contemporary Claudette Colbert allowing anyone to stick her in the rump with a pin to "teach her to scream" as Oscar does to Lily, but Lombard carries off the harebrained scene with aplomb.

Twentieth Century isn't as manic as some of the screwball comedies that came later. There are no implausible cases of mistaken identity or multiple wives or any of the clichéd conventions of the genre. Instead, the movie thrives because of fast paced (for the day) farce that employs outrageous physical comedy, snappy dialogue and two lead actors who relish every second of it.

Availability: On DVD

"I'm not afraid of you, you king-sized cigarette lighter!"
— CARY WEST (HANS CONRIED)

THE TWONKY (1953)

Before Milton Berle came along and ruined everything Arch Oboler had a good thing going. A busy radio producer, he was the ears behind many radio classics including the innovative *Lights Out,* a horror anthology show that displayed his genius for audio dynamics.

Then Berle and the cathode ray tube appeared and supplanted radio as America's favorite home entertainment and Oboler was out of a job.

His revenge came in the form of a strange movie called *The Twonky*, a curious story about how television destroyed one man's life. Oboler knew he was waging a losing battle against television, but wanted to make his point. When his star Hans Conried pointed out that the unusual film would likely lose money, Oboler replied, "That's all right. I need a tax write-off this year anyway."

Based on a short story by *Last Mimsy* author Henry Kuttner, *The Twonky* begins when Professor Cary West's (Conried) wife gives him a television set to keep him busy while she is out of town. He doesn't really want the newfangled contraption in his house, but also doesn't want to hurt her feelings, so he reluctantly accepts the gift. When the delivery guy asks for a $100 deposit, West is embarrassed. He only has five dollars on him, and even that has been misplaced. Searching for the fiver he discovers a neatly arranged group of bills on his living room floor in front of the television.

"It's money," says the amazed delivery guy as he greedily counts out the cash, which adds up to $100.

"My wife, she must have left it," says a confused West.

The professor soon realizes that there is something strange about his new appliance — it's alive! Not only does it do the housework and light his pipe with a magic beam, but it also slowly starts to take over his life, choosing what he should read and write. It hobbles around the house on stout wooden legs, marching to military music, completely running West's life all without ever being plugged in.

He confides in his neighbor, a boozy football coach (Billy Lynn) who at first believes the set's behavior is a hallucination, the result of over-work. Later, after a number of glasses of homemade hooch he mumbles, "That television set isn't a hallucination, it's a Twonky. I had Twonkies when I was a child. A Twonky is something that you do not know what it is."

Whatever the case, the Twonky slowly drives West mad. Using laser beams and its agile antennas it fights off treasury agents sent to investigate the counterfeit fives, hypnotizes anyone who might do it harm, orders a female companion for West from the telephone company and slowly exerts its grip on the teacher, changing his tastes from highbrow books to lowbrow television entertainment.

Soon West and his neighbor decide that the Twonky must be an alien life form trapped inside the television.

"It assumed the form of a television set when it fell out of its dimension of time into ours," speculates the coach. "It fell into a television production factory line or into that television shop. With its super intelligence it knew at once where it was and the danger to it and it immediately changed its form into something we could understand — a form that would be quite safe and acceptable. Who knows what it really looks like?"

Fearing for their lives (and sanity) they must get rid of the device, but that will be easier said than done. "I told Carolyn not to buy anything on the installment plan," West sighs as he tries to figure a way out of the mess.

Oboler isn't subtle in his diatribe against television. Three decades before David Cronenberg created *Videodrome*, another dyspeptic view of the cathode ray machine, the former radio producer made his point loud and clear — television isn't an innocuous form of entertainment but a dangerous gadget that has an evil effect on American society. Although *The Twonky* may seem like a silly movie — its low-fi special effects don't help that perception — it actually functions well as social satire, examining 1950s hot button topics like fear of technology, consumerism and even gender roles.

Television was new technology when Oboler made *The Twonky* in 1953, and much of what he predicts in the film has come to reality. The idiot box has taken over many homes, becoming the prime source of entertainment, favoring a steady flow of lowbrow reality shows in lieu of educational or dramatic offerings. A decade after *The Twonky* bombed at the box office FCC chairman Newton Minow echoed

Oboler's sentiments calling television a "vast wasteland." Worse, however, according to Oboler is the effect it has on people's psyches.

The difference between radio and television is elementary and dramatic in Oboler's eyes. Radio allowed for the use of imagination as the listener conjured up pictures in their minds to go along with the words coming from the speakers while television requires nothing more than slavish adherence to it. To hammer home this point, Oboler has the Twonky force the professor to rewrite an essay on individualism and personal freedom, and West, powerless to disagree, acquiesces.

The Twonky did nothing to slow the popularity of television, but Oboler had one more trick up his sleeve in the battle against the box. Hoping that 3-D technology would inspire people to abandon the boob tube and flock to the movie theaters he made the first 3-D color film, *Bwana Devil*. While successful, 3-D was a short-lived fad and didn't have the effect he wanted.

Ironically *The Twonky,* a movie to which the word obscure scarcely does justice, isn't available on DVD or VHS so you'll have to keep an eye open for it, that's right, on the late, late show on television.

Availability: Hard to find

My Favorite Movie You've Never Seen

Short Circuit: "John Badham directed this 1986 film, which starred Ally Sheedy and Steve Guttenberg. It struck just the right note of balance between science fiction and comedy, a light and delicate touch that disappeared in a sequel, *Short Circuit 2*."
— Herschell Gordon Lewis, director of 1963's seminal *Blood Feast* and the filmmaker known for creating the splatter film

VENUS IN FURS (1969)

- - - - - - - - - -

Venus in Furs has one of the most confounding family trees of any movie of the 1960s. Confusingly, the film shares its name, but not its storyline, with the famous Leopold von Sacher-Masoch erotic novel. It's also just one of three movies in the '60s to have the name, although some distributors muddied the waters even more by attaching a series of aliases such as *Paroxsysmos* and *Black Angel* to it. To top it all off director Jess Franco directed almost 200 films, but changed names so many times you'd need a slide rule to keep track. The Internet Movie Database lists no less than 69 pseudonyms ranging from names borrowed from jazz greats like Clifford Brown and American actors like James Gardner to made-up monikers like the bizarre Rosa Maria Almirall and Lulu Laverne. As such, it's hard to get a grip on his varied resume.

The movie's strange pedigree has made tracking down a copy akin to searching for the proverbial needle in a haystack, but it's worth the hunt. *Venus in Furs* is an unhinged trip into the twisted psyche of its director, with cinematic detours to Russ Meyerland and Fassbinder Alley.

James Darren (Moondoggie from the *Gidget* movies) is Jimmy Logan, an American jazz trumpeter working in Istanbul. One night while strolling on the beach he finds a dead body that has recently washed ashore. In a strange coincidence he recognizes the corpse as the beautiful Wanda Reed (Maria Rohm), a woman he last saw being abused at a wild party by three sadomasochists led by millionaire playboy Ahmed (Klaus Kinski). Thinking they were simply playing sex games — "Man, it was a wild scene," he relates, "but if they wanted to go that route, it was their bag . . ." — he didn't interfere. Now he is troubled by his decision.

To clear his mind he goes to Rio to throw himself into his music. He starts an affair with singer Rita (Barbara McNair), who performs while lying flat on the floor. All goes well until the night Wanda's doppelganger walks into the club, clad in a fur coat. He becomes obsessed with the strange woman even though she warns him to stay away. When two of the trio of torturers from the party wind up dead, Logan is thrown into crisis. Who is this woman? Is Wanda really dead?

Venus in Furs is unadulterated erotic Euro horror. Sure, style trumps substance in every frame of this film, but what style it is! Franco front-loads the movie with lesbian vampires, good-looking people — the clean-cut television idol Darren uses his slick good looks to channel Chet Baker, while Rohm is perfectly cast as the mysterious femme fatale. There are great images, including McNair singing on the floor and shots of Kinski's piercing eyes. Much of it is unforgettable, if slightly incomprehensible, stuff.

Franco's greatest achievement here is creating a dreamlike aura of menace. The story doesn't make a great deal of sense, often drifting off into existential tangents, but the movie's tone and style are a great keepsake of freewheeling Euro cinema of the 1960s.

Availability: On DVD

VIVA LA MUERTE (LONG LIVE DEATH) (1971)

Filmmaker Fernando Arrabal's troubled childhood haunts his first and most famous surrealist film, *Viva la muerte*. The framework of the story of Fando (Mahdi Chaouch) whose father has been arrested for treason in Franco-era Spain was based, in part, on true events.

Born on the cusp of the Spanish Civil War, Arrabal was just a child when his father, an officer in the Spanish Army, was sentenced to death for trying to assassinate the head of the Popular Front government. His punishment was later commuted to life-in-prison. When Fernando was nine, however, the elder Arrabal broke out of jail and was never heard from again. The loss of his father informs much of Arrabal's work, but none so much as *Viva la muerte*, a movie called one of three "perfect surrealist films" by digitalbits.com, along with *Un chien andalou* and *El Topo*.

The movie begins with some very strange yet striking opening credits. Superimposed over a childlike theme song sung by French schoolchildren Arrabal has layered Hieronymus Boschian etchings (by *Fantastic Planet*'s Roland Topor) of torture and sexual deviancy. It's a grabber of an opening but the weird ride has just begun.

Episodic in nature, it's a nightmarish coming of age story for Fando, who — despite his father's execution for "political crimes" and his mother's assertion that the father wasn't executed, but actually committed suicide — clings to the belief that his father is alive and well. Fando soon realizes that his life is part of a web of lies when he learns that his mother was the one who turned his father in to the authorities. In reaction to the mounting pressure from everyone in his life to renounce his Communist father, Fando conjures up a series of increasingly twisted Oedipal fantasies.

What follows is not for the weak of heart. Decades after the film's release, these multicolored scenes still have the power to cause shock and awe. Arrabal not only pushes the envelope, he tears it in half, showing disturbing and scatological scenes of Fando's father being beheaded by his mother, his mother making love to his captors and, later, the mother wearing a freshly slaughtered ox like a coat. I would say most certainly that Arrabal can't guarantee that no animals were harmed during the production of this picture, and while he would never be able to get away with the butchering of the ox (or the beetle that is sliced in half or the decapitated lizard, for that matter) on film today, it is a vivid image.

Viva la muerte's jumble of surrealism and autobiography is a potent mix, made more effective by Arrabal's unwavering use of disquieting imagery. Good taste is certainly not on the menu, but the dream sequences are unforgettable. In one scene Fando urinates over the side of a building while imagining that the entire town below is drowning in a sea of his urine. In another he imagines Arabesque men playing polo with his father's disembodied head. These are strange and unsettling images that take us further into the psyche of young Fando. He has been lied to, mistreated by those closest to him and in the end his only refuge is in the dark recesses of a tortured mind.

Viva la muerte is the very definition of "not for everyone." It is risky and upsetting viewing, but in the avant-garde descriptions is a beautifully crafted — although completely gonzo — portrait of a young person in mental anguish.

Availability: On DVD as part of the the Fernando Arrabal Collection

"Are you sure you saw a man talking to Caroline this morning?"
— SHERIFF BEN KELLOGG (RICHARD ROBER) IN *THE WELL*

THE WELL (1951)

Quote whoring is the practice of lower-rung film critics and media types of supplying the effusive blurbs you often see on movie advertisements in your Saturday paper. They usually contain words like "funniest" and "exciting" or phrases like "I smell Oscar" and are punctuated with lots of exclamation points. In return for these brassy quotes reporters are often given access to the film's talent via junkets which are paid for by the studios.

Not all people who supply quotes are whores. Roger Ebert isn't trawling for a free hotel room and a four-minute interview with Zac Efron when he supplies a sentence or two to be reproduced in an ad, but many are. You can usually tell a quote whore by the number of times you see their name on ads. If they're on more than two ads in one week, chances are they're using their words and whatever credibility they have to pimp for the studio. If their quote is in huge letters but their name is in hard to read tiny type, they're likely a small outlet hoping to exchange a quote for favor with the studio.

Quoting can be a dirty business — most quotes are meaningless hype sarcastically known as "advertorials" in the biz — but occasionally a few words on an ad or the back of a DVD can grab the eye. Such is the case with *The Well*, a forgotten 1951 drama endorsed by no other than former First Lady Eleanor Roosevelt. "An exciting movie, filled with drama and tension," she called it, "None of you will want to miss it!" Her quote had all the usual characteristics — the exclamation point and use of the word exciting — but the source was so unusual that the DVD leapt out of the rack at me.

It's not hard to see why Mrs. Roosevelt lent her name to *The Well*. As an early leader in the Civil Rights movement she would have been attracted to the movie's take on racism and how community cooperation can overcome adversity. This examination of race in America has been unfairly overshadowed by its successor *To Kill a Mockingbird*, but take it from Eleanor: it's worth a look.

The Well begins with an attention-grabbing scene in which an adorable African-American kindergarten child (Gwendolyn Laster) falls into an abandoned well on her way to school. Her parents (Maidie Norman and Ernest Anderson), unaware of their daughter's predicament and fearing that she has been hurt, seek the help of Sheriff Ben Kellogg (Richard Rober), who assures them that he will leave no stone unturned in his search for their daughter.

His investigation begins with Claude Packard (future *M*A*S*H* star Henry Morgan), a stranger in town and the last person seen with the girl. It turns out that Claude isn't some undesirable, he's actually the nephew one of the town's big wheels, construction boss Sam Packard (Barry Kelley).

Sam tries to throw his weight around and bully the Sheriff into taking the heat off the nephew, while at the same time trying to coerce Claude into falsifying an alibi. The drama builds as both men defy the powerful construction boss and unrest grows in the community.

As time goes on the African-American townsfolk begin to believe that justice will not be served because of Claude's powerful family connections, and when a small scuffle is blown out of proportion a full-on race war explodes in the streets. Fueled by years of resentment unrelated to the missing girl, the town's previously peaceful facade is shattered. When the news arrives that the girl wasn't made off with, that she is actually trapped in the well, the community pulls together to come to her rescue.

Clocking in at an economical 85 minutes, *The Well* doesn't waste time establishing the frantic pace of the film. Oscar-nominated montages by editor Chester W. Schaeffer effectively show the spreading of racial poison by hotheaded white citizens who play broken telephone while dispersing untrue gossip about the "uppity" blacks of the town. By the time we get to the race riot the film has ceased to be about the young girl and morphed into a riveting portrayal of the seething hatred that plagues small minds — in the midst of the street fighting a messenger runs up to the leader of the white mob and says, "They found the kid." The leader's so wrapped up in his loathing he says, "What kid?"

The tone of the movie changes abruptly after the young girl is found to be alive, but even the town's reconciliation and feel-good ending can't wipe away the vividly portrayed hatred of the hysterical riot scenes. Played mostly by non-actors, some of the acting is iffy, but that doesn't detract from the effectiveness of this sequence. In 1951 this was raw stuff; racial tension had rarely been portrayed in such a brutal way before on screen.

Availability: On DVD

"We have no right to do what we're doing, unless we're prepared to answer with our lives."
— **TONY FENNER (JOHN GARFIELD) IN *WE WERE STRANGERS***

WE WERE STRANGERS (1949)

We Were Strangers should have been a classic, or at least a well remembered historical footnote for any number of reasons. Instead it has been consigned to the delete bin of Hollywood history, forgotten by most, seen by very few.

Based on the Robert Sylvester novel *Rough Sketch*, it was John Huston's first independent film, wedged between his considerably more successful outings *Key Largo* and *The Asphalt Jungle*; it was the film that almost gave Marilyn Monroe her first lead role and, on a more sinister note, may have been one of the triggers that pushed Lee Harvey Oswald to assassinate John F. Kennedy.

Set in 1933 Havana — seven years after Cuba's independence — the action begins when beautiful bank clerk China Valdés (Jennifer Jones) discovers that her brother Manolo (Tito Renaldo) has joined a revolutionary anti-government cell. The country has been under the oppressive thumb of President Gerardo Machado and Manolo and his compatriots are looking to end his reign of terror.

China becomes involved after Manolo is savagely murdered by secret policeman Armando Ariete (Pedro Armendáriz) on the steps of the local university. Vowing to avenge her brother's death she joins the anti-government movement and allows her home to be used as ground zero for a scheme cooked up by ex-patriot American Tony Fenner (John Garfield).

His elaborate plan is multi-pronged. First the small group of rebels will dig a tunnel under a local cemetery. Then they will assassinate a high-ranking member of the senate who will later be buried at the same cemetery. During the funeral, which is sure to be attended by El Presidente and high-ranking members of the government, they will ignite a bomb hidden in the tunnel and wipe out the evil regime in one fell swoop.

Everything goes according to plan until several members of this political underground start to crack under pressure, driven to distraction by the ghoulish details of the dig and the repercussions of the entire scheme.

We Were Strangers took a roundabout way to the screen. Independently produced by Huston and Sam Spiegel under their Horizon imprint, the film was courted by two studios who wanted to sign production deals. The pair almost co-produced with MGM but backed out when the studio insisted on placing Gene Kelly in the lead. Columbia Pictures offered more money and allowed Huston to cast his first choice for the lead, Garfield. Huston had wanted to cast the actor in the role of Curtin in *Treasure of the Sierra Madre*, but Garfield was unavailable. Active in liberal political and social causes, the actor was eager to do *We Were Strangers*, a movie whose politics appealed to his libertarian bent.

Huston didn't get his first choice for female lead, however. Originally planned as a vehicle for Marilyn Monroe, the film had to be recast after the producer Sam Spiegel refused to pay for a screen test for the young starlet. Instead, Huston cast Jennifer Jones, the raven-haired former model who had picked up a Best Actress Oscar in 1943 for *The Song of Bernadette*. She wasn't keen on taking the role — she didn't want to cut her hair or speak with a Cuban accent — but she was loaned out by producer David O. Selznick and had little choice in the matter.

For extra authenticity Huston shot much of the second unit footage in Havana and wisely rounded out the rest of the cast with the cream of the crop of Latin actors in Hollywood. Perfectly cast as the villainous Ariete, a corrupt government official with the hots for Jones's character was Pedro Armendáriz. He was a handsome green-eyed man with a business degree who turned to acting when he was discovered by director Miguel Zacarías while reciting Hamlet's "To be or not to be" monologue to an American tourist in a cafeteria in Mexico City. He went on to star in many Mexican and Hollywood movies, including *The Conqueror* with John Wayne and *From Russia with Love*. His work in *We Were Strangers* is among the best of his career as he effortlessly steals every scene in which he appears.

Also top billed was Mexico-born actor, and former silent movie heartthrob, Ramon Novarro, back onscreen after an absence of seven years. As a Cuban freedom fighter — it was his first supporting character role — Novarro was almost unrecognizable from the matinee idol that had burned up screens in past years. He was 20 pounds heavier, with thinning grey hair. To top it off he grew a scruffy beard, wore unattractive glasses and spoke in a high pitched, nasally voice.

"It was a small but important role," he said. "Something I had never done before, but a chance for real acting. Huston gave me the part without testing. He was very gracious." *Variety* praised his performance, and Novarro credits it with reigniting his stalled career. "This role was in a sense a test," he said. "Out of it came a bigger role in *The Big Steal* — that of Colonel Ortega, a Mexican police official who is very proud of his knowledge of the English language."

Novarro may have been pleased with the results of the film, but virtually no one else was. Critics from the left and right crucified the film's politics. Dubbed communist propaganda by the *Hollywood Review*, who called it "the heaviest dish of Red theory every served to an audience outside the Soviet," it was conversely slammed as "capitalist propaganda" by the Marxist newspaper the *Daily Worker*. The movie couldn't win with mainstream critics either. Bosley Crowther of the influential *New York Times* called it "passionless" and "written poorly and clumsily played" while others dismissed it outright, citing its lack of action and abundance of radical ideas.

Huston intended *We Were Strangers* to be a metaphor for the American government's anti-communist investigations during the Red Scare years, but audiences didn't get the deeper meaning, instead, focusing mostly on its support of armed revolutionary terrorism, even at the cost of innocent lives. For perhaps the first time ever in a Hollywood film, the terrorists were the good guys. After just a couple weeks of anemic box office it was withdrawn from theaters.

Huston immediately disowned the film — in a 1972 interview he claimed not to have seen the film since he made it — and it disappeared for many years, only occasionally popping up on television or at rep cinemas until its release on DVD in 2000.

That should have been the end of the story for *We Were Strangers* and its legacy but in 2000 author John Loken suggested that the movie may have been one of three "trigger films" (with *The Manchurian Candidate* and *Suddenly*) that motivated Lee Harvey Oswald to commit the most talked-about and studied assassination of the twentieth century. In the days leading up to the shooting of John F. Kennedy, Oswald watched *We Were Strangers* twice in one 24-hour period in mid-October

1963. It is Loken's theory that Oswald, known to be an impressionable young man, was taken with the idea of martyrdom as portrayed by one of the characters.

"I would admit that *We Were Strangers* works as a motivator whether or not you believe in conspiracy," Loken told *Filmfax Magazine*, "but if you accept Oswald's 'copy-cat' motive, you don't need the conspiracy allegations. In fact, you could argue that *We Were Strangers* takes the place of a co-conspirator. Rather than Oswald relying on co-operation from a real person or persons, you have this movie running over and over in Oswald's mind. It's easy to imagine that he received a lot of emotional support from mentally replaying this movie.

"If this film provided just 5 or 10 percent of Oswald's motivation, its impact would still be enormous."

We'll never definitively know if *We Were Strangers* was one of Oswald's inspirations (Jack Ruby saw to that), but what is for sure is that the film has aged well, acquiring a deepness that resonates in a post-9/11 world. Huston took a chance in 1949 making a film sympathetic to the Cuban insurrection, but today the movie seems even more daring, more subversive and timelier for its use of pro-terrorist themes. It's as controversial today as it was when it was first released and its ability to make you think about the nature of revolution and the morality involved is the very thing that makes this such a riveting film.

Availability: On DVD

My Favorite Movie You've Never Seen

"There is a Canadian film that I really love that was made by someone named Mike Rubbo which is called *Waiting for Fidel* (1974). It was a great inspiration for me. Mike Rubbo had gone to Cuba to meet Fidel Castro whom he never actually meets. He does a very amusing and very funny insightful piece about Cuba, and he and the crew are stuck in this hacienda on the outskirts of Havana and the head of the TV station paying for it is very impatient that Mike Rubbo should get on it and get this interview with Castro . . . and what questions is he going to ask him and so on and so forth, and you get all that sort of comedic tension and although you never meet Castro you learn all about the shenanigans going on there and it's very, very funny. I don't think it's ever been released properly theatrically but I think that soon Castro will die and it will be a great occasion to release that film."

– Nick Broomfield, BAFTA winner and the director of
Aileen: Life and Death of a Serial Killer and 29 other films

> "I wonder if there's any radiation about."
> **— JIM (JOHN MILLS) IN *WHEN THE WIND BLOWS***

WHEN THE WIND BLOWS (1986)

In this chilling animated feature from director Jimmy T. Murakami, Jim and Hilda Bloggs (John Mills and Peggy Ashcroft) are an elderly couple living out their golden years in the English countryside. World War II is a distant but vivid memory for the dear old pair, English to the core, who live a quiet life doting on one another and drinking tea by the gallon. Their idyllic existence is turned upside down when Jim reads a story in the newspaper and announces, "It looks like there is going to be a war, dear."

The couple, having survived the big one, don't quite grasp that World War III, a showdown between the United States and the Soviet Union, will be played out with nuclear weapons. "Well, if worse comes to worst, we'll just have to roll up our sleeves, tighten our belts and put on our tin hats until it's VE day again," says Hilda through her stiff upper lip.

With nostalgic memories of World War II and "the greatest generation" rattling around their heads they build a bomb shelter with the help of government-issued leaflets like *The Householder's Guide to Survival*, since, according to Jim, the government always knows what's best.

Their worst fears are confirmed when war breaks and a bomb is dropped. The couple survive the nuclear blast, but don't seem to understand the gravity of the situation. Leaving their shelter for the first time after the blast Hilda notices a strange burning smell. "Like roast meat," she says.

"I expect people are having their Sunday dinners early this week due to the unexpected circumstances," reasons Jim, unaware that the real reason is much more sinister.

Firm in their belief that the government will provide help for them, they wait patiently for things to return to normal, unaware that they are slowly being poisoned by fallout radiation and will not survive.

When the Wind Blows is a remarkable mix of dark and light — the subject matter and animation style — and has the impact of a live action drama without losing the whimsy of the animated form. Further drama is added by a theatrical score by Pink Floyd's Roger Waters.

Japanese-American director Jimmy T. Murakami, the former art director at Roger Corman's New World Pictures, uses a mixed bag of textures to tell the story. There's hand-drawn animation, three-dimensional tableaus, stock black and white news footage and some crude computer generated imagery. Based on British cartoonist Raymond Briggs graphic novel, the movie's deceptively sweet look lulls the audience into a false sense of security before walloping them with a strong and emotional anti-war message.

The movie has a dark satiric edge, playing the naiveté of Jim and Hilda — simply and plainly voiced by Mills and Ashcroft — against the bleak specter of nuclear war. Their optimism never dims, even post bombing when their gums bleed, and their hair falls out. When they start to develop splotches on their skin they write off all the infirmities to the effects of aging, not radiation.

When the Wind Blows is an unsettling anti-war film that uses the small personal details of Jim and Hilda's life, pre- and post-blast, to draw the viewer into the much larger horror story of nuclear terror.

Availability: Out of Print VHS

THE WILD DOGS (2002)

- - - - - - - - - -

Hanging Garden director Thom Fitzgerald initially traveled to Romania to make a low-budget, hired-gun horror movie called *Wolf Girl*. Drawn by easy access to shooting locations and an agreeable exchange rate on the dollar Romania had become a mecca of sorts to filmmakers looking to save a few bucks.

Shooting *Wolf Girl* was not an entirely happy experience though, as Fitzgerald had to deal with pushy producers who insisted, among other things, that the sweaters of the female cast members be skin tight. During production, however, Fitzgerald met and befriended several homeless people who hung around the set. These individuals were the inspiration for his next film, *The Wild Dogs*.

This film's title refers to the canines that were left homeless in Bucharest, Romania, when Dictator Ceaușescu decided to level the city and rebuild it in his vision. After years of unchecked breeding, the initial population of perhaps 2,000 stray dogs has multiplied to as many as 200,000. Fitzgerald uses scenes of the dogs snarling and fighting as a metaphor for human behavior.

He weaves three main plot lines together: an ineffectual dogcatcher (Mihai Calota) fears he will lose his job; Victor, a decadent, terminally ill ambassador (David Hayman) takes advantage of his position of power, while his pampered wife (Alberta Watson) begins to understand the crushing poverty that exists all around her; and a reluctant Canadian pornographer named Geordie (Fitzgerald) comes to town to scout for young inexpensive "talent" willing to strip down for his camera.

It's Geordie's story that holds most of the film and viewer's attention as he tours the city with his three-foot-tall tour guide Radu (Marcel

Ungureanu). Once on the streets the photographer loses interest in the young women he came to exploit and has a moral rebirth as he becomes involved with the physically challenged homeless people he meets. His redemption lies with a disabled man he tries to rescue. Known as Sour Grapes (Visinel Burcea), he crawls through traffic begging for change, his abnormality — reverse jointed legs — the result of an intentional deformation at birth to improve his usefulness as a beggar.

The movie comes to an emotional high ground when a disfigured boy (Nelu Dinu) follows Geordie to a chic charity cocktail party thrown by the ambassador and his wife. The boy's presence at the party causes a stir, to say the least.

Meanwhile, in another part of the city the dogcatcher's dangerous attempt to rescue a pack of wild dogs backfires with surprising results.

It's a complex narrative, but Fitzgerald manages to bring it all together, blending the stories and timelines effortlessly. It's the film's imagery that really has an effect. Shot on digital video Fitzgerald packs the film with unforgettable sequences. His camera unblinkingly follows the ambassador's wife as she goes about her daily routine of pampered excess while being shadowed by Dorutu (Nelu Dinu), the legless young boy whose sole means of transportation is a single roller-skate. In sequences like this Fitzgerald fills the frame with social commentary, all without the aid of dialogue. It's accomplished filmmaking, and although some may find the tone of the film downbeat it should be noted that Fitzgerald also blends in dry humor and pathos to take some of the sting out.

Even the film's sly cultural criticism and social commentary is occasionally presented with humor. When the dogcatcher, faced with a near Sisyphean task of hunting down the strays, finds himself inside the city's dilapidated opera house, he wonders aloud why the once beautiful building hasn't been restored.

"We have CNN now," says a co-worker, referring to the public's shifting tastes away from highbrow entertainment.

The film has a documentary, almost Dogme feel as Fitzgerald pulls loose performances out of a cast made up of pros and talented first-timers.

The weakest casting is Fitzgerald in the lead role of the pornographer. I found myself wondering what a more accomplished actor might do with this role. Don McKellar or Tom McCamus could have pulled this off, but I would have liked to seen Callum Keith Rennie take on the part. He has the toughness to make us believe he could be involved in something unsavory and the acting chops to show us the character's salvation. Fitzgerald's section is still effective, just not the emotional powerhouse it could have been.

"I wanted to give a voice to some fascinating people," Fitzgerald told the *Montreal Mirror*. In *The Wild Dogs* his expert visuals and interesting script speak loud and clear about the role of compassion in a place where kindness is scarce.

Availability: On DVD

"Why with everybody else? Why with every slob . . . and not me?"
— LARRY SHERMAN (SAL MINEO) IN *WHO KILLED TEDDY BEAR?*

WHO KILLED TEDDY BEAR? (1965)

Five years after his second Academy Award nomination for Best Supporting Actor, 26-year-old Sal Mineo made a film he says landed him "on the weirdo list," triggering a 10 year career free fall.

In Hollywood the years between 1934 and 1967 marked a period of rigid adherence to the Production Code (also known as the Hays Code), a set of guidelines governing the moral content of movies.

One of the films that helped chip away at the Code's hold on Hollywood was Joseph Cates' (father of actress Phoebe) 1965 film *Who Killed Teddy Bear?* This lurid story, jam-packed with insinuations of pornography, lesbianism, drug-taking and masturbation all framed by a boy-stalks-girl scenario, shattered several of the Code's guiding principles, including "references to sex perversion," not upholding the sanctity of marriage and the big no-no, which read, "no film shall be produced that will lower the moral standards of those who see it."

This one would have made Code founder William Harrison Hays' puritanical head explode. Described by Kenneth Anger in *Hollywood Babylon* as "a prim-faced, bat-eared, mealy-mouthed political chiseler," Hays' idea of the endless torments of hell would probably include nightly screenings of *Who Killed Teddy Bear?*

Shot on location in Manhattan in the mid-'60s, the film opens with a startling voyeuristic sex scene. Writhing bodies, partially obscured by a filmy haze and the opening credits, undulate onscreen as a young girl cowers in the doorway, watching and clutching a teddy bear. Horrified by what she sees she recoils and falls down a flight of stairs. As the film's title credit flashes on the screen the camera moves in on a dramatic close-up of the girl's face and the crumpled body of the teddy bear.

It's a grabber of an opening, but pales in comparison to the scenes that follow. A shadowy figure in tight white shorts gets out of bed, suggestively adjusts himself in the mirror before making an obscene phone call.

"I know you don't know me," he says, "but I know you very well."

At first the object of his "affections," Norah Dain (Juliet Prowse), a DJ and bartender at a seedy midtown discotheque, isn't concerned by the unwanted attention. Used to dealing with rough drunks hitting on her at the bar, she assumes the anonymous call is harmless.

"It was *just* a phone call," she says.

When Dave Madden (Jan Murray), a sarcastic police detective who specializes in sex crimes, becomes involved the situation deepens. The calls continue, and Madden, whose wife was killed by a sexual predator, becomes obsessed with cracking the case. Norah tries to lead a normal life, but when the club's lesbian owner, Marian Freeman (Broadway legend Elaine Stritch) is killed while wearing one of Norah's coats in front of her apartment building she turns to a co-worker for solace.

Her new friend is Larry (Sal Mineo), the club's busboy, a lonely, quiet man with a proclivity for wearing jeans so tight they look painted on. When he isn't cleaning up spilled beer or mopping toilets he cares for his mentally challenged younger sister, Edie, who looks a lot like the girl in the film's opening credits.

What Norah doesn't realize, until it is too late, is that she is now face to face with her stalker. In the end Larry goes on the lam in Manhattan with Detective Madden and the NYPD in hot pursuit.

The shocking power of *Who Killed Teddy Bear?* hasn't dulled in the 40 years since its release. Despite being marred by a terrible soundtrack (faux rock and roll songs by former Four Seasons backup singer Charlie Calello), some melodramatic moments and poor lighting, the implied incestuous relationship between Larry and Edie, the sheer creep factor of the phone calls and the flashbacks of child abuse are effectively rendered and haven't lost their punch over time. It can make for some uncomfortable viewing, but does provide a fascinating insight to the burgeoning sexual ethos of the era.

Also interesting is the insight the film gives us on 1965's New York City. Shot in glorious black and white by Joseph Brun and assistant cinematographer Michael Chapman (who 10 years later would shoot *Taxi Driver* for Martin Scorsese), *Who Killed Teddy Bear?* features great unvarnished shots of the Times Square sex shops, the Central Park Zoo and theater district passageways. The documentary feel of the on-location sequences adds a tangible feeling of realism to the movie.

New York not only provides a backdrop for the action, but actually helps feed the story. The claustrophobia of the city is effectively used to add an air of paranoia. What if your stalker lived next door, close enough to peer through your bedroom window? In the high density Big Apple presented in the film, this scenario seems likely and deadly.

Who Killed Teddy Bear? met with mixed critical reaction. Some called it edgy, while others labeled it unwatchable, but it was likely the movie's unabashed mix of sexuality and violence that kept the film from finding its audience. Once word got out that the movie contained sexual, but not sexy content, not even sensational advertising taglines like "Peeper Ogles Strip Dancer Taking Bath" and "Anonymous Calls Lead to Attack" could lure people into the theaters.

The only common ground between divided reviewers was the performance of Sal Mineo, which was praised for its intensity and bravery. Years before *Taxi Driver*'s Travis Bickle wondered, "Are you looking at me?" Mineo's portrayal of the handsome but troubled Larry seethed with a similar kind of bottled-up sexual energy. Too bad his performance got lost amid the controversial aspects of the film.

"You see, in some of the shots while I was on the phone they wanted to suggest that I was masturbating, but I couldn't be naked," Mineo said a decade after the film flopped in theaters. "So I was wearing jockey shorts. It turned out that that was the first American film where a man wore jockey shorts. They always had to wear boxer shorts onscreen. So I got hit with all this, and I'm laughing about all this controversy about what is considered obscene. Imagine. And only a few years later we've got *Deep Throat.*"

At least one of Mineo's co-stars had no regrets taking part in such a controversial film. "I was a lesbian owner of a disco who fell in love with Juliet Prowse and got strangled on Ninety-third Street and East End Avenue with a silk stocking by Sal Mineo," said Elaine Stritch. "Now who's *not* going to play that part?"

Mineo's career nosedived post *Who Killed Teddy Bear?* It's as if producers were put off by the overtly sexual posturing of that movie, and after 1965 he was rarely offered any significant screen work, mostly being relegated to the stage and guest roles on television. The odd time he was offered a studio picture, his talent was seldom showcased. Playing a talking chimpanzee in *Escape from the Planet of the Apes*, the second sequel in the series, didn't exactly signal an upturn in his career or win him any new fans, but did help pay the rent.

Eleven years after the release of *Who Killed Teddy Bear?* Sal Mineo was murdered in West Hollywood while returning home from a rehearsal for a stage show that he hoped would be his come-back. The obits that followed his death trumpeted his Oscar-nominated work in *Rebel Without a Cause* and *Exodus*, with nary a mention of *Who Killed Teddy Bear?* He was finally off "the weirdo list."

Availability: Hard to find

"Everything happens in the yellow Rolls-Royce!"
— **ADVERTISING TAGLINE FOR *THE YELLOW ROLLS-ROYCE***

THE YELLOW ROLLS-ROYCE (1964)

The cinematic sub-species of portmanteau was birthed with the 1948 movie *Quartet* based on stories by W. Somerset Maugham. The idea of creating one omnibus style feature consisting of different short films based on some kind of connective tissue — usually a person, place or thing — seems irresistible to filmmakers who, over the years, have followed the life and times of everything from a $20 bill (*Twenty Bucks*) and a 300-year-old violin (*The Red Violin*), to world class cities (*New York Stories*; *Paris, je t'aime*) and unusual people (*Four Rooms*). A classic, but little-known portmanteau film is 1964's *The Yellow Rolls-Royce* written by Terence Rattigan, once the world's highest paid scenarist. The film boasts an all-star cast and consists of three separate stories connected only by the ownership of a chic Phantom II Rolls-Royce.

In the first segment foreign office bigwig Lord Frinton (Rex

Harrison) buys the car from a West End dealership as an anniversary present for his pretty French wife (Jeanne Moreau). Soon afterward Fritton's horse wins the Gold Cup at Ascot. Excited, he searches for his wife, only to discover she is nowhere to be found. A bit of infidelity later the car is placed on the market along with other artifacts from the couple's crumbled marriage.

The next time we see its unique yellow visage we're in Genoa in the 1930s. This time it is purchased by an American gangster (George C. Scott) as a present for his current flame, hat-check girl Mae Jenkins (Shirley MacLaine). Once again the car's back seat is the scene of some illicit sexual hijinks, this time between Mae and street photographer Stefano (Alain Delon), and soon the car is once again placed on the market.

The auto takes its last spin around the block in a story set in 1942. Now in the northeastern Italian port city of Trieste, the Rolls has seen better days when it is purchased by American millionaire Gerda Millett (Ingrid Bergman), who plans on driving to Yugoslavia at the invitation of the royal family. Hitler is attacking Yugoslavia, but that is not going to stop her from fulfilling her social engagement. As she prepares to leave she is approached by Davich (Omar Sharif), a magnetic Yugoslav partisan who convinces the woman to smuggle him into the wartorn country.

The duo of director Anthony Asquith and scriptwriter Rattigan had tread this territory before. The year previous they had teamed to produce *The V.I.P.s*, another all-star omnibus of stories about a group of travelers thrown together by chance as they wait in the VIP lounge of London Airport, hoping for the fog to lift so they can board a plane to New York. That film grabbed audience's attention, whereas *The Yellow Roll-Royce*, despite an all-star cast, an amazing polyglot theme song called "Forget Domani," and first-class production values, didn't make an impression.

It's a shame people didn't see *The Yellow Rolls-Royce*. Each segment has its own personality — the first wistful, the second exuberantly comedic, the last romantic and dramatic — but Asquith handles the material skillfully, artfully weaving the three separate stories into one continuous whole. Particularly strong is his work on the third piece. The story of wartorn romance could easily have fallen prey to melodrama and maudlin sentiment, but he keeps it on track and even draws a rare comedic performance from Bergman.

Rattigan's dialogue shines, from the refined haughtiness of Lord Fritton to the brash, "My baby wants a Rolls-Royce . . . my baby *gets* a Rolls-Royce!" *braggadocio* of Scott's gangster.

The Yellow Rolls-Royce is a wild ride through several decades and many different characters, but is held together thematically by the strong vision of its director and writer.

Availability: Hard to find

"Attention space adventurers, Zathura awaits. Do you have what it takes to navigate the galaxy? It's not for the faint of heart, for once you embark upon your journey there's no turning back until Zathura is reached."
— WALTER (JOSH HUTCHERSON) READING GAME INSTRUCTIONS

ZATHURA: A SPACE ADVENTURE (2005)

Zathura is more than just a *Jumanji* wannabe. If that sentence doesn't make any sense to you, it's because you've forgotten about the 1995 movie *Jumanji* starring Robin Williams. Both movies are based on Chris Van Allsburg books and both are flights of fantasy centered on board games that come to life.

Beyond that they have little in common. *Jumanji* was a big-budget CGI spectacular that I felt let the effects overwhelm the story. *Zathura* is about the Budwing brothers (played by Jonah Bobo and Josh Hutcherson) and a mysterious board game, but *Iron Man* director Jon Favreau never lets the human element of the story get washed away by the effects. He carefully manages to integrate the numerous fantastic elements of the story into the movie without allowing the balance to tip in favor of the sci-fi. Even though there are black holes, menacing robots, evil lizardlike space creatures named Zorgons and a cryogenically frozen sister, he wisely keeps the spotlight on the boys and their relationship.

This story focuses on two battling brothers, Danny (Bobo, who lost four teeth during filming and had to wear fake teeth for continuity) and Walter (Hutcherson), who discover a magical board game. As soon as they start to play, it's obvious this isn't Monopoly. More like Trouble, but as the old jingle said, "this kind of trouble is lots of fun." At least it is for the viewers.

Instead of the wild animals unleashed in *Jumanji*, *Zathura*'s game board hurtles the boys, their house and terminally bored sister into outer space: the rings of Saturn, to be precise. The two siblings realize that if they ever want to get home in one piece they must learn to cooperate and keep playing, despite the danger conjured up by the game at every turn.

A movie like this relies on special effects to keep the eye entertained, but Favreau didn't take the easy way out and cram *Zathura* with fancy CGI. Instead he chose to create the eccentric creatures and planets produced by the game with old-school special effects instead of high-tech computer generated imagery.

"I'm a bit of a nostalgic filmmaker so working with practical effects [i.e. not computer-generated] just makes it more fun for me," Favreau told writer Rebecca Murray. "On *Elf* we did stop-motion animation. We did forced perspective in camera. And I find that the challenges of presenting the crew with the mission statement of trying to work with practical effects makes it a much more collaborative and creative experience.

"On most movies you just shoot the actors, you shoot green screen, and you know everybody sort of says, 'Okay, we did our jobs. I can't wait to see what it looks like.' And then months and months are spent with digital houses. We did some of that in this movie, but it's so fun to actually shoot real spaceships or have a real robot running around on the set, or real Zorgons built by [Oscar-winning makeup and special effects man] Stan Winston. It gives the actors, especially young actors, so much to work off."

Favreau's use of practical special effects imbues *Zathura* with a handmade feel that gives the movie an old-fashioned patina, somewhat akin to the cheapo space opera serials that used to run before features in the Golden Age of Hollywood. It's a nice nostalgic touch that adds depth to the movie's visual storytelling.

Favreau has said he also used more traditional effects in hopes of appealing to the parents who would be watching this movie with their kids.

"Hopefully adults will have an experience that reminds them of the experience that they got when they were younger watching the movies that we grew up with," he told *Dark Horizons*. "You know, hopefully they'll appreciate the effort that was put into the filmmaking, using the practical effects and using the older techniques — and also the older style of storytelling."

That nostalgic, timeless style suits the story perfectly. Too many children's movies use frenetic video games as a reference point. *Zathura's* style is more like pinball. Old-fashioned perhaps, but engaging nonetheless. It is also a rare action-oriented family film without the gross-out elements that are so often a part of children's entertainment.

Availability: On DVD

BIBLIOGRAPHY

Alexander, Chris. "Bava On Bava: Five Films of Blood." *Rue Morgue.*
    May 2007: 52–53.
———. "Kids vs. Monsters." *Rue Morgue.* July 2007: 16–24.
Anger, Kenneth. *Hollywood Babylon II.* New York: Plume Books, 1984.
Aulier, Dan. *Hitchcock's Notebooks: An Authorized and Illustrated Look
    Inside the Creative Mind of Alfred Hitchcock.* New York:
    HarperEntertainment, 1999.
Barbour, Alan G. *Humphrey Bogart: The Illustrated History of the
    Movies.* London: W. H. Allen Ltd., 1974.
Baxter, John. *De Niro: A Biography.* London: HarperCollins Publishers,
    2002.
Biskind, Peter. "Midnight Revolution." *Vanity Fair.* March 2005.
Bona, Damien. *Inside Oscar 2: 6 New Years of Academy Awards History:
    1995–2000.* New York: Ballantine Books, 2002.
Brooks, Ken. "Did *We Were Strangers* Trigger an Assassination?"
    Filmfax Plus. September 2007: 86–89.
Brown, Peter H., and Jim Pinkston. *Oscar Dearest.* New York: Harper
    & Row, 1987.
Canby, Vincent. "Is *El Topo* a Con?" *Film 71/72 — An Anthology.* New
    York: Simon & Schuster, 1972.
Corman, Roger and Jim Jerome. *How I Made a Hundred Movies in
    Hollywood and Never Lost a Dime.* New York: Random House, Inc,
    1990.
Dalton, Stephen. "Absolutely Fabulist." *Uncut.* December 2005: 40–44.
———. "For a Few Dollars Less." *Uncut.* September 2004: 84–87.
"Disastrous, Disgraceful or Just Plain Dumb: The 50 Most Disturbing
    Moments in Movie History." *Premiere.* November 2004.

Divine, Christian. "Freaks and Geeks: An Interview with Actor-Playwright Austin Pendleton." *Shock Cinema*. Number 33: 8–14.

Edmonds, Ben. "No Exit." *Mojo*. June 2002.

Fierman, Daniel. "Kings, Queens and Wild Things." *Entertainment Weekly*, Issue 793. November 19, 2004.

Fortnam, Ian. "Hollywood Rocks." *Classic Rock*. October 2007: 37.

Frascella, Lawrence, and Al Weissel. *Live Fast, Die Young: the Wild Ride of Making* Rebel Without a Cause. New York: Touchstone, 2005.

Fredrik, Nathalie. *The New Hollywood and the Academy Awards*. Beverly Hills: Hollywood Awards Publications, 1974.

Gardetta, Dave. "Mr. Indelible." *Los Angeles Magazine*. February 2005.

Graham, Jamie. *Adventures in Movieland*. London: Total Film Publishing, 2007.

Grey, Rudolph. *Nightmare of Ecstasy: the Life and Art of Ed Wood Jr.* Portland: Feral Press, 1994.

Harmetz, Aljean. *The Making of* The Wizard of Oz: *Movie Magic and Studio Power in the Prime of* MGM *— and the Miracle of Production #1060*. New York: Delta, 1977.

Heard, Charles, Mank, Gregory William and Nelson, Bill. *Hollywood's Hellfire Club*. Los Angeles: Feral House, 2007.

Higham, Charles. *Brando: The Unauthorized Biography*. New York and Scarborough, Ontario: The New American Library of Canada, 1987.

———. *Charles Laughton: An Intimate Biography*. New York: Doubleday & Company, 1976.

Hoberman, J., and J. Rosenbaum. *Midnight Movies*. New York: Harper & Row, 1983.

Jacobs, Jay. *Wild Years: The Music and Myth of Tom Waits*. Toronto: ECW Press, 2000.

Johnstone, Nick. "Force of Nature." *Uncut*. April 2001: 68–72.

Jordan, Rene. *Clark Gable: The Illustrated History of the Movies*. London: W. H. Allen Ltd., 1974.

———. *Marlon Brando: The Illustrated History of the Movies*. London: W. H. Allen Ltd., 1973.

Juneau, James. *Judy Garland: The Illustrated History of the Movies.* New York: Jove Publications, 1974.

Kinn, Gail and Jim Piazza. *And the Oscar Goes to . . . The Academy Awards.* New York: Black Dog & Leventhal Publishers, 2002.

Kleiner, R. "Alexandro Jodorowsky." *Penthouse.* June 1973: 60–64.

Konow, David. "Behind, Beside and In Front of the Camera!" *Filmfax Plus.* September 2007: 78–82.

Levy, Emanuel. *All About Oscar: The History and Politics of the Academy Awards.* New York: Continuum, 2003.

Love, Damien. "America's Most Wanted." *Uncut.* September 2004: 68–71.

———. "Hollywood's Best Kept Secret." *Uncut.* June 2003: 68–72.

Mann's Chinese Theater. C.P., 1992.

McGilligan, Patrick. *Alfred Hitchcock: A Life in Darkness and Light.* New York: Regan Books, 2003.

Moser, Margaret, Bertin, Michael and Crawford, Bill. *Movie Stars Do the Dumbest Things.* Los Angeles: Renaissance Books, 1999.

Moss, Robert F. *Karloff and Company: The Horror Film.* London: Pyramid Publications, 1973.

Nashawaty, Chris. "Fight Club." *Entertainment Weekly*, Issue 803. January 28, 2005.

O'Neil, Tom. *Movie Awards: The Ultimate, Unofficial Guide to the Oscars, Golden Globes, Critics, Guild & Indie Honors.* New York: Perigee Books, 2003.

Peretz, Evgenia. "The Sky's the Limit." *Vanity Fair.* December 2004.

Pond, Steve. *The Big Show: High Times and Dirty Dealings Backstage at the Academy Awards.* New York: Faber and Faber Inc., 2005.

Price, Michael H., and George E. Turner. *Forgotten Horrors: Early Talkie Chillers from Poverty Row.* Guerneville, California: Eclipse Books, 1986.

Queenan, Joe. *If You're Talking to Me Your Career Must Be in Trouble.* New York: Hyperion, 1994.

Rhodes, Gary D., and Richard Sheffield. "Lugosi, Vampira & Ed

Wood's Atomic Bride." *Filmfax Plus*. April/June 2007: 54–61.

Salisbury, Mark. "Cannes is Burning." *Premiere*. September 2004.

Sandford, Christopher. *McQueen: The Biography*. New York: HarperCollins Entertainment, 2001.

Schruers, Fred. "Women in Hollywood: Angelina Jolie." *Premiere*. October 2004.

Seal, John. "They Came From the Basement." *Videoscope*. Fall 2007: 33–34.

Skal, David J., and Elias Savada. *Dark Carnival: The Secret World of Tod Browning, Hollywood's Master of Disguise*. New York: Anchor Books, 1995.

Staggs, Sam. *Close-Up on Sunset Boulevard: Billy Wilder, Norma Desmond and the Dark Hollywood Dream*. New York: St. Martin's Griffin, 2002.

Stein, Jean, and George Plimpton. *Edie: An American Biography*. New York: Dell Books, 1982.

Strangis, Jason. "The Roar of the Pussycat! The Tale of Tura Satana." *Filmfax Plus*. September 2007: 83–85.

Taraborrelli, J. Randy. *Once Upon a Time: Behind the Tale of Princess Grace and Prince Rainier*. New York: Rose Books, 2003.

"The Total Film Readers' Awards 2004." *Total Film: The Ultimate Movie Magazine*, Issue 96. December 2004.

Tranberg, Charles. "The Remarkable Fred MacMurray: He Was Tops!" *Films of the Golden Age*. Fall 2007: 21–37.

Wiley, Mason and Bona, Damien. *Inside Oscar: The Unofficial History of the Academy Awards*. New York: Ballantine Books, 1986.

Wulf, Steve. "Oscar 2005: Morgan Freeman." *Entertainment Weekly*, Issue 804/805. February 4, 2005.

Wynn, J. Scott. "Shock Cinema Talks With Film Auteur Extraordinaire Russ Meyer." *Shock Cinema*. Number 13: 25–27.

Yanni, Nicholas. *W. C. Fields: The Illustrated History of the Movies*. London: Pyramid Publications, 1974.